the
GOOD MOVl

© The Good Move Guide Ltd. 1996

First Issue 1996
First Edition 1996

Published by: 'The Good Move Guide Ltd.'
Registered Address: 'Tanglewood',
Holmbury St. Mary,
Surrey RH5 6LQ
Company Registered in England No. 3066289

Typeset by: J.T. Huckin & Co.,
2a Thornton Road, East Sheen, London, SW14 8NS

Printed by: Seven Corners Press Ltd., Penmark House, Woodbridge Meadows, Guildford, Surrey GU1 1BL

© 'The Good Move Guide Ltd.' 1996

All written material and hand drawn maps
are by the author: Susan de Launay

The Author asserts the moral right to be identified
as the author of this work.

All Rights Reserved. No part of this publication
may be reproduced, stored in a retrieval system,
or transmitted in any form or by any means, electronic,
mechanical, photocopying, or otherwise, without the
prior permission of the copyright owner.

Great care has been taken throughout this guide
to be accurate, but the publishers cannot accept
responsibility for any errors that appear, or their
consequences.

ISBN 0 9526922 0 1

British Library Cataloguing in Publication Data.
A catalogue record for this book is available from the
British Library.

To advertise in future editions of this Guide
please contact the publishers.

'The Good Move Guide' logo designed by:
Steve Diederich, *Graphics and Design Consultant*
Front Cover designed by:
The Brochure Works, Capel Rd, Rusper, Sussex

AUTHOR'S NOTE

First inspiration for this guide was simple - my own experiences and those of others, which revealed that moving home was always exhausting, often precarious and normally much more expensive than first thought. With the best 'will-in-the-world' the amount of organisation could be daunting, even for the most energetic and enthusiastic. What's more, some important research was never actually covered at all because, it became clear, most people fit moving home around an already busy schedule. Pitfalls and stumbling blocks could appear without warning, creating unexpected problems and dashing hopes. Even amongst the most sensible and conscientious of us, some things were simply left to luck.

With all this in mind, I felt most people moving home would benefit from an appropriate aide-memoire, a sort of handy local reference book focused to suit their point of view. At best then, this might help reduce some of the risks, by making the unknown more familiar - as they say 'forewarned is forearmed'.

So whether you are new to the area or already local, I hope you find this guide displays an accurate and revealing insight into the neighbourhood, highlighting all you need to know.

                              HAPPY HUNTING!

                              Susan

WITH SPECIAL THANKS
to the following:

Simon Ball,
The Brochure Works,
Stammerham Business Centre,
Capel Road, Rusper, Nr. Hosham,
West Sussex RH12 4PZ
Tel: 01306 713489

Peter Cliff,
The National Association of Estate Agents,
Arbon House,
21 Jury Street,
Warwick CV34 4EH
Tel: 01926 496800

Peter Huckin,
J.T. Huckin and Co.,
2a Thornton Road,
East Sheen,
London SW14 8NS
Tel: 0181 876 4186

Richard Trendall,
Cowing Balmforth Trendall,
18-24 Westbourne Grove,
London W2 5RH
Tel: 0171 221 1819

Tad Zurlinden,
Association of Relocation Agents,
Premier House,
11 Marlborough Place,
Brighton, BN1 1UB
Tel: 01273 624455

friends:
Steve Diederich
Nicky MacKenzie

and husband, Craig

CONTENTS

GENERAL SECTION
Page

FIRST THOUGHTS ON MOVING
AND GETTING STARTED 13
To Buy or Rent - that is the question?
Second thoughts and a final word of warning
To Sum Up
So You Really Want to Move?
Testing the Water!
Taking the Plunge!
To Sum Up - Ten Commandments for Moving Home
Step by Step

BUYING AND SELLING 19
(A Summary for Purchasers and Vendors)
Purchaser's Considerations
Timing
The Area
The Price
The Type and Condition of Property
Other Types of Purchase
The Offer to Buy
The Time Delay
Exchange of Contracts and Completion
Moving In
Vendor's Considerations
Timing
The Best Price
Finding a Buyer
Advertising Your Own Home Yourself
Showing People Round
Moving Out

RELATED FINANCIAL AND LEGAL MATTERS 29
Purchaser's Responsibilities
The Mortgage
Where to get the Best Advice?
The Cost of the Mortgage
The Legal Fees
The Valuer's and/or Surveyor's Fee
Stamp Duty
Land Registry Fee
Local Authority Searches

Page

Purchaser's Responsibilities *Continued ....*
Exchange of Contracts
The Deposit
Countdown to Completion
Removal Expenses
Vendor's Responsibilities
Estate Agent's Commission
Advertising
Solicitor's Fee
Mortgage Redemption
Exchange and Completion
Removal Expenses
Capital Gains Tax
LETTING AND RENTING 39
(A Summary for Landlords and Tenants)
Landlord's Considerations
Can I let?
How Do I let?
The Inventory
To Sum Up
Tenant's Considerations
The Priorities
Research
Tenancy Agreements
Assured Tenancies
Shorthold Assured Tenancies
Rent Increases
RELATED FINANCIAL AND LEGAL MATTERS...................43
Landlord's Responsibilities
Advertising Expenses
Agent's Commission
Inventory
Tenancy Agreement
Maintenance and Management Expenses
Buildings and Contents Insurance
The Mortgage or other loans secured on the property
Ground Rent
Tenant's Responsibilities
The Deposit
References
The Rent
Preparation of Tenancy Agreement
Check In and Check Out Charges

                                                                    Page
Tenant's Responsibilities *Continued ....*
Utilities including Council Tax
Cleaning, Replacements and Repairs
Contents Insurance
Access to the Property

HOMES OF INTEREST 47
Listed Buildings
Thatched Homes
Semi-detached Homes
Building your own Home
Repossessed Homes
House Boats

WHERE TO FIND AVAILABLE HOMES 51
National Newspapers
Local Newspapers
Other Newspapers/Circulars
Glossy Magazines and Periodicals
Estate Agents
Auctions
Property Registers
Relocation Agents
Computer Technology

ESTATE AGENTS' SERVICES 55
The National Association of Estate Agents
The Royal Institution of Chartered Surveyors
The Incorporated Society of Valuers and Auctioneers
The Vendor's Point of View
The Obvious Choice?
Which One?
Their Services
Their Charges
Terms and Conditions
Letting Agents

The Purchaser's Point of View 61
Research
Property Particulars
Other Services
Sunday Opening
Letting Agents

	Page
VIEWING AND RESEARCH	65

Thoughts Before You Look......
Location
Country Living
Town Living
Location Priorities
Analysing Available Homes
'Armchair Research'
Viewing - What to Take
Getting the Most from Viewing
Tips On Viewing

Hidden Problems	71

Weather Conditions and Seasons
Your Journey to Work
Potential Building Construction
Nuisances or Advantages
Different Times of the Day
Next Door
Neighbours
Crime and Rowdyism
Pollution
Contaminated Land
Further Afield

MOVING CHECKLIST	75

(1) Moving Out
'Notify Change of Address' Checklist
'Organise' Checklist
(2) Moving In
'Reminder' Checklist
(3) General Moving Advice and Tips
(4) Crime Prevention and Fire Safety

LOCAL SECTION

ABOUT SURREY	83

Fig. 1 The County of Surrey - Administrative Boundaries
Location
Origins
Potted History
Industry
Leisure
Buildings and Gardens

                                                                    Page
Road and Rail Communications 88
Fig. 2 The County of Surrey - Major Roads
Fig. 3 The County of Surrey - Rail Connections
Rights of Way - 'Off Road'
The North Downs Way
The Greensand Way
The Downs Link
Airports
Business Investment
New Homes
House Prices

INFORMATION CENTRES 98
Tourist Information Centres
Surrey County Council Information Centres

SURREY COUNTY COUNCIL 100
Local Information and Contact Telephone Numbers
Surrey County Council Publications

MOLE VALLEY DISTRICT COUNCIL 102
Local Information and Contact Telephone Numbers
Council Tax Bands and Charges 1996 - 1997

TOWNS AND VILLAGES
'At-a-Glance' 104

Photo **Dorking High Street** *(Courtesy Surrey County Council)* 108

TOWNS AND VILLAGES
of the Mole Valley 109

Dorking. *Fig. 4* **Dorking Map** 111
(Similar Paragraph Headings are included for all the Towns)

Location, Opinion, The Town and Surroundings,
Local Telephone Books
Transport: Roads, Rail, Buses
Shopping, Council Offices,
Commercial, Leisure, Schools,
Night Life, Hospitals, Police Station
Football Pitch, Recreation Ground, Allotments,
Cemetery, Sewage Works, Refuse Tip, Gipsy Sites,
Aircraft and Traffic Noise, History

                                                                    Page

Leatherhead   *Fig. 5* **Leatherhead Map** 125
Ashtead   *Fig. 6* **Ashtead Map** 135
Great Bookham   *Fig. 7* **Great Bookham** 143
(including Little Bookham and Fetcham)
Photos **Abinger Hammer and Leigh** 148
(Courtesy Surrey County Council)

THE RURAL VILLAGES 149

of the Mole Valley *(See the Mole Valley Map)*
Parish News Magazines
Public Houses and Local Shops
The District"s Country Lanes
Horses
Modern Utilities

Abinger (Abinger Common) 151

(incl. **Abinger Bottom, Broadmoor, Friday Street, Sutton and Wotton**)
(See Mole Valley Map)
Location, Opinion,
The Village and Surroundings
Local Telephone Books
Transport: Roads, Rail, Buses
Shopping, Schools, Noise,
Parish Council Information, History

Abinger Hammer

(Similar Headings as above are included for all the Villages)
(See the Mole Valley Map for all the Villages) 154
Betchworth (incl. Buckland) 158
Brockham 161
Capel 165
Charlwood 169
Coldharbour and Leith Hill 172
Headley 176
Holmbury St. Mary 180
The 'Holmwoods' (incl. **Beare Green**) 186
Leigh 190
Mickleham 193
Newdigate 196
Ockley 199
Westcott 203
Westhumble (incl. **Ranmore**) 206

                                                                  Page.
SCHOOLS INFORMATION 211
State Schools
Independent Schools
Local Pre-School Child Care

PRE-SCHOOL LOCAL NOTICE BOARD 213

LOCAL SCHOOLS INFORMATION 217
Local Education Office

State Schools Selection
Primary and Middle
Middle
Secondary

Independent Schools Selection
Pre-Preparatory
Preparatory
Senior

Adult Education Centres
Leatherhead
Dorking

SPORTS AND LEISURE FACILITIES 227
General, Sports Councils, Sports Clubs, Badminton,
Bowls, Bridge, Cricket, Cultural Activities, Cycling,
Entertainment, Fishing, Football/Rugby, Gymnastics/Judo,
Ki Aikido Clubs, Libraries, Polo, Pony Clubs, Riding and Livery Stables,
Riding Instruction, Societies, Shooting, Stoolball, Sub-Aqua, Swimming,
Table Tennis, Tennis and Squash, Youth Hostels

GOLF COURSES 235

LOCAL ATTRACTIONS 236

NEWSAGENTS 237
Around the Mole Valley

LOCAL ESTATE AGENTS 241
Ashtead
Fig. 8 Ashtead Estate Agents 241
Visiting Amenities
Bookham
Fig. 9 Bookham Estate Agents 245
Visiting Amenities

	Page
Fig. 10 Dorking Estate Agents	249

Visiting Amenities

Leatherhead
Fig. 11 Leatherhead Estate Agents 253
Visiting Amenities

CHURCHES 256

TEMPORARY ACCOMMODATION 258
Hotels, Motels, Self-catering, Pubs, Farm and Guest Houses
Dorking and District
Leatherhead and District

USEFUL ADDRESSES AND TELEPHONE NUMBERS 261

ADDENDUM

BUDGET CHANGES AND THE OUTLOOK 263
Glossary 264
Notes Pages 265
Floor Plan 268/9
Index to Advertisers 270/1

INSIDE REAR COVER:
Fig. 12 FOLD OUT - Mole Valley Map

Hand drawn maps
Fig 1.   The County of Surrey 82
Fig 2.   Surrey's Main Road Network 89
Fig 3.   Surrey's Main Rail Network 90
Fig 4.   Dorking Map 110
Fig 5.   Leatherhead Map 124
Fig 6.   Ashtead Map 134
Fig 7.   Great Bookham Map 142
Fig 8.   Ashtead Estate Agents 240
Fig 9.   Bookham Estate Agents 244
Fig 10. Dorking Estate Agents 248
Fig 11. Leatherhead Estate Agents 252

Key to Maps
T .... Toilets
P .... Parking
PO .... Post Office

FIRST THOUGHTS ON MOVING AND GETTING STARTED

WHY MOVE?

People do it all the time, don't they? But beware, it can be exciting! So be careful not to let the enthusiasm for the idea over-rule the logic! It seems perhaps, more serious thought is often given to less important matters. In reality moving is expensive, sometimes painful and always hard work - but people do it and enjoy it!

On a serious note, moving is renowned to be one of life's most stressful events and will undoubtedly require a considerable amount of your time and energy. It can be fun, but equally it can be really disappointing. Finding the right home will need much thought, and a little luck! Almost without exception some compromises will have to be reached, no matter how fortunate you are in your search. Beware that like in most things, where there are winners there are losers, stop to think - and be sure not to rush in where angels fear to tread.

Consider the expense

First consider carefully the expense, the actual cost of the move may be much more than you think, let alone the ongoing financial commitments. The physical upheaval and the legwork needed can be exhausting and then there are the numerous people who will need to be informed of your change of address.

Reduce the stress

An organised approach is essential to reduce some of the stress. Above all be prepared for unexpected disappointments, such as the house you really want 'falling through', your buyer letting you down, or the lengthy legal and financial processes producing obstacles. Try to avoid the common, but precarious situation of falling in love with a home you view! Remember 'love is blind' and you may well make an appalling fool of yourself, which will cost you. Be patient and perhaps a bit more fatalistic than usual, it could save you breaking your heart!

Remember, consider your options and be certain your reasons for moving are valid. Make the time to write a list, identifying your priorities about why you want to move - it will be useful to refer to later, especially if you have second thoughts.

Currently the market shows that many people are choosing to 're-mortgage' their homes at the moment. Some of these people may not have wanted to move home in any case, but some may have decided this to be the favourable alternative. For them 'staying put' may have proved to be the better idea once the whole picture was taken into account. Try and make sure therefore that moving home is what you really want, possibly it may not be the best answer and then you certainly will have saved yourself much time and money.

To buy or rent - that is the question?

Renting a home can be preferable to buying in many circumstances, everyone's requirements are different, only you can honestly weigh up the balance of your own needs and priorities. Obviously if you rent, the property is not your own and cannot be treated as such, it can never be your investment, and you may never feel truly settled. However the big advantage is that you are not tying up a large capital sum or committing yourself to a purchase you may be uncertain about. Renting can give you more flexibility and choices in your lifestyle allowing you to spend a larger part of your savings and income on other important things.

Factors affecting your decision may be purely personal considerations, e.g. the time you anticipate being in a particular home and your own financial position, more recently the importance of thinking of outside influences have come into play. It would be true to say that people once convinced that buying a home was the best answer have changed their views and rented instead. Property can never be guaranteed to be an investment, especially short term and the total cost of buying a home, over many years, is often staggering looked at in the cold light of day. The recent recession has generally meant falling house prices, so tenants rather than owner/occupiers, have probably faired better in many instances.

Second thoughts and a final word of warning

So you decide to move and start your research, it may be now that moving proves not to be such a good idea - but beware, looking at new homes does become exciting! The disadvantage then is that everything may gather momentum too quickly, affecting your better judgement. Estate agents and other professionals, have a vested interest in encouraging your move. Take extra time considering any second thoughts you may have. Bear in mind if you enter the property market on a whim, it could be the most expensive mistake you ever make. I mention these pitfalls and experiences to remind you of the saying: 'A wise man learns from his mistakes, an even wiser man learns from other peoples'!

To sum up: Be organised. Be cautious. Be realistic. But be optimistic!

SO YOU REALLY WANT TO MOVE

Of course, in reality many people do move home successfully - and so can you! The best way to get started can be difficult to decide and will always depend on your own position. If you have a home to sell first before you buy another, this is the most tricky situation!

If you intend to rent a new home some of your considerations are of a different nature, you will still want the best home at the best price and you will need to research the market. However possibly your selection will be easier and the very large financial commitment at the outset, in comparison with those buying, will not be one of your major concerns.

For those looking to buy, many of you will also have a home to sell. Normally you will be aiming to complete the sale of your old home on exactly the same day that you purchase the new one, inevitably this 'ideal timing' can raise problems. Obviously you don't want to be rushed into buying, so you may have to come to terms with selling your home first and finding temporary accommodation during the interim period. This may seem a big disadvantage and will undoubtedly lead to extra trouble and expense at first. However to recommend it, you then become the ideal purchaser with nothing to sell and perhaps bargains to be found!

Testing the water!

Whether buying or renting begin to have a general look at the market and see if the sort of home you want can be afforded. Be realistic and keep your feet on the ground, nearly everyone spends more than they want to, this can then mean years of working all the hours God sends to make ends meet - beware! At this stage make as much use as you can of advertisements in newspapers, gathering information. Don't be tempted to get on estate agents mailing lists too soon. If you do there is a danger they may try to rush this important research stage by being very keen to get your instructions (to sell your present home as well). Take as long as you like, this may be the last time you stay totally in control!

N.B. If you have to sell your home as well, as a general rule, my best advice would be to get it on the market *as soon as you are certain you want to move*. How you do this is a choice for you. This will allow you to get a feel for what your property is really worth - probably an essential factor. You will then be generally taken more seriously as a potential buyer, by the vendor of a property and/or their possible agents. The further along the process you are of selling your own property, the greater your bargaining power to purchase. Naturally the best situation to be in, is the 'cash buyer' with no home to sell, then you can be more ruthless in your offers and 'call the shots' - beware though you too can fall in love with a particular property and pay too much!

Taking the plunge!

Preferably this should be a gradual process, however it is easy to get swept off your feet! Once you are in the market the ball starts rolling and the speed is not easy to control. It can be too fast, or equally too slow, in comparison with your own expectations; stopping it altogether can be very much more difficult than starting it. Often the speed of proceedings is just luck, although you should be able to exert some influence, there may always be elements of surprise. Remember that there will be a lot of people involved in the transaction, financial and legal matters take time and people can change their minds! If you need more time for any reason, insist you get it and consider very carefully the advice that you are given, *especially by professionals acting for you.* Last, but not least - Good luck!

To sum up: Don't be rushed

Don't pin your hopes too high

Don't give up!

STEP BY STEP

Ten Commandments for Moving Home!

1) Analyse carefully your reasons for moving

2) Decide on exactly what you can afford

3) Make a list of the priorities for your new home

4) Identify areas where you are willing to compromise

5) Consider whether to buy or rent

6) Start your research looking at local property papers

7) Put your own home on the market early on

8) Contact estate agents and spread your research to other corners of the property market and private advertising

9) Stay optimistic, despite disappointments, often something better is round the corner

10) Never throw caution to the wind!

Equestrian Country Home Insurance

If you keep your horses on your own property, we have the policy for you. Cutting the cost, and even more importantly, giving you the cover that you really need in one convenient policy, payable if required, by monthly direct debit

Extensive research has produced the Equestrian Country Home Policy which enables you to select the level of cover you need for:

- Home – buildings and contents
- Stables, barns and all outbuildings (full cover available)
- Garden and field machinery (including tractors)
- Hay, straw, feed and tack
- Third party, employers and property liabilities
- Livestock

This policy is available for both commercially and privately used properties.

CALL FOR DETAILS
01708 850000
and ask for Jacky Smith

SOUTH ESSEX
INSURANCE BROKERS

BUYING AND SELLING
A SUMMARY FOR PURCHASERS AND VENDORS

PURCHASER'S CONSIDERATIONS
Timing

The timing of your move will be personal to you, but try not to let it coincide with other important happenings like having a holiday or even a baby! You will be taking on a stressful situation anyway just moving, ideally try to plan for it to take place during a period of calm and stability!

Beyond personal considerations, if you are a first time buyer *you* will be most influenced by the state of the property market. On a 'rising' market, as fast as you save for a deposit you may never catch up the gap, the home you want ever increasing in price. With prices stable or falling you can take all the time you like, saving as much as possible and really looking for bargains.

With a home of your own to sell, remember overall prices will mean that if yours isn't as valuable as you thought, you should also find one relatively inexpensive to buy. In other words the gap in prices between homes will generally stay the same. Now might be a good time to stress, that if you make a 'wrong move' in a stable or falling market you are very likely to be stuck with it, or lose a lot of money. With prices rising a mistake is not so critical and can probably be rectified by moving again soon, perhaps even without losing capital!

The Area
Without question **this is the single, most important choice to be made,** where your home is located will always reflect its value, more than any other factor.

The location cannot be changed by you, other matters like the size and condition of the property often can be. This priority therefore, should be given more thought than anything else. If you already know exactly where you want to move this is advantageous, *the more you know about the location the better* (hence this publication!). However, quite often the exact area is flexible in people's minds, sometimes places are not known at all and yet still come within the general boundary considered possible.

Remember: 'The right house in the wrong place is the wrong house'.

The Price

Give careful consideration to the size of the commitment you are taking on and remember the horror stories we have all heard. Nasty things don't always happen to other people, overstretching yourself financially can seriously damage your health and your relationships. Buying a home isn't covered by a government health warning, but it should be! After all, it is the government and the Bank of England who will determine the variable monthly cost of your home with their 'interest rate' policies. There is so much uncertainty about the future, you must leave yourself room to manoeuvre, or suffer the consequences. Mortgage lenders should take into account your whole financial situation and only lend responsibly, in the end they may be the only people to save you from yourself, but even they cannot predict a sudden illness or loss of job. Nevertheless in the long-term, your property should be a good investment and to many a source of great joy and pride. Owning a home of your choice is a solid base from which to extend the rest of your lifestyle, it should be a pleasure to come back to after a hard day at work! This ideal is generally what drives buyers on and, if accomplished, your home can become one of life's greatest rewards.

The Type and Condition of the Property

The type of home you wish to find and its condition must next be borne in mind. Although it is always best to remain flexible, someone who is thinking of buying a new property will have very different considerations from someone purchasing an older home. It is difficult for a new building to have the same 'atmosphere' as an older home, but there are many advantages as can be seen:

Advantages of a New Property

* Major repairs and redecoration should be unnecessary in the first few years
* Most new houses will come with a ten-year NHBC* warranty
* If the house is unfinished, your own modifications might be incorporated by the builder
* The finances to be arranged can come in an 'attractive package', sometimes meaning a smaller deposit than normal, sometimes including a part-exchange deal on your old home
* Security is more likely to be 'designed in' to your new home as it is high on the list of requirements in most people's minds

Disadvantages of a New Property - Mostly 'teething troubles'!
* The completion date can be uncertain and extends beyond initial expectations
* There may be temporary problems such as new plaster drying and creating cracks
* The approach roads and gardens may not be finished
* The rear garden can be a 'sea of mud' and left entirely to you
* Check that fixtures and fittings are those you agreed
* Responsibility for drains, roads and boundaries need to be clarified
* The price of a new house is seldom negotiable

Advantages of An Older House
* Most older houses will have more of a sense of 'character' and even 'history'
* You cannot buy a new 'period' property, and people love them!
* The building, grounds and surroundings are there to be seen - for better or worse!
* Often comparably larger rooms than found in new homes, at the same price
* Often thicker internal walls, reducing noise between rooms
* Often built on bigger plots of land

Disadvantages of An Older House - Mostly expense!
* Possibly larger than expected expenses in repairs and maintenance
* Hidden costs in replacing electrics, plumbing, damp-course, windows etc.
* Lengthy wait for planning permission and building regulations before making improvements
* Older kitchens may often be smaller than required
* Generally there may be too few bathrooms or washing facilities
* Additional hard work of cleaning and probably redecoration to your tastes
* Listed properties need special considerations (see our special section).

Other Types of Purchase
Apart from the general type of home-buying in the open market, there are other types to be mentioned such as:

Buying from a Local Authority
Tenants who have lived in a council house for three years or more have 'a right to buy' at a substantial discount. A leaflet *'Your Right to Buy Your Home'* is available from the Department of the Environment (Tel: 0171 276 0900).

Buying from a Housing Association

This scheme was established to help people buy 'a percentage' of the property, then as they could afford more, they could buy more, known as 'staircasing'. When selling in this position, the percentage share could be sold on to a new purchaser. More information may be obtained from the Housing Corporation (Tel: 0171 393 2000).

Where To Find Available Homes

This big subject has its own separate section of the same name.

Viewing and Research

Again there is a separate section for this subject.

The Offer to Buy

When you are happy that you have found the home of your choice now comes the offer to buy, you may do this before the property is surveyed or afterwards. Remember that you may also apply for planning permission on property which does not belong to you. This may be a relevant factor if considering purchasing a home you would like to alter, thereby making sure *before purchase*, that alterations will be approved. Remember too that you are under no obligation to buy until 'Exchange of Contracts' which will be some way off. However it has been normal practice to pay the estate agent an initial deposit in the region of £250 as a 'token of intent' when the offer is made. Establish if this is refundable before agreeing to pay, it is not legally binding. Use the time delay between your offer and 'Exchange of Contracts' to your advantage, by carrying on checking and double checking your decision is the right one. Changing your mind after putting in an offer might be costly, but listen carefully to your professional advisers and your own second thoughts, ignoring them could be far more costly.

Your initial offer: This will be influenced by the following considerations and perhaps others:

The vendor's position: Are they keen to move out? Is there vacant possession? Is there a 'chain'*? Are other purchasers truly in competition with you? - (not always easy to establish). What does the price include?

Your position: Likewise the offer may be influenced by your own position. How keen are you to move? Are you in a strong position to bargain? Are you happy to risk losing this property? How might you feel about starting all over again? If you are selling as well, is your buyer reliable?

The state of the property market: Generally this may also affect your offer, sometimes there is a distinct 'buyers' or 'sellers' market. If there are similar properties nearby, see how well their asking prices compare.

It is wise to make the offer 'subject to survey and contract', verbally and then in writing. It may be made in person, or through the agent, if there is one. Estate agents are often keen to negotiate and stress the importance of their role at this point in proceedings. It is a matter for you, in each case, whether you approach the vendor directly or not. I have known agents positively discourage free access and communication between vendor and purchaser, preferring always to act as intermediary. This can be helpful, or very annoying, depending on the personalities involved, all I would say is resist being dominated by them!

Financial and Legal Matters

The next section covers these main points to be considered.

The Time Delay

There are often many frustrations surrounding the progress of the transaction, no two cases are ever the same, just be prepared to accept this from the outset. There are many stories such as people disappearing on holiday just when contracts are due to be exchanged, let alone allowing for solicitors, surveyors, mortgage lenders and others to take their time.

Exchange of Contracts and Completion

The last two 'big steps' and then your next home is legally your own, covered more fully in the next section, 'Financial and Legal Matters'.

Moving In

See the 'Moving Checklist' section to help you as an 'aide-memoire'.

VENDOR'S CONSIDERATIONS

Timing

As with buyers, this will be personal to you, but there are traditionally better times of the year to sell than others. The spring is the obvious favourite and there is often a 'lull' in the summer holidays and during the Christmas period. It can be argued that if you market your property at the most popular times of the year, there is likely to be the most competition, but equally 'out-of-season' times can be very slow. I would say go ahead anytime of year. We viewed a house once on the 23rd December. On that occasion the timing was perfect for us and we completed the purchase soon after. Above all, try to avoid the situation of being rushed or forced to sell.

The state of the general property market may well influence you too. However remember that although you may not get as good a price as you were hoping for your own sale, most other homes will be following the same trend. Once you are on the 'property ladder' your home's position on it will more-or-less stay the same.

The Best Price

Naturally you will want to achieve the best possible price. If there are a few minor jobs that need doing to make the property look much more appealing, now would be the best time to get them done. It is surprising how much better a tidy up and a coat of paint can make! However, if the property you have needs a lot of up-dating, there is an argument to leave it as it is, there are many purchasers who want to take on this work themselves.

When you have decided on the price you will accept for your home, make the original 'asking price' higher. How much higher will be in proportion to the original cost, possibly *at the most* about 10% i.e. a home worth £350,000, might first try an asking price of £375,000 or even £395,000, by the same principle a home worth £50,000 might only ask £55,000 or £57,500. It would be wise to have an open mind on the figure you hope to realise, you may well find that you will change your opinion as time passes whilst your property is on the market.

Recently we know that most 'mainstream' properties have been only selling at very 'realistic' prices, your home is only worth what someone else will actually pay for it. Over-pricing it too much will result in little interest and then advertising will be a waste of money. Try not to allow it to 'stagnate' on the market as buyers will become more suspicious, ideally you should aim to get a firm buyer *at least within six months*. So, if you wish, start with the higher price for a short period, you can always lower it.

Finding a Buyer

The majority of owners probably decide to sell their homes through estate agents (see their separate section), but there are other ways. You may certainly consider advertising and selling yourself and then there are 'Property Registers', auctions and even raffles! Sometimes prospective purchasers advertise if they want to buy a home in 'Property Wanted' columns. Also don't underestimate the power of 'word-of-mouth', many desirable homes sell before they ever reach the open market.

Advertising Your Own Home Yourself

The Advantages

The cost of you advertising your home successfully may well be a great deal less than an estate agent's charges. Why not take on the marketing of your own home? After all you are normally the person who knows it best anyway. If you have the time to market your home and carry out the necessary research, this could be your best and most economic move!

The Mechanics!

You will need some particulars of your home to send to interested parties and keep as a reference for yourself, especially when answering the phone. It is not difficult to describe your property as well as an estate agent, why not pick up a few ideas from them? First look at particulars they produce, preferably on a similar type of property and use them as a guide. Also read the 'Estate Agents' section of this book it will help you. Notice they concentrate on room sizes, radiators, windows, sockets and fitted cupboards for each room. Room sizes may be measured in feet and inches and/or metric, most people will still favour the old measurements. Be as accurate as possible, in any case to the nearest 3 inches, measuring from one internal wall surface to the other. Remember to include where a room narrows. The kitchen normally takes the most time to describe. ***Don't include anything in your description that is not included in the sale or cannot be proved.*** Carpets and curtains may be subject to negotiation later, but fixtures and fittings always form part of the property to be sold. Outside, the garaging and room for car parking must be mentioned as well as approximate garden measurements. Remember to mention the utility services connected to your property. Optional information might include which way the garden faces, or if any of the property has a shared right-of-way, i.e. a driveway etc. There might be quite a lot more you know about your own home that you could sensibly describe, but stay factual, only including what you know to be true.

Honesty is always the best policy in your description, ***'The Property Misdescriptions Act 1991' makes it a criminal offence to mislead a prospective buyer.***

Tip: When thinking of selling your property it becomes apparent just how important it will have been to keep a written record of any improvements that have been made. Get in the habit of keeping a sort of 'log book' for your home. Receipts and guarantees will need to be produced to prove what work has been done over the years. Like estate agents, you are not allowed to describe any improvements in your property, without the written evidence to support it.

Last, but not least, there is nothing so important as a colour photograph, (or colour laser copy) preferably taken on a sunny day and after you've tidied up and done the gardening! Obtain at least a dozen copies to include on your particulars and don't forget the obvious like the address, good directions and contact phone numbers.

If your home is so placed that a 'For Sale' Board would be useful, make a good job of one and erect it somewhere safe and prominent on your own property. This will surely be your cheapest form of advertising and it might well do the trick!

Postcards in local newsagents windows can also be surprisingly successful and, of course advertise in your local newspaper(s). National newspapers and magazines are worth considering, but are often too general and very expensive - a matter for you. There are other ways to advertise, the more people that know the better; the separate section 'Where To Find Available Homes' should help you with ideas.

The publicity you have worked on must be matched by a good answering service when you expect enquiries, don't time your advertisements to come out on a weekend you are away! If you cannot be in for a while, make sure of a good answer phone message (or better still a message answering service) people will quickly get fed up if they have to ring more than once. Be prepared for questions when people view your home, so do some homework. More serious buyers may like to see evidence of the general running costs, guarantees on work done, servicing on central heating etc. and even if you've never needed to before, find out about the local bus route and schools etc.!

The Disadvantages

The biggest disadvantages of selling your own home are the 'immediate' costs of the advertising and the feeling of 'going-it-alone'. It may take a lot of confidence to be positive about selling your own home yourself, especially if you don't get the interest you expect. However, if you are prepared to take the time and make the effort, you will lose little and stand much to gain by at least giving it a try first. Even if you are not successful and consequently instruct an estate agent, you will feel happier about paying their commission!

Don't forget you can still do some of your own marketing, even having instructed an estate agent. Just be careful that there isn't a conflict with them over whose advertising brought the introduction of any prospective buyer.

Showing People Round

Whether through an estate agent or not, make sure you are 'happy' with the people viewing your home. Especially when advertising yourself, follow a few simple steps to maximise security for you and your property.

* Make a double check on enquirers' details, at least take their name and telephone number, ring the number back, you can always make an excuse why you had to! (Estate agents should have these details of their clients)

* When showing people round make sure that you have hidden small valuable items from view and, if you are doubtful, don't arrange appointments when you will be alone
* If they arrive in a car, discreetly record the registration mark
* In short, don't invite crime by being thoughtless, careless or over trusting. Viewing your home is a wonderful way for a criminal to see exactly what there is to steal

Moving Out

Hopefully you will have your next home (whether temporary or permanent) arranged well in advance of this stressful day itself. Refer to the 'Moving Checklist' section for an 'aide-memoire'. Remember it will be very useful indeed for your purchasers if you leave them a note along the following lines:

* Local services - i.e. milk and newspaper deliveries - where from and when
* Refuse collection - which day of the week, where to put the dustbins
* Post - the local post office, nearest post box and normal delivery times
* Local servicemen recommended - i.e. window cleaner, plumber etc.
* Immediate neighbours' names - who you'd like to introduce!

The Good *move* Guide always welcomes news, views and interesting stories from its readers, share some of your 'moving experiences!' The next edition will include the best of these on a 'Readers Page', all those printed will receive a £20.00 cash prize.
So get writing!

FINANCIAL AND LEGAL

PURCHASER'S RESPONSIBILITIES
The Mortgage

Arranging the right mortgage will be the most important consideration of all, but listing and explaining all your choices is not a subject covered here. There will be many professionals only too willing to help you, as lenders and brokers will earn money from the deal in one way or another. Remember to compare only the *A.P.R.* Interest Rates* and ensure that you get the *'best advice'*.

For the life you don't yet know.

Allied Dunbar can help plan your finances - now and in the future. Using their Personal Financial Planning Service, I can highlight those areas you need to consider to ensure you achieve your financial goals.

Contact me for your financial review - there is no obligation. We can examine:

- Life Assurance for your family security
- Special cover for critical illnesses
- Pension planning for maximum retirement benefits
- Mortgage services
- Financial services for your business
- Income protection for sickness or disability
- Healthcare needs for your family
- School fees planning, investment and savings opportunities
- Inheritance tax liabilities and their mitigation
- Will writing services

Tony Birtwell Financial Adviser. Allied Dunbar House, Chilsey Green Road, Chertsey, Surrey KT16 9HB. Telephone: 01932 568888 Daytime. Home: Upper Lodge, Holmbury Hill Road, Holmbury St Mary, Surrey RH5 6NR Telephone: 01306 730894 evenings.
Representing only the Allied Dunbar Marketing Group, which is regulated by the Personal Investment Authority, in relation to life assurance, pensions and investment plans bearing Allied Dunbar's name.

Where to get the Best Advice?

There are really *two* different types of financial advisers that can offer you their services; *'tied agents'* who are allied to major financial institutions and alternatively *'independent mortgage brokers'*. *Both* types are able to search for the best mortgage on the market to suit you. The difference is that *'tied agents'* will earn most of their commission from the policies they sell with the mortgage, whereas *'independent mortgage brokers'* receive most of their income from selling you the actual mortgage they arrange.

It is important to remember that moving home is normally a very appropriate time to review *all* your finances. Your new home is likely to be just one of a whole range of financial commitments you will have in the future, so taking time at this vital stage will help avoid long-term mistakes. With expert advice, it may be that you are pleasantly surprised by the many choices you have. Nowadays mortgages and investment policies can be arranged in all sorts of ways, but be prepared for such a review to take more time than you thought!

For example, it may be advisable to arrange a mortgage before you even start to look around the property market. A mortgage offer can be reserved in advance of you finding the right property, but the funds put aside will have a time limit. So by thinking ahead you can give yourself a crucial head start.....sometimes this may even be the difference between you buying the home you want or not!

For your further information a list of bone-fide independent brokers in each appropriate area may be obtained by writing to the British Insurance and Investment Brokers Association, BIIBA House, 14 Bevis Marks, London EC3A 7NT (Tel: 0171 623 9043).

Tip - Remember that some other professionals offering advice on where to obtain mortgages, perhaps estate agents or even your own bank, are rarely independent. After all it is noticeable that estate agents are often owned by insurance companies, banks or building societies

---

WHEN RESPONDING TO ADVERTISEMENTS
PLEASE MENTION THE 'GOOD *move* GUIDE'

INVESTING FOR
GROWTH

TAX
PLANNING

PLANNING FOR
RETIREMENT

PRIVATE/ FURTHER
EDUCATION
FEE PLANNING

INVESTING
FOR INCOME

BUYING
A HOME

FINANCIAL
PLANNING

ETHICAL
INVESTING

INCOME
PROTECTION

WHAT ARE YOUR FINANCIAL INTERESTS?

Friends Provident have been successfully helping clients in many of these areas for over 160 years. Currently Friends Provident manage assets approaching £13 billion and over 2½ million policies. Friends Provident First Call works on a salaried basis ensuring a professional approach.

A Comprehensive and quality range of pension plans and investments, competitive protection products, and the first and largest portfolio of ethical investment funds in the UK.

All of this means that whatever your financial interest, Friends Provident can help.

At every stage of your life, Friends Provide.

To find out more please contact:-

**Friends Provident First Call Limited
Ground Floor
APP House
100 Station Road
Horsham
West Sussex RH13 5XA**

Tel: **01403 271100**

REPRESENTATIVE ONLY OF THE FRIENDS PROVIDENT MARKETING GROUP,
WHICH IS REGULATED BY THE PERSONAL INVESTMENT AUTHORITY,
FOR LIFE ASSURANCE, PENSION AND UNIT TRUST BUSINESS

The range of pension, investment and protection plans is provided by Friends' Provident Life Office.
The range Unit Trusts and PEPs is provided by Friends' Provident Unit Trust Managers Limited.

The Cost of the Mortgage

The initial cost will be made up of the following in all cases:
* the lender's valuation fees
* the lender's legal fees
* your own legal fees (unless you are doing your own conveyancing)

In addition, these further fees may be incurred:
* the cost of advisers or brokers (see above)
* mortgage indemnity policy (often required if your loan is a very high percentage of the price of the property, see below)
* mortgage protection insurance (policies to ensure that your mortgage continues to be paid for a limited period if you fall on hard times, or paid off in full if you die)

Mortgage Indemnity Policy

Reputed to be one of the mortgage industry's best kept secrets (and sometimes called different names) don't be caught out wondering what this extra expense is and who benefits from it.

The lenders take out this insurance to cover themselves against the risk involved in advancing larger loans, it covers the costs of repossessing and reselling a property should a borrower default. In particular, it is used to meet any shortfall between the outstanding loan and the price the lender gets for the property. However, although it is the lender who benefits from the insurance, it is the borrower (the homeowner) who pays the bill. Even more horrifying is the fact that if the insurance is paid out to a lender, the insurance company can then chase the original homeowner for reimbursement, at any time over the following twelve years. Mortgage Indemnity Policies are associated with loans normally over 75% (occasionally 80%) of the property's value, so if a purchaser is able to raise at least 25% of the purchase price they will not apply.

Mortgage Interest Relief

The first £30,000 interest repayments on a mortgage borrowed to purchase your home (not a second property) is currently subject to 15% tax relief. In other words the government assists the borrower a *little* up to this limit.

ADVERTISEMENT FEATURE

THE GOOD, THE BAD AND THE ENDOWMENT

Arranging a mortgage involves being faced with a startling array of choice. You have to choose a lender (a **Bank** or **Building Society**), an interest rate (**fixed, capped, variable** or **discounted**) *a*nd finally a way of paying back the mortgage (**interest only** or **repayment**).

So what's best for you?

Your choice of lender and interest rate depends on your preference. How you repay your mortgage, however, depends on your attitude to risk, your circumstances and how much you know about how the two methods work. With repayment mortgages, part of the money paid to the lender each month pays off the loan and the rest pays the interest on the amount outstanding. Separate life assurance is generally required to repay the loan should the borrower die during the mortgage term.

With interest only mortgages, the whole amount paid to the lender each month pays the interest because the loan itself remains at the same level for the entire mortgage term, at the end of which the original amount borrowed must be repaid with funds accumulated in a separate savings policy (this is typically an **endowment** policy, hence the term **'endowment mortgage'***)*.

With an endowment policy, some of your money will be put into a 'pot' or fund of your choice - this might be a **With Profit Fund** which allocates regular bonuses to your plan depending on the size and distribution of profits made by your insurance company, or a **Unit Linked Fund**, in which your premiums purchase 'units', the value of which will go **up and down** depending on the underlying investment performance of the fund chosen. It will also provide life cover which should be equal to the mortgage amount.

Endowment plans have suffered from a great deal of criticism in recent years: consumer watchdogs, financial journalists and the Office of Fair Trading have all had their say, usually bad!

Is the criticism fair?

One of the main criticisms of the endowment is whether it gives value for money - it is pointed out that, in the first few years of its life, an endowment will almost certainly pay back less than has been paid in if it is 'cashed in' or 'surrendered'. This does not mean that repayment mortgages necessarily provide better value for money.

5An endowment policy is a long term contract, which usually runs for 25 years (the normal mortgage term) so it is certainly not a good idea to surrender any endowment policy as only by allowing it to run full term will you fully benefit from this type of investment.

In the first few years of a repayment mortgage, the interest portion of the premium paid to the lender each month is so high, there is little left over to pay off the loan and so a borrower paying off a 25 year repayment mortgage in full after, say, 5 years would be mistaken if he expected the loan to have reduced by 20%.

continued/..................................

Recent falls in this tax relief from 25% to 15% indicates that perhaps it may not continue at all very much longer.

To clarify what this is: Tax relief at 15% means with every £10 owed in interest, the borrower will only pay £8.50 (and the government £1.50) up to the limit of £30,000. Any part of the loan interest above this is paid in full by the borrower. Most mortgages are within the MIRAS* scheme so this all happens 'At Source' and you will not particularly notice it.

The Legal fees

You will normally instruct a solicitor or 'licensed conveyancer' to oversee the legal formalities. Conveyancing is possible to do yourself, but is not a subject covered here. If you do not have a preferred solicitor or conveyancer already, get estimates from any that are recommended, there are so many from which to choose. Remember this fee, like that of the valuer or surveyor, is subject to VAT at 17.5%.

The Valuer's and/or Surveyor's fee

This will amount to a substantial figure, depending on the price of the house and what type of survey is completed. If you are borrowing money to buy your home, at the very least the lender will insist on someone valuing it and you will be responsible for the valuer's charges.

For your own peace of mind you may well consider it worth the extra expense of additional advice on the soundness of your potential home. You may do this by having a *house buyer's report* which is coupled with the valuation. This will tell you more (and cost you more) than a straight valuation, but it may give you the extra peace of mind you wanted.

A *full structural survey,* carried out by a surveyor, will give you the most information possible and although it will cost you the most, it may save you the most as well. Any defects found by it will put you in a strong position to discuss with the vendor that your original offer should be reduced accordingly to allow for the costs of repairs. The scales of charges you may expect, are set out in booklets obtainable from the Royal Institution of Chartered Surveyors.

ADVERTISEMENT FEATURE   continuation/.............

Another criticism of endowments is the uncertainty about their ability to repay mortgages, because of poor equity investment returns in the early 1990s giving rise to lower maturity payouts on Unit Linked and With Profit endowment plans. Although it cannot be guaranteed that an endowment plan will pay off your mortgage, endowments generally perform better then deposit based investments over the longer term and have regularly repaid mortgage loans AND provided their owners with a **cash surplus** at maturity to spend as they wish (a 'bonus' you will **never** achieve with a repayment mortgage).

25 years is a long time and although past performance is not necessarily a guide to the future, the long term trend of equity investment, even including the worst of all the stockmarket 'crashes' has been up. By making conservative assumptions about future investment returns from the start of a plan, endowment premiums are set at a realistic level that should ensure a sufficient fund at maturity to repay the mortgage. Insurance companies will normally build in review dates to the plan to check on its growth and advise policyholders of any potential shortfall. This allows time to make up any difference by paying additional premiums into their endowment.

Choosing the right insurance company for your mortgage endowment is obviously important as, regardless of how the stockmarket is performing in the short term, you need a company that has historically provided good long term results on this type of investment. Friends Provident, established in 1832, has just such a reputation. As well as providing excellent returns on a range of products (including endowments) through expert fund management and prudent investment strategies, they are today one of the most successful insurance and investment companies in the United Kingdom, managing nearly £13 billion of money worldwide.

First Call, the financial planning arm of Friends Provident, is able to offer advice on what type of mortgage is best suited to you and how to apply for it. If you are confused as to which mortgage to apply for, or would like some guidance on the house buying process, please contact your local Friends Provident First Call office.

Friends Provident First Call is a representative only of the Friends Provident Marketing Group, which is regulated by the Personal Investment Authority, for Life Assurance, Pension and Unit Trust business.

Past performance is not necessarily a guide to the future. For Unit Linked policies, the value of a plan depends on the underlying investment performance of the fund chosen and the value can go down as well as up and is never guaranteed. For With Profit policies, the value depends on the profits that Friends Provident makes and on the decisions it takes as to their distribution.

Your home is at risk if you do not keep up repayments on a mortgage or other loan secured on it.

Friends Provident First Call can provide written mortgage quotations on request.

Tip - Advice on the selection of a Chartered Surveyor in any part of the United Kingdom and information about the Institution of Chartered Surveyors may be obtained from:

> The Royal Institution of Chartered Surveyors,
> 12 Great George Street,
> Parliament Square,
> London SW1P 3AD   Telephone: 0171 222 7000

Stamp Duty

This is the tax payable on the purchase price of a home costing above a certain figure (currently 1% if the price is over £60,000). For example: Price £75,000 - stamp duty £750.

Land Registry fee

This is paid on a scale related to the purchase price, for most properties it may be anything up to a few hundred pounds. It finances the searches made into the title and ownership of the property, again subject to VAT at 17.5%.

Local Authority searches

Charged for checks on planning permission in the area, not a large sum in comparison to other costs.

Exchange of Contracts

When all the searches have been completed and the 'Enquiries Before Contract' questions answered, the relevant documents are physically swopped over between purchaser and vendor. In other words the contracts signed by both relevant parties are exchanged. The sale then becomes a legal agreement from which neither side can withdraw and is supported by the purchaser's deposit. The date for completion of the sale is agreed and stipulated in the contracts. *Responsibility for insurance of the building also normally passes to the purchaser at this stage.*

The Deposit

Traditionally this has been a figure of 10% of the asking price required at the time of 'Exchange of Contracts'. These days it may be possible to pay less, so establish what is expected early on with your solicitor. The figure of 10% should be allowed for in normal circumstances. If you are selling at the same time as buying, it may be possible to get a bridging loan* for this deposit from your bank. This is then repayable on the completion of the sale of your present home, which would normally be only 4 weeks from the date of exchange. A bridging loan is very expensive and is generally not recommended for longer periods.

Buildings and Contents Insurance

Responsibility for the building insurance lies with the purchaser normally at the exchange of contracts. Check to see what is expected.

Countdown to Completion

This is a useful time to confirm your arrangements for moving and a busy time for the legal matters to be finalised. Normally about 28 days after 'exchange', completion is the day when the purchaser pays the vendor the balance of the price for the property and the vendor must move out. The deeds and keys are now handed over to the purchaser.

Removal Expenses

These can be determined by you to a certain extent. If you are using a professional firm, allow plenty of time and get several different quotations before you make your choice. If property needs to go into storage at all, this should be thought about at the same time. Some companies now offer containerised packaging at source, so there is minimum handling of your furniture. Even 'doing-it-yourself' is fairly expensive, hiring a large van and possibly some help.

VENDOR'S RESPONSIBILITIES

Estate Agent's Commission

If you employ a 'traditional' estate agent, their commission on the sale of your home plus VAT will probably be your largest cost for which to budget. As explained earlier there are estate agents who charge on a different basis, but their fees will still always run into hundreds of pounds at a minimum. Very recently, some estate agents linked to Building Societies are offering a free service to vendors if they undertake to mortgage their new home with the relevant society. So costs in this respect can be different and are worth investigating.

Advertising

If you do not instruct an estate agent, other forms of advertising will obviously cost you any amount of money and only you will be able to control how much!

Legal Fees

This will be your only other major cost and will vary in accordance with the price of your home for sale and the time spent upon the transaction.

Mortgage Redemption

There may be a redemption penalty to pay on your mortgage when you cancel the contract by selling your home. If you take out a new mortgage for your next home with the same bank or building society, this is often waived, but bear in mind this cost and the restrictions in choice it places upon you to avoid it.

Exchange and Completion

As discussed above 'Exchange of Contracts' makes the transaction legally binding and 'Completion' normally follows some 28 days later. It should be emphasised here that the keys to the property should never be handed over early to the prospective purchaser, only on the day of completion.

Removal Expenses

As with the buyer's responsibilities you too will need to consider this cost and to budget for it.

Capital Gains Tax

If the property has been used as your main or sole residence no capital gains tax will be payable on any net profit. If the property has been an investment, my advice would be to instruct an accountant to help you. Normally the sale of investment property is subject to Capital Gains Tax, but there are exceptions in certain circumstances.

LETTING AND RENTING
A SUMMARY FOR LANDLORDS AND TENANTS

LANDLORD'S CONSIDERATIONS

Can I Let?
Before you think of renting your property at all you must make sure that you can! If the property is mortgaged or has other finance owing on it, the lenders will need to know. This may be your first stumbling block, some will not agree to it being rented at all, others only if certain conditions are met, e.g. new accommodation being provided with a new job. If you already rent your home it is unlikely that you can 'sub-let' it again. The terms of your buildings and contents insurance will also be affected, although this is normally quite a simple matter to sort out.

How Do I Let?
Remember you may seek free estimates on the property's likely rental value from lettings agents without obligation. Think about renting the property unfurnished, partly furnished or fully furnished and what you expect to realise as income.

Early on you must come to terms with the fact that someone else will be in your home and that necessary wear and tear will occur, if not other accidental damage or worse. Unlike selling and making a clean break, with renting your home, it will remain your responsibility. There is always a danger of something going wrong, which ultimately you will have to sort out. These risks must be minimised with the best preparation by you and your agent and with the most

appropriate tenancy agreement being agreed. In every case, insist on seeing a number of references concerning your potential tenant's character and financial status.

By understanding what the tenant will be considering in the next section, if you wish to let your property successfully, make sure you have the relevant answers to hand. You may tackle renting your home yourself, if so it would normally be advisable to have the assistance of a solicitor. It may be that

you know someone who would like to rent your property or who sees it through your own private advertising.

However, more commonly, you may instruct a letting agent, when a commission will be required on a 'tenant finding' or 'full management' basis. If you choose a reputable letting agent, their experience and familiarity with the proceedings may negate you having to take independent legal advice - they will draw up the necessary tenancy documents, explain and help you through the proceedings.

The Inventory

It is always advisable to make an inventory of your property's contents before the beginning of the tenancy, this can then be agreed at the outset and referred to later in the event of any disagreement. You may do this yourself, through the appointed agent or by using an independent specialist. **N.B.** Recent legislation requires that landlord's furnishings must be fire resistant under the Furnishings (Fire and Safety) Regulations.

To sum up:
*Can you rent your property?
*What amount of income can you expect?
*Unfurnished/partly or fully furnished?
*Duration and type of tenancy?
*Buildings and contents insurance?
*Advertise for tenants
*Compile inventory
*See references first

DON'T FORGET TO RETURN
The Good *move* Guide Market Research Questionnaire
A few minutes of your time could win you a prize worth £200
2nd prize is a £20.00 voucher for dining at 'Pizza Piazza',
third prize will be FREE entrance to one of Surrey's main
attractions Hampton Court Palace (valid for up to 5 people).

TENANT'S CONSIDERATIONS
The Priorities

Your first considerations will be very different from the landlords, you will need to identify the priorities for your new home and you should at least be prepared to compromise on the less important points. This will give you the best chance to find a suitable property fairly quickly. Consider very carefully the 'pros and cons' of renting as opposed to buying, in individual circumstances it may, or may not, be a simple choice. The obvious big advantages are not having to commit to a big initial outlay or an indefinite long-term obligation. Normally you will consider most of the following:

* The maximum rent payable
* Duration and type of tenancy
* Minimum size of accommodation
* Furnished/Unfurnished
* Location (transport, schools, shops, recreation etc.)
* Parking and garden requirements

Research

Look in local papers for your initial research, you will probably need to contact a number of letting agents in the area for the best selection. First dismiss properties that obviously do not suit you from the choice available and then make a short list of the rest. If you can, view the location and outside of those you like before asking to see their interiors, this may save time for everyone concerned. Then go ahead and pick the best options to view fully, the more you see the better you will be able to judge value for money yourself. Remember to establish the terms regarding the following points:

* Maintenance and management responsibilities
* Insurance of building and contents
* Furnishings and fixtures included
* Deposit required
* References required
* Inventory
* Financial liability for 'utilities' bills and council tax
* Length of rental/possible variations

TENANCY AGREEMENTS

Lettings under the Housing Act 1988

Part I of the Housing Act 1988 came into force on 15th January 1989. Most new lettings made on or after that date by private landlords, who do not live in the same property as their tenants, will be **assured tenancies** or **assured shorthold tenancies**. It is always advisable to enter into a written agreement; if a reputable letting agent familiar with dealing in these matters is not involved, then a solicitor's services should be considered.

Assured Tenancies

The tenant will have long-term security of tenure and he does not have to go unless the landlord has grounds for regaining possession which he can prove in court. There are both mandatory and discretionary grounds that a court may consider before granting the landlord repossession of the property. The tenancy may be fixed in the first place for a number of months or years when it is called a **fixed term tenancy** or it may be for an indefinite period when it is called a **contractual periodic tenancy**.

Shorthold Assured Tenancies

This is the more usual tenancy agreement preferred by landlords as it offers them a guaranteed right to repossess their property at the end of the tenancy.

*A first shorthold tenancy must be for a fixed term of at least six months.

*The tenant must be told that it is a shorthold tenancy prior to commencement.

*At least two month's notice is required from the landlord to bring the tenancy to an end.

*Another shorthold tenancy can be agreed to extend the period of the let, or if the landlord has not served notice that the tenant must leave, then that tenant may stay on in the property. At any time after the fixed term, the landlord may serve two month's notice to recover possession if he wishes, but the agreement can continue indefinitely if it suits both parties.

Rent Increases

Generally rents cannot be increased in the case of a **fixed term tenancy** until the end of the term, and in the case of a **contractual periodic tenancy** until the end of one year. Exceptions may be where a specific written contract exists allowing the landlord to increase the rent prior to the end of these periods. Some Assured Tenancy agreements will contain a 'rent review clause' which will state how and when your rent will be increased. Under a **shorthold assured tenancy** the landlord will charge a market rent for the fixed term, which will not increase during that term.

Further reading on **Assured Tenancies** *may be found in* **Housing Booklet Number 19** *produced by the Department of the Environment and available from HMSO (telephone no. 0171 873 9090 / 0171 873 0011) and some council information offices. There are also several other similar booklets on various landlord/tenant subjects including 'Repairs', 'He wants me out', 'Notice that you must leave', 'The rights and duties of landlords and tenants', 'The management of flats', all of these and more may be obtained in the same way.*

FINANCIAL AND LEGAL

LANDLORD'S RESPONSIBILITIES

Advertising Expenses

This initial outlay is always met by the landlord when advertising privately. If a letting agent is instructed then they bear the cost of normal advertising of your property, within their quoted commission to you.

Agent's Commission

If a Letting Agent is employed then the landlord pays his commission for services to find the tenant and if necessary for the management of the property as well. This will be based on a percentage of the rental income over the agreed period. Typical rates for this are in the region of 10% for 'tenant finding' and 15% for 'full management'. Agents may add a small charge, say 3%, if they are required to collect rent for the landlord after the 'tenant finding' service.

Tip - Agents may require payment of their commission in different ways, sometimes you will be expected to pay this as a lump sum at the start of the tenancy and sometimes as the rent is collected. Remember, in either case this figure is also subject to VAT at 17.5%.

Tip - Even if the tenant leaves the property earlier than the expiry of the tenancy, the landlord is still liable to pay the full tenancy period's commission to the agent.

Inventory
This is normally completed at the landlord's expense, by an independent service or by the agent.

Tenancy Agreement
The cost of drawing up the agreement may be shared with the tenant.

Maintenance and Management Expenses
All running costs for the normal on-going maintenance of the property is expected to be met by the landlord, e.g. general servicing of appliances and upkeep of the property itself. The landlord will also be responsible for the management of the property and its costs, either in his own capacity or through his agent.

Buildings and Contents Insurance
Insurance of the building and personal contents is the landlord's concern, however he is not liable for the contents belonging to the tenant.

The Mortgage or other loans secured on the property
The tenant will be expecting to live in 'quiet enjoyment' in the property once it is let to him, it is therefore obviously the responsibility of the landlord to ensure the mortgage is paid and that the tenant will be able to remain for the duration of the tenancy agreement without fear of any repossession.

Ground Rent
If applicable, would be the responsibility of the landlord.

TENANT'S RESPONSIBILITIES
The Deposit
The main deposit should be agreed and paid in advance by the tenant, as a figure it will often be equivalent to approximately one month's rental. The tenant pays this to show that there is money available, at the outset, to compensate the landlord for possible repairs and breakages. In most normal circumstances therefore, the balance is returnable to the tenant.
Tip - Check in whose account the deposit will be held and to whom the interest will be payable (this may be the landlord's account or his agent's).

References
References will be required by the landlord or his agent upon your status, income and character. The best people to provide these therefore will be your employer, accountant, bank, present landlord or similar person.

The Rent
Whether a letting agent is involved or not, normally rental is collected monthly, although this may vary to suit all parties. Whatever the decided period, it should be expected that the first installment be paid in advance of the tenancy commencing and then continue to be paid in advance. In the normal course of events this should be arranged by a standing order. See also the paragraph 'Rent Increases' above.

Preparation of Tenancy Agreement
There is normally a charge for the preparation of the legal documents required at the outset. This may be your responsibility, the landlord's, or shared jointly, check to see what is expected.

Check In and Check Out Charges
There may be an extra charge for checking you into and out of the property when an inventory will normally be gone through, this can be quite time consuming.

Utilities including Council Tax

As the utilities payments are usually the responsibility of the tenant, including council tax and water rates, it is important to contact the relevant companies yourself even if the landlord does this as well. They need to know your personal details for billing and confirmation of the date of your take-over. If there is a garden, the tenant is normally responsible for its upkeep.

Cleaning, Replacements and Repairs

At the end of the tenancy there may be a charge for depreciation, cleaning, replacements and repairs.

Contents Insurance

The landlord is expected to pay for his own buildings and contents insurance, however insurance of the tenant's belongings is the tenant's own responsibility. Often letting agents will have a policy especially suitable for this or refer to your normal insurance company.

Access to the Property

In order to ensure that the property is being kept in good order and for

---

The Good *move* Guide
always welcomes news, views
and interesting stories from its readers,
share some of your 'moving experiences!'.

The next edition will include the best of these
on a *'Readers Page'*,
all those printed will receive a £20.00 cash prize.
So get writing!

HOMES OF INTEREST

Listed Buildings
The Department of National Heritage is obliged to maintain 'lists' of buildings of 'special architectural or historical interest' and in so doing the Department acts on advice from English Heritage.

There are currently some 500,000 individual buildings listed in England alone, of which 95% are listed grade II. There are 9,000 grade I buildings and 18,000 grade II* buildings. The grading reflects the relative importance of the buildings, but has no legal significance. In addition to this, local authorities maintain a non-statutory list of buildings of local interest, sometimes referred to as grade III, but they are not 'listed buildings' as such. Within this listing are other structures such as important street furniture e.g. milestones and pumps.

Advantages and Disadvantages of Ownership

An important point to remember is that when a building is 'listed' it is listed in its entirety even though some parts of it are likely to be more important than others. This should be taken into account by the authorities when any application for alteration is made. Some buildings are listed just because their facades are important and not their interiors, but even to change the colour of a coat of paint on an interior door may not be allowed without permission. The law in this respect may be relaxed within a government 'green paper' whereby the interiors of such buildings may be 'de-listed'. One has to balance therefore the advantages of owning a listed building as opposed to the disadvantages. The advantages lie mainly in the 'cachet' and pride of ownership, as set against the disadvantages of the bureaucracy, the prejudices imposed and the lack of freedom to make alterations.

Grants for the works on listed buildings *may* be obtained from English Heritage and County Councils, but application should be made prior to any works being commenced. VAT will apply at zero rate against 'approved alterations' work, but is not applicable against work of a general maintenance or repair nature.

For advice and guidance on all aspects of the survival of buildings which are old and interesting, you may find it useful to contact: The Society for the Protection of Ancient Buildings (SPAB), 37 Spital Square, London E1 6DY. Telephone: 0171 377 1644.

Thatched Homes

Thatched cottages have a special appeal of their own and even more often now, we are again seeing new homes benefitting from the charm of a thatched roof. Owning a thatched home presents its own problems though, especially in the costs of renewing the thatch which is expensive and in finding the best reed, which is often in short supply. If the house is also a 'listed' building the local authority may dictate the type of reed used.

However, on a good note, whereas once the insurance figures were quite prohibitive, nowadays because of the use of modern flame retardant materials, the insurance figures have been reduced. One big advantage of thatch is that it keeps a home relatively cool in summer and warm in winter.

The Thatching Advisory Service of Reading, Berkshire, (Tel: 01734 734203) can help with advice on insurance, may provide thatch surveyors and has a list of registered thatchers.

Semi-detached Homes

As different in style, size and price as any other types of homes, the traditional 'semi' is one of Britain's most prolific and best loved. The 'semi's' history goes back as long ago as the 1600s in the shape of farm cottages and then saw a rise in numbers some 200 years ago. Their biggest advantages over detached homes, were the speed in which they could be built and their saving in land area and costs.

By the 1850s every self-respecting town had middle-class suburbs where the semi's numbers quickly expanded, but it was not until the 1880s that these homes began to have bathrooms when mass-produced enamelled cast-iron baths were first available! Millions more 'semis' were built in the

1920s and 1930s which often included large room sizes, bow windows and mock timbering. Builders realised that the semi offered the 'ideal' and affordable home to many, with space to breathe, access from front to back and efficient use of land. Originally the cost of such a three bedroom semi was as little as £350 - £550, how times change!

Building your own Home

This market has done very well recently with over 20,000 individual homes being built last year. According to NHBC* figures, this represents one in three of all new detached houses and bungalows built in the UK. The advantages are obvious in that you are able to design exactly the home you want and the costs can be cheaper than buying a new home from a developer. The most important step, of course, is finding the right plot and recently there do seem to be more available for the private purchaser in the wake of the recession. *'Individual Homes' is the monthly magazine covering each county, which is a major source of reference for buyers.*

Repossessed Homes

Repossessed homes have received much publicity because of the fall in the value of homes, especially over recent years. They may come in any shape, size or value, but they all have one thing in common: they are all homes that have been repossessed by lenders of mortgages (or other loans), where repayments on those mortgages have not been met. Any borrowing secured on a property which is not repaid, may make that property subject to repossession, whether someone's home or not. Once repossessed, the lenders then aim to recover their losses by selling the properties on to a new buyer.

The lenders then have the right to transfer 'absolute ownership' to the new owner and, in this sense, these homes are no different from any other. However, they will be empty and very often in a poor state, sometimes vandalised deliberately by previous occupiers. It may be that fitted kitchens and doors are missing and their value will be substantially less for this reason. So remember they may not be the 'big bargain' they might at first appear.

Lenders are required, by law, to obtain the best available price, but they will want to sell their asset as soon as possible to recover the debt. Sometimes selling through 'auction'* or by 'tender'* achieves these objectives sooner than other means. However, you may still find these properties on estate agents' books, as usual, especially in the early stages of their marketing.

In London and Surrey the following are companies who specialise in listing such properties:
    'The London Repossession List' (Tel: 0171 376 1100)
    'The Property Unit' (Tel: 01428 656556)
Up-dated lists will be sent to you upon payment of a subscription, you may find they duplicate many properties you can find elsewhere, but normally there will be others included in the list of which you may not be aware.

House Boats

Romantic and unusual, but often with all the comforts and amenities associated with bricks and mortar, a house boat is the answer for a growing number of people. Coming in all shapes and sizes, a house boat's intrinsic value is in its mooring which needs to provide mains power, drinking water, sewerage, rubbish collection and a permanent berth. Canal and river frontage is often prime development land and unoccupied moorings are virtually non-existent, so buying a 'homeless' boat is inadvisable unless a nomadic existence is possible.

Be particularly vigilant therefore about the rights of the mooring and the relevant ownership or lease. The ideal purchase will be well considered and unrushed, remember surveys need to be carried out on boats, as with houses before a purchase, and marine mortgages are available for finance. In many cases then, for the price of an ordinary small flat or starter home, a house boat can provide a unique and often beautiful place to live.

Further information on this subject is obtainable from the 'Residential Boat Owners' Association' which publishes a specialist guide to living afloat, write to:
The RBOA, PO Box 181, Macclesfield, Cheshire, SK11 0NT.

WHERE TO FIND AVAILABLE HOMES

NEWSPAPERS
National papers often advertise new developments and some private sales, but generally they are not a good substitute for the local area's property papers which will give a much fuller picture of the market. National papers carry 'Property Sections' on certain days of the week, most are listed below.

National Daily Papers

Property Sections on following days each week

The Daily Telegraph
Wednesday, Saturday

(Sunday Telegraph)
Sunday

The Times
Wednesday, Saturday

(Sunday Times)
Sunday

The Independent
Saturday

(Independent on Sunday)
Sunday

The Daily Mail
Friday

(Mail on Sunday)
Sunday

The Mirror
Saturday

The Express
Friday

(Sunday Express)
Sunday

The Daily Star
Wednesday

Mole Valley Newspapers

Circulated on the following day each week:

Surrey Advertiser *Friday*

Surrey Mirror *Thursday*

Surrey Comet *Friday*

Leatherhead Advertiser *Thursday*

Dorking Advertiser *Thursday*

Epsom and Ewell Herald
Wednesday

OTHER NEWSPAPERS/CIRCULARS

Free publications such as estate agents' own *'in-house'* papers and the weekly issues of the popular *'Property Weekly'* (Wednesdays) and *'Property Guardian'* (Thursdays) give a good indication of properties and market prices. Of course there are others, both national and local, such as *'Daltons Weekly'*, *'Loot'*, and *'Hot Property'*. Some properties advertised in this way might catch your eye, but like national papers generally they cannot replace the much more comprehensive choice represented in local newspaper advertising.

GLOSSY MAGAZINES AND PERIODICALS

'Country Life' in particular and other similar magazines carry a selection of homes for sale or let. Some other specialist sport magazines will also carry property sections such as *'Horse and Hound'*, both these publications mentioned are issued weekly so properties advertised here are very much up-to-date. *'What House?'* magazine contains current information on new property developments, county by county and news of the latest deals being offered.

Estate agents themselves periodically issue their own glossy magazines to promote the sale of properties on their books normally across a wide area. However, remember the actual properties featured will not be the most up-to-date available, some may have been sold already and others will have come onto the market. These magazines are produced as much to attract possible instructions from prospective vendors as well as to sell the actual properties contained therein.

ESTATE AGENTS

Still the most popular and obvious place to find available homes, like private advertisers they too will use newspapers (almost religiously) and other media to promote properties on their books. Another section in the book covers this subject extensively.

AUCTIONS

Buying a property through an auction is an alternative to the normal 'private treaty*' sale, although both types of sale may be advertised in estate agent's windows and newspapers. There are fundamental differences that must influence whether this is suitable for your sort of purchase. Some properties have to go to auction for legal reasons and others simply as the vendor's preference. A 'reserve' price is usually agreed with the auctioneer by the vendor, so the property cannot be sold beneath this figure in the auction room. Whether buying or selling it is normally essential to seek the assistance of a professional. The Incorporated Society of Valuers and Auctioneers is certainly one organisation which offers advice.

As a purchaser, at auction, you will be expected to pay a deposit straight away if yours is the successful bid, normally 10% of the selling price. Being committed to the purchase at this point, every previous stage of necessary research, surveying and financing must be completed prior to walking into the auction room to bid for the property. When the hammer falls it is an effective exchange of contracts, with an agreed completion date normally 28 days later.

Be sure to have a ceiling price before attending an auction and be prepared to accept disappointment rather than be tempted into a price you cannot afford. *(Like all wise advice this is easier said than done!)* For this reason, amongst others, it may be advisable to instruct a professional to act for you, who at least can be dispassionate. Purchasing a property at auction is obviously not for everyone, for such a large commitment probably most of us prefer a less pressurised environment. However, if you do all your homework and preparation (seeking professional help where necessary) then there is no reason why you shouldn't feel confident! Good luck, obviously there are nice properties and bargains to be found.

Further information may be obtained from: The Incorporated Society of Valuers and Auctioneers, 3 Cadogan Gate, London SW1X 0AS. Telephone: 0171 235 2282

PROPERTY REGISTERS

These are a relatively new and easy concept, brought about more and more by the ever increasing computer age. They offer both buyers and sellers a 'matching service', a bit like computer dating for couples, but this time for homes and potential new owners. Normally free to buyers, the companies charge the sellers to advertise properties and hold their details on a computer data base for a given length of time. The properties are then matched to the requirements of the potential buyer.

It is left up to the parties involved to arrange their own follow up once the introduction has been given by the Property Register. *Their service ends with the introduction.* There is no guarantee of a sale of course, or even how many introductions will be obtained. Although a good idea, I personally find that it is all too remote and uncertain for most people's tastes. There is something much more satisfactory in physically seeing your property advertised in a local estate agent's window, or even in a newspaper, rather than on a data-base. *In my opinion I think they have yet to catch-on to be as successful as some of the companies would wish.*

RELOCATION AGENTS

Relocation agents or 'property search agents' offer the service on the other side of the coin from estate agents. In acting in the *buyer's interests they research the property market* and should be able to assist with many practical aspects of the transaction for their clients. They charge for their services in different ways and they are not cheap, but when it comes to reducing the stress of moving they can also be an excellent investment!

In this day and age relocation agents are becoming more and more popular, although they would still be seen as an expensive 'luxury' for most people moving home. However, for some home finders they offer an absolutely essential service and if you are short of time or at a distance from where you wish to move, they could prove to be a *'God send'*. More purchasers would be well advised to use their services, especially people moving around the country, foreigners, 'ex-pats' and purchasers with limited time. For your peace of mind, the more experienced and long standing will be members of the *Association of Relocation Agents* who will be happy to advise you (Tel. 01273 624455).

COMPUTER TECHNOLOGY

As technology rapidly progresses, computers are bound to increasingly solve the problems which arise in searching for a home. So much information is available now through the *Internet*, just watch this space!

ESTATE AGENTS' SERVICES

THE NATIONAL ASSOCIATION OF ESTATE AGENTS

This National Association was formed in 1962 to represent the interests of estate agents, especially those not otherwise professionally qualified, and to *raise their professional standards*. It now has more than 9,500 members in 49 branches in the UK and it is widely recognised throughout the profession. All NAEA members must adhere to strict rules of conduct and the Association provides recourse through its disciplinary procedures. It also operates a guarantee bonding scheme - to protect purchase deposits (either pre-contract or contract) held by a member - and a referral network of member agents throughout the UK and overseas, called 'Homelink'.

The Association believes that the public must receive competent and honest service and advice, including protection against fraud, misrepresentation and malpractice. It aims to make apparent to the public that they are likely to receive this from a member by the general standard of presentation of the member's office and conduct of the staff.

The most obvious way in which the NAEA protects consumers is by admitting to membership only those estate agents who have undergone thorough assessment of their knowledge of estate agency law, practice and ethics. The NAEA publishes a range of informative leaflets, all of which are available from their Warwick headquarters. When using an estate agent, members of the public can identify a member of the NAEA by the Association logo, shown below.

The National Association of Estate Agents are located at:
Arbon House,
21 Jury Street,
Warwick
CV34 4EH
Tel: 01926 496800

THE ROYAL INSTITUTION OF CHARTERED SURVEYORS

This well recognised and long established Institution now has about 60,000 members many of whom, past and present, have been the backbone of estate agency for many years. It is common to find estate agents with at least one partner, or senior member of staff, who is a registered Chartered Surveyor. All Chartered Surveyors are qualified by examination and experience and they may use the designatory letters FRICS or ARICS.

Nearly half of all Chartered Surveyors value, sell and manage property of all kinds and as estate agents they are a familiar presence in every high street. As well as selling residential property, the Chartered Surveyor will be appointed to carry out mortgage valuations and structural surveys. The profession's Information Centre in London provides further information and advice and can be contacted at:

The Royal Institution of Chartered Surveyors,
12 Great George Street,
Parliament Square,
London
SW1P 3AD
Tel: 0171 222 7000

THE ROYAL
INSTITUTION
OF CHARTERED
SURVEYORS

THE INCORPORATED SOCIETY OF VALUERS AND AUCTIONEERS

This society, which is also well known and widely respected, has existed for seventy years, since the First World War. As with the R.I.C.S. above, members can be identified by the appropriate designatory letters after their names FSVA or ASVA. Further information about the society, its services and its membership may be obtained from:

The Incorporated Society of Valuers and Auctioneers,
3 Cadogan Gate,
London
SW1X 0AS
Tel: 0171 235 2282

ISVA

*The professional
Society for Valuers
and Auctioneers*

THE VENDOR'S POINT OF VIEW
The Obvious Choice?

When it comes to selling houses estate agents must be the obvious choice in many ways, but they are expensive! If you decide to give them your instructions, first choose several local agents to view your property, usually they are only too happy to make this a free service. They can advise you on both an expected market value and the overall sales strategy they will use for your home. Ask as many questions as you like of them at this stage, try and assess who will be your best representative and which agent offers you the most favourable deal. Influencing factors will normally be the *commission they charge, their range of services, their qualifications, the situation of their offices and perhaps last, but not least their advertising schedule.* Try to make sure that the estate agent is prepared to advertise from each of their closest branches to your home. The ideal would be for your property to be central in the area of their main advertising, not on any periphery. They will have a normal 'advertising block' (i.e. the newspapers and publications they use) that they should readily explain to you, any further advertising you want them to do would require separate negotiation and they may often insist it is funded by you in addition to their final commission.

Which One?

Estate agents often specialise is 'market segmentation' in other words being 'best known' for selling certain types of properties i.e. prestige or mainstream. Preferably choose an agent who seems to have the best understanding and the most experience in the marketing for your type of home. Finally you will probably be able to find out easily their reputation locally by speaking to friends and neighbours. It hardly matters to you normally, if they are an 'independent' local agent or one branch of a large, well known chain of agencies. Both types will offer the same services by and large, it is up to you to decide what is most important to you. Remember as well, that you can always try negotiating the commission rate they first offer, they may be adamant that they cannot lower it, if they don't you have lost nothing by trying, but some just may do, there is a lot of competition out there!

Tip - Don't automatically instruct the agent who advises on the highest asking price for your property, this can be an obvious ploy to flatter you - be careful.

Most agents will claim to be open seven days a week, an important point as many would-be purchasers look for homes at the weekend. However, do not expect a full-service from them especially on Sundays when it is very unusual to find a negotiator prepared to accompany any prospective purchasers around. Make sure they know if you are prepared to show people around yourself, in particular at weekends, it may well increase your likelihood of a sale.

Their Services

Estate agents act for you, the vendor, and their loyalty is to you, but they will assist purchasers as well to help to bring the transaction to a satisfactory conclusion as soon as possible. Remember their vested interest is in getting to the completion of the sale, when they normally receive their payment (see below).

First of all they will visit the relevant property and advise on a sale price. Subsequently, if they are then instructed to act as agents, they will spend some time measuring up, taking photographs and finding out as much as possible about your home. They will expect to take a set of spare keys to enable accompanied, or if the property is empty, sometimes unaccompanied viewing. They should then work quickly to produce accurate 'property particulars' (with colour photographs), allowing you to see a draft copy for approval and signature, before distributing them to interested parties. The standard of presentation of these particulars may vary considerably, but the standard of accuracy in content should be consistent and flawless.

As estate agents normally have more than one branch, they circulate these details to all of their appropriate offices, nowadays more are doing so using a computer data base. Appointments 'to view' are then made through the agent who should at least offer to both parties that a negotiator be present. Once any offers to purchase are received by the agent, all of them must be divulged to the owner along with other essential information which is now a statutory requirement.

N.B. It is interesting to note that despite this era of Information Technology, computers are still not yet universally popular or widely used amongst estate agents, so don't be surprised to find that 'old fashioned touch' - it obviously still works!

Tip - As the vendor it is *particularly useful to know one ongoing contact* at the agents to whom you can address your specific questions. Naturally this will often be the negotiator who originally viewed the property and measured up.

Tip - It is also interesting to realise that experience shows estate agents that the greatest opportunity of selling your property is generally within the first four weeks of it going onto the market. There is no doubt that they normally invest a fair amount of time and money to reach this end, especially if they are sole agents, when they have a good chance of obtaining their commission without competition. You may be forgiven for thinking that if your house sells within a few days then perhaps it was under priced. Equally you may feel the commission you will be charged is hardly proportionate to your agent's efforts, but 'spare a thought' - perhaps you should be congratulating, not criticising, them!

Their charges

Most estate agents receive their income in the form of a commission which is based on a percentage of the agreed sale price of your home. There are several different rates.

    1) 'Sole Agency' Most estate agents will offer you *'Sole Agency'* commission rates around 1.5% of the final sale price, i.e. £1500.00 (plus VAT) for a sale price of £100,000. They will often request on a *'Sole Agency'* basis, that they have a set minimum period of time (i.e. 8 weeks) to sell your home prior to you withdrawing your instruction from them, perhaps in favour of a competitor. *Remember you are then tied to that one agent to sell your home for that period, if any other agent introduces a prospective purchaser during that agreed time, you will be in breach of your contract and you will be at least committed to paying both agents' commission.* The trouble is that you may often be approached by other agents seeking to sell your property through their own introductions. **Do not** be persuaded by them, sit-tight with your instructed agent otherwise the whole transaction could get messy and very expensive.

2) 'Multiple Agency' Agents will quote a figure higher than their *'Sole Agency'* for *'Multiple Agency'* rates, when they acknowledge they will be competing with other agent(s) you may choose to instruct. *In the event of a sale, you will only pay commission to the estate agent who has made the successful introduction, none of the others.* For this reason some agents may not invest as much time and money into the sale of your property than they would if they were sole agents. It may appear to potential purchasers that you are desperate to sell your home if they see it in every estate agent's window! Again a matter for your consideration along with the extra expense.

3) 'Joint Sole Agency' More unusual is the *'Joint Sole Agency'* where two agents jointly share the commitment to sell your home, commission rates may be different again and would normally fall between 'Sole Agency' and 'Multiple Agency' rates. Instead of being in competition, the agents will co-operate and divide the commission between themselves upon a sale.

4) 'Special Deals' It may be possible to find estate agents who offer their services free of commission charges if the vendor promises to take out any new mortgage required with their associated Building Society. Be careful of this apparently excellent deal, you may be committed to a lack of mortgage choice which could cost you dearly in the long-term.

5) 'Lump sum Payments' There are a few estate agents who offer the alternative of charging a 'lump sum payment' upon your instructions initially, therefore not depending on the sale of your home to receive their income. Sometimes the flexibility built into their systems of payment even allow part 'lump sum' and part 'commission'. They obviously try to offer a cheaper service than the traditional 'full commission' based agents. They are not common and if you can find such an agent, only *you* can then decide if they are a better choice.

Estate agents traditionally become entitled to the commission from a sale upon exchange of contracts, although it is normal practice for this to be paid upon the completion. Their account is usually submitted to your solicitor or conveyancer, for the account to be settled upon this day. Remember all charges, whether lump sums or commissions, are subject to VAT at 17.5%.

Terms and Conditions

With all agents, be very careful at the outset to establish what 'Terms and Conditions' they are putting into their contract with you. For instance, don't agree to *'Sole Selling Rights'* which means that the agent would claim his commission even if you genuinely sold your home yourself. Also bear in mind that if you choose to advertise your home for sale on *'Property Registers'* when you have already instructed a *Sole Agent,* check that for commission purposes, they are *not* regarded as other 'agents'.

Letting Agents

Much of what has been said above equally applies to letting agents, many of whom will be estate agents as well. Your property 'For Let' may not have such extensive details taken as those 'For Sale', but in many other ways the services provided are very comparable.

N.B. It is also interesting to note that estate agents must disclose 'personal interests' under the Estate Agents Act 1979 and subsequent Orders. This means that an agent is required to disclose if he or she (or a connected person) has a beneficial interest in the property or the proceeds of the sale.

THE PURCHASER'S POINT OF VIEW

Research

Look in as many estate agents' windows as you can in the time allowed that cover your area of interest. This will give you the best idea of the type of properties they have for sale, many more will be inside. Go in and introduce yourself and your property requirements, they will offer to put you on their mailing list and take day-time contact numbers. At first registering with them can be quite enjoyable, but repeating the same information to them all, soon gets tedious and very time consuming. Be prepared to find that what you thought might be a 'quick look' round them all, easily becomes several hours and in a large area, several days or even several weeks! Also you will find that despite being put on their mailing lists, you can rarely rely on them sending you details of homes that you would be interested in, without further prompting by you.

Property Particulars

The details of the properties estate agents have on their books is generally of a high standard and accurate, recent legislation has sought to stop flamboyant claims and inaccuracies in descriptions. This is covered under *'The Property Misdescriptions Act 1991'*. From the purchaser's point of view, nothing should now be claimed on the particulars which cannot be proved. However there is no law against describing the property in the best possible light, without being misleading, or taking photographs with a wide-angled lens giving the appearance of it being bigger than it really is.

Particulars generally include:
* Tenure - i.e. freehold or leasehold
* Colour photograph(s) - traditionally the front elevation, sometimes internal or others
* Situation - including the exact address and immediate locality
* Description - the type of house - i.e. terraced, semi, bungalow
* Age of the property
* Measurements and basic description of interior rooms
* A floor plan - sometimes reserved for higher priced properties
* Outside - what is within the boundaries
* The services connected
* Local Authority
* Post code
* Council Tax Band
* Price
* Accurate Directions

Other Services

Estate agents don't just stop at presenting properties and showing people around. You will find they are more than helpful in recommending solicitors, surveyors and other professionals to assist you with your purchase. They may also provide maps and other helpful literature, however the information may not be up-to-date and is unlikely to be very comprehensive or to show detrimental features! Once an offer is made they will assist in the progress of the sale right up to completion and will act as intermediaries where necessary.

Sunday Opening

Many estate agents will claim to be 'Open on Sundays', but they rarely like to tell you that there is only a 'skeleton' staff in the office and therefore their services are exceptionally limited. I have frequently found offices all locked up despite showing longer hours on the door. For the same reasons very few viewings are arranged for Sundays, as a rule there are few negotiators (if any) available to accompany any prospective buyers. Another disadvantage is that the staff that are available on Sundays are often only temporary and may not show the interest, knowledge and professionalism of their full-time colleagues.

Letting Agents

Many estate agents are also letting agents, but those which offer both services are not always located in the same office. It is normal for most agents to carry 'rental particulars' in their local sales offices, but they may refer you to their specialist or central office for the most up to date lists and then for further enquiries. You will see from the 'Local Estate Agents' section that this is frequently the case and that the centralised lettings offices generally cover a wider catchment area than the sales offices. Specialist letting agents as well normally cover larger catchment areas.

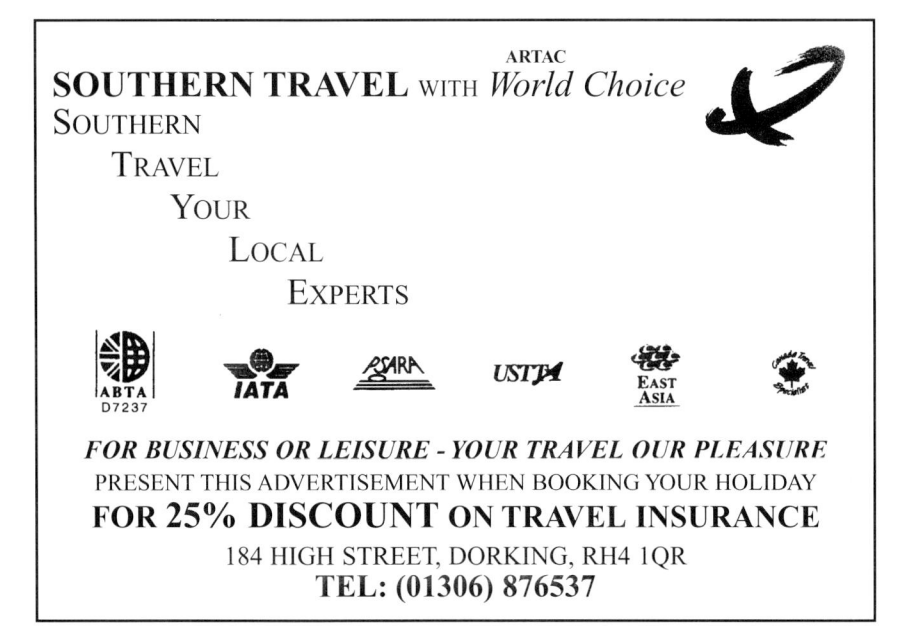

ARTAC
SOUTHERN TRAVEL WITH *World Choice*
SOUTHERN
　　TRAVEL
　　　　YOUR
　　　　　　LOCAL
　　　　　　　　EXPERTS

ABTA D7237　　IATA　　PSARA　　USTPA　　EAST ASIA

FOR BUSINESS OR LEISURE - YOUR TRAVEL OUR PLEASURE
PRESENT THIS ADVERTISEMENT WHEN BOOKING YOUR HOLIDAY
FOR 25% DISCOUNT ON TRAVEL INSURANCE
184 HIGH STREET, DORKING, RH4 1QR
TEL: (01306) 876537

BRITISH GAS TIPS when BUYING or RENTING a NEW HOME

If you are moving, tell us at least a few days before you move so that we can arrange to read the meter.

Points to check
When you move into a new home everything should be in order, but it's a good idea to make sure for yourself. Use the following checklist:

✓ If you smell gas, phone the emergency service, listed under GAS in the British Telecom Phone book.

✓ Keep a note of the meter reading.

✓ Make sure you know where your main gas tap is and that it is easy to turn off.

✓ If your meter is in a meter box, make sure that you have a key and that it works.

✓ Make sure that all gas points (the points on gas supply pipes where appliances can be connected) which you are not using are sealed off before you turn on the main gas supply.

✓ Check that all gas appliances look in good condition and that everything works. For example, check that the outer case of a fire and the wall next to it are not stained or discoloured.

✓ Check to see that wall or window vents are not blocked. Before having a gas fire fitted, you must have the chimney brush-swept.

✓ If you live inside the gas supply area and your home does not have gas, we can advise on the charges for a new gas supply. if you are very close to a suitable main you may be connected **free of charge**.

✓ British Gas has developed a wide range of payment methods. **DirectPay** is the easy convenient way to settle your gas bill and can save you money on subsequent bills. **OptionPay** can give you savings when you settle your bill promptly. There are now over 19,000 places to pay your gas bill. Most of these are Post offices which accept gas bill payments **free of charge**.

✓ We are here to help if you are experiencing difficulties in paying your bill. Remember you must call us. The sooner we know there is a problem, the sooner we can help you.

Useful Gas telephone numbers:
  For gas accounts and moving details 0645 801802
  For gas escapes, ring the number shown under 'G' for Gas in the phone book. If the phone book is not available, ring 0345 581 071
  For central heating installation and servicing 01372 726130
  For new gas supplies 0645 555 806
  For a DirectPay application 0500 620 620
  For information on OptionPay 0500 520 520

VIEWING AND RESEARCH
THOUGHTS BEFORE YOU LOOK

Location
You may be considering a change in your lifestyle with your next move. Many people wish perhaps that they could live in the country or near the seaside, but beware that this may be an idealistic view with as many things against it as for it. When you are deciding where to move, apart from the type of lifestyle you would most like, think how important being close to friends and family is to you. Often what you are most familiar with is the best alternative, but you may not always appreciate it, remember *'the other man's grass is always greener'*!

Country Living
Advantages*:* *The country may well provide you with a healthier and safer lifestyle than city living, away from overcrowding and other town problems. Generally the air is much less polluted and there are greater facilities for walking, riding and other outdoor activities. It is often quieter than the town with plenty of space for car parking and a safer environment in which to bring up children. There is often more social life and 'caring' between residents in villages than there is in large towns and a slower pace of life for relaxation.*

Disadvantages: Services of all kinds may be much more remote such as transport, shops, schools and hospitals. The weather may cut off routes (and electricity!) more often. You are much more likely to need your own car and the cost of transport considerably increases. Many local roads, don't have pavements or lighting. Often no mains gas is laid on or even mains drainage. Modern living choices taken for granted in town, are not always available, such as cable TV. Social life, especially night life, is restricted with few alternatives. Sometimes it is just too quiet for people!

Town Living
Advantages*: Their is much more choice in types of homes such as flats and terraced properties. Many more services are available and immediately on hand. There are normally much better facilities for transport, shopping,*

social life, and entertainment. For elderly people in particular, many more essential facilities are close by.

Disadvantages: Overcrowding and a lack of space and privacy. Noise levels, traffic, pollution, crime and stress are greater. The pace of life is faster leaving little time for 'old fashioned' politeness. Car parking may be very difficult and all types of insurance costs are often greater. Property in town is often smaller in size for the same price as in the country. Sizeable gardens and garages are frequently very expensive luxuries.

Location Priorities

This book has been almost wholly conceived with this important subject in mind and is focused to help you know as much as possible about the area before deciding on your next move. *Location is the single most important factor when considering moving, closely followed by the number of bedrooms required in your new home.* Once these two priorities are satisfied normally other compromises may be made. Ideally your home should be in a location that does not give you cause for concern in any respect. *It is especially important to try and avoid something detrimental becoming apparent which was not realised before moving.*

Obviously some properties are in more desirable places than others, which will nearly always be reflected in their price. For instance, if you really don't mind noise and are prepared to move somewhere on a main road, then make sure you are compensated by paying less in the first place than for a comparable property in a quieter location. Be careful that something that you might dismiss as unimportant at the outset, might eventually be a continuous source of irritation over a prolonged period of time. *The biggest dangers are not the obvious handicaps that may be easily seen, but ones that are less apparent and you may have to spend sometime discovering the truth!*

Tip - 'Out-of-sight' is not always 'out-of-mind', remember you have five senses - hearing and smell are equally as able to be offended as sight! Noise levels are probably one of the greatest causes of stress to people, ideally therefore, noise should be avoided wherever possible in choosing your next home.

ANALYSING AVAILABLE HOMES

'Armchair Research'

Research as much as you can about the 'available home' before you view, in the comfort of your own home. This will save you so much time, effort and disappointment. Travelling round the countryside looking at homes is very tiring, especially with the addition of children. Your time is probably very precious too, so using up every spare weekend viewing, though often enjoyable at first, can easily become a complete chore. If you don't know the locality well, apart from referring to this publication, the most up-to-date 'current affairs' about the area will be found in the *local newspapers* probably alongside the properties for sale - read every page! An easy way of obtaining these papers is to telephone or go to a good local newsagents in the relevant area and place an order for copies of the papers as they come out. They should be able to mail them to you with appropriate arrangements. The local Council will also be full of readily available further information affecting the local community.

Buy a good, latest edition, ***A-Z Map*** of the area and study it very carefully, I recommend the 'Premier Street Atlas of Surrey' in full colour and based on the Ordnance Survey 1:10,560 maps. It is obtainable from normal local stockists price £11.50 *(Geographers' A-Z Map Company Head Office Tel. No. 01732 781000).*

To know more about 'public rights-of-way' the original **Ordnance Survey maps** will show you their routes. This may quickly solve any doubts you may have about rights-of-way over the land, before instructing solicitors and incurring further expense. Ordnance Survey maps will even show you contour lines for heights, remember the higher your home the more exposed to changes in the weather and often a little cooler all year than neighbouring low-lying areas. Valleys may be river flood plains and prone to fog, as opposed to higher ground suffering the extremes of weather and perhaps low cloud cover, especially in winter.

Most ***'property particulars'*** from estate agents will give you accurate directions to an 'advertised home', by reading these carefully you may even be able to see exactly where in the road the property is, the likely shape and size of the garden and which way it faces.

Tip - After the question of location, generally next on the list in deciding on your future home should be identifying the minimum number of bedrooms required, it is no good needing four bedrooms and then being enticed and distracted by a lovely three bedroom house that cannot be extended. You will find yourself soon thinking of moving again!

Tip - Once on your 'short list' of 'possibles' really read carefully the particulars sent. At first glance a home may appear to be worth viewing, but save your time and energy by especially noting room measurements. A property claiming to be five bedrooms, may only be three bedrooms, one box room and an attic conversion for instance and remember the minimum size for a double bedroom should be about 11' x 11'. Some homes claiming to have five bedrooms may even be 'top heavy' with inadequate sized accommodation downstairs to match, ideally five or six people need some generous living space too!

Also a room measuring 25' x 11' may look big, but it will be more like a 'tunnel' and perhaps difficult to furnish and heat. Last but not least, by looking at measurements, see if your largest and/or most precious furniture is likely to fit into the home! Sensible 'arm-chair' analysis of the particulars will save much of your precious time in the long run.

VIEWING - WHAT TO TAKE

Things To Take With You
1. This publication!
2. Your faithful new map(s)
3. The property's details
4. Pen, paper and your grid (see above)
5. Torch, binoculars and compass
6. Wellington boots and umbrella
7. A mobile phone, or card/change for a public phone
8. Refreshments!

Things Not To Take With You!
Distractions in the shape of:
1. Young children!
2. Your dog!
3. Your mother-in-law!
   (unless you are looking for her granny annexe too)!

GETTING THE MOST FROM VIEWING

When you have the time and several properties you want to view, you might like to make a grid, so you can make notes and compare them easily. You can make your own headings and include whatever comments you like alongside them. For example:

Headings	Address 1	Address 2	Address 3.
Price			
Type/Style			
Condition			
Position			
Gen. Locality			
Bedrooms			
Recept'n Rooms			
Kitchen			
Utility			
Bathrooms			
Other rooms			
Garages			
Outbuildings			
Parking			
Garden			
Public Transport			
Local Schools			
Shops			
Leisure			

TIPS ON VIEWING

Inspecting The Property

1. Try to be punctual for appointments, letting people know of alterations or cancellations
2. Note which way the property faces, traditionally lounges should be sunny, kitchens should be cool, gardens should face (or bank) south
3. Concentrate on the amount of light in various rooms and notice the sizes of windows
4. Study the kitchen carefully on layout and space for appliances
5. Try to visualise furnished homes without the furnishings
6. Note ceiling heights, thickness of internal walls, signs of damp or cracks
7. Walk all round the garden, paying special attention to the boundaries, it's often revealing (and surprising) what you might find or see

If more interested, (at the time or later)

8. Make a rough floor plan (if one isn't supplied) it can be surprisingly difficult to recall layout after leaving, especially if viewing several homes. *You can use the squared pages at the end of this book!*
9. Ask to see relevant bills on maintenance, utilities, council tax etc.
10. Request proof of guarantees and planning permission on building work where appropriate
11. Bring up the question of carpets/curtains/furnishings that might be included in the price
12. Request to provisionally test the heating or other fixtures e.g. showers and taps
13. Note the type and number of electric sockets, note the type of heating
14. Ask about the age of plumbing, wiring, damp course etc.
15. Discover if TV and Radio reception is good in the immediate area
16. Check the exact postal address, obviously useful in any case, this may be essential to know when homes are on council (or postal) boundaries. Sometimes the address itself may affect the price of a home or there may be a significant difference in council tax charges.
(Tip - Postcodes may be double checked by telephoning the Royal Mail on 0345 111222)

Remember the vendors of a property will not always willingly tell you of detriments to their home!

HIDDEN PROBLEMS?

Weather Conditions and Seasons

Whatever time of year you are viewing try and imagine what the property will be like in the different seasons, in terms of light and screening by trees etc. Traffic noise may be louder in winter when foliage from trees has gone. Is the property overlooked, and if so what by? Is the drive or any approach steep, which may be very hazardous in winter? Is the property likely to suffer from poor insulation on a cold draughty day?

Your Journey To Work

What affect does the property's location have upon your journey to work? Usually this will be a very significant factor, but possibly one that's importance could be under-rated at first. Carefully consider the implications of extra time and expenses.

Potential Building Construction

If there is a lovely view from the property, try to make especially sure that this valuable asset is not likely to change in the near future or that any other nearby building work may soon be carried out to the property's detriment. Construction of new roads will be revealed by searches your solicitor makes, but try to establish everything you can think of sooner rather than later, so less of your time and money are wasted.

Nuisances or Advantages

Some nearby buildings may be regarded as either a nuisance or an advantage by you, such as shops, schools, hospitals, garages, police, fire and ambulance stations. Whatever creates parking problems, noise or smell must be accounted for and realised. Even sports and leisure facilities on your door step, from football pitches to swimming pools may enhance or disadvantage your property.

Large trees may be lovely, but they may be the source of problems as well. If they are too close to the property they may cause unwanted shade or even affect drains or foundations. Be careful of covenants and rights imposed over the property which may last indefinitely, even if they are many years old it is not wise to ignore them.

Different Times of Day

However handy a map may be to expose potential problems, it cannot tell you what the location is like at different times of the day. Once decided on the home you most like, carry on with your research right up to exchange of contracts, you are not committed to the purchase legally before this date.

Even if you think you know the location well, you cannot be too careful. I once heard of a family moving into a property they thought they knew. Having been previously owned by friends, they had often visited the house in the evenings or at weekends. Little did they suspect that during 9am-5pm weekdays, the property took on quite a different character. The quiet road outside then became a road full of accident damaged cars waiting to go into a car-breakers which was out-of-sight down the road. Traffic and parking was chaotic, the ambience was ruined and much stress and annoyance resulted. So whenever possible make more than one or two visits at different times of the day and on different days of the week. Your chosen, quiet side road might be a rat-run for rush hour traffic or a busy car park for local commuters.

Next Door

If you share anything like an adjoining wall, boundary or drive, this is an especially important subject. Try to establish the condition of the relevant building and land and, without being intrusive, do what you can to find out about your neighbours!

Neighbours

This must be one of the most difficult subjects to cover, because they can change! By this I mean 'change' in personality and 'change' by moving away. Neighbours will influence the happiness of your home environment probably more than anything and yet you have no easy control over them! There are laws that can be enforced about such problems as noise, obstruction and boundaries, but living in harmony and with respect for each other is really the only way to be happy.

Be especially careful that your neighbours seem like *reasonable people* (this is very difficult of course!), but the outward appearance of the properties themselves will give you lots of clues. Ask yourself if the properties are well kept, eg. are there curtains at the windows, what state is the garden in, if people come and go do they have the appearance of a family, or could it be a refuge, bail hostel or even a squat? Another possible indication are the types of cars driven by the occupants and probably parked outside the property. Do they display 'road tax' and are they cared for? You may be able to think of other clues and, if you are concerned, you might find out more from the local council. There is little else left to be said about this then, it is very much the luck of the draw and you may not be able to either spend the time investigating this or afford the luxury of checking on every neighbour who might affect you! My only really positive advice is try to be a good neighbour yourself!

Crime and Rowdyism

Does your new choice of home make you vulnerable? So much misery may be inflicted by burglary, other crimes and general anti-social behaviour that this factor must be borne in mind. Homes close to public houses, night clubs, bail hostels, squats and sprawling council estates may be more obviously vulnerable than others. Even if you have never been a victim of crime before *don't be naive* about the future possibility.

If you have a car which needs to be left in the street, naturally it will be much more vulnerable than if you have a garage or even driveway. Crime Prevention advice is free from your local police who will help you decide on the most effective ways to spend your money on home security. The advice may be free, but the products are expensive, so look carefully at security when viewing a property, several hundreds of pounds may have already been invested this way or may have to be invested by you. Beyond the structure of the building itself you must ask yourself whether the layout of the property and its immediate environment gives you confidence about your own safety at all times of the day and night? If not, seriously reconsider your potential mistake.

Pollution

This is an example of an 'out-of-sight' hazard that will effect your quality of life and must therefore be given consideration. For example, you should discover if your home is within the prevailing wind direction of a local factory's chimney, let alone whether it is close to busy roads. We have all been made aware of people claiming their health has been seriously affected by living close to nuclear power stations, these are highly publicised cases, but there may be many more of us putting our health at risk without really thinking first.

Unfortunately pollution may be carried quite some distances by air or water, so the source may not be immediately apparent. I include this heading just to make a point, I am not naturally an alarmist, but it must be sensible at least to think about this.

Contaminated Land

There are policies proposed to operate a register of contaminated land, so that it is possible to find out if the house has been built on the site of a municipal rubbish tip. Even if this is not in force as yet, you will probably be able to establish this by making enquiries of the local council.

Further Afield

Consider that there may be more unusual places within the general locality that you may consider undesirable, such as sewage plants, gipsy sites, bail hostels and electricity pylons, as well as the obvious motorways, airports and railway lines. Be prepared to find that the smell from sewage can be especially bad in some weather conditions, whereas at other times it may be unnoticeable. *N.B.* Some sewage works shown on maps are not actually *foul* sewage treatment works, some may be general water works and pumping stations, investigate further should you be concerned.

WHEN RESPONDING TO ADVERTISEMENTS
PLEASE MENTION THE 'GOOD *move* GUIDE'

MOVING CHECKLIST

See also 'USEFUL ADDRESSES AND TELEPHONE NUMBERS'

(1) MOVING OUT
You must notify change of address to the following people:
(In most cases - as soon as possible)
N.B. Any annual bills, such as water rates and council tax will be subject to 'apportionment' i.e. you will be responsible for payment up to the date of completion at your old address and from the date of completion at any new address.

Tick boxes when done.
- [ ] BANK (S) *(Consider change of branch)*
- [ ] BUILDING SOCIETIES, PREMIUM BONDS
- [ ] *COMPANY SHARE(S) REG. OFFICES*
- [ ] HP FINANCE (Other loans and finance)
- [ ] *CREDIT CARDS STORE CARDS*
- [ ] DRIVER VEHICLE LICENSING (Vehicle Reg. Doc(s) and Driving Licenses)
- [ ] INSURANCE *(home, car, life policies, other)*
- [ ] TV LICENSING (Address at back of book)
- [ ] MAIN UTILITIES *(Water, Electric, Gas)*
- [ ] TELEPHONE(S) (**N.B. Remember** mobiles/pagers and that you can keep the same tel. no. in the same exchange area

- [ ] *COUNCIL TAXATION OFFICES*
- [ ] CLUB MEMBERSHIPS
- [ ] *SCHOOL (S)*
- [ ] DOCTOR(S)
- [ ] (DENTIST Optional)
- [ ] *SECURITY ALARM CENTRAL STATIONS*
- [ ] Post Office ('Keepsafe' & 'Forwarding Mail' Service) Optional

Organise:

DISCONNECTION OF UTILITIES (Or where possible 'take-over' arrangements with new occupiers)
REMOVALS - PROFESSIONAL OR DIY
DISPOSAL OF UNWANTED BELONGINGS (Remember the contents of your loft, shed and garage! Think of charity shops, car boot sales etc.)
SETTLING OF ACCOUNTS (Milk delivery, newspapers etc.)
ORDER NEW AREA TELEPHONE DIRECTORY/YELLOW PAGES
ELECTRICIANS/PLUMBERS (To disconnect appliances, where necessary)
LABELS FOR PACKAGING, BOXES etc.
DEFROST/EMPTY FREEZERS, FRIDGES etc.
SURVIVAL KIT FOR DAY OF THE MOVE (Food and drink, string, scissors, marker pen, pad, coins/cash, first aid, road map, torch, soap, toilet paper, plugs, light bulbs, basic tool kit)

To benefit new occupiers:

CLEARLY MARK KEYS, GIVE SET TO EST. AGENT (Label keys to garage, windows, shed, as well as doors etc.)
LEAVE AVAILABLE INSTRUCTIONS AND GUARANTEES (Re: location of water mains stop cock, mains electricity switch and fuse box and guarantees for appliances, building works, any security/fire equipment etc.)
DOMESTIC SERVICES (Leave a list of days and times of milk deliveries, post, refuse collection and perhaps recommended local plumbers etc.)
NEIGHBOURS (Give a written introduction and even warnings where necessary!)

(2) MOVING IN

CONNECTION OF UTILITIES (**N.B.** Whenever possible remember it is sensible to arrange to *take over* the supply of the utilities/services rather than disconnection and reconnection which is often unnecessary and costly).
TELEPHONE NUMBER(S) If applicable, establish early on whether the old phone number is being kept by the previous occupier (or not) so you can arrange 'change of address' cards sooner rather than later.
SECURITY AND SAFETY ('New Home-New Dangers', think locks, alarms, stairs, kitchens)
ARRANGE NEW KEYS COLLECTION POINT AND TIME
THINK ABOUT TEMPORARY FLOOR COVERING (Carpets in an entrance hall may particularly suffer during a move)
REMOVAL MEN (AND FRIENDS) may want a tip!

(3) GENERAL MOVING ADVICE AND TIPS

a) Try and pace yourself leaving as little to do as possible towards the moving date.

b) Sort and clear out unwanted items from your old address, thereby giving yourself time to wisely dispose of these things, e.g. at auction, car boot sales, charity shops etc.

c) Packing always takes much longer than you think, try not to have anything left to do on moving day that you could have done before.

d) Look for packaging materials well in advance, e.g. collect boxes from supermarkets, find/buy plastic bin liners, newspaper etc. Mark what is fragile appropriately.

e) When removing items around the house (from hanging pictures to kitchen appliances), tape their hooks/screws/bolts/plugs etc. where possible to the object themselves, so that they are easily found again on your arrival.

f) If you have surplus stocks of domestic oil, firewood etc., see if you can negotiate selling the surplus to the purchaser, or run the supply right down.

g) Be especially careful when moving certain domestic appliances e.g. electric cookers will need an electrician to disconnect, fridges should be kept upright and washing machines should have their revolving drums immobilised before moving. Remember other machines and equipment may also be sensitive to being turned and moved. *Mark* all these items appropriately.

h) Don't *'double handle'* - a useful removal man's 'tip', meaning once anything is lifted ideally it should not be put down again until it is at its destination, this saves a lot of time. To help with this, boxes should be labelled to show to which room they should be taken.

i) Don't forget to make suitable arrangements for children and pets.

j) Finally remember 'Rome wasn't built in a day' and neither will your new home look in order straight away - be patient and give yourselves plenty of time!

(4) CRIME PREVENTION AND FIRE SAFETY

Take a look at your new home and its surroundings, is it as secure and safe as you would wish? Look at some of the tips below to help you:

a) Gates and boundary fences

Identify any weaknesses and consider topping with trellis for climbing plants. Thick hedges are good security, especially if the bushes are prickly.

b) Outbuildings, sheds and garages

Put ladders inside if possible. Use good locks, such as padlocks or mortice locks.

FIGHTING FIRE AT HOME

Buying a home is probably the biggest single purchase you are ever likely to make and it follows therefore that you would want to protect your investment and ensure the safety of your family and yourself.

By following a few simple guidelines you can help reduce the risk of fire at home and help us to help you should you ever have the need to call us out:-

If smoke alarms have been fitted, replace the battery and vacuum the inside of the detector to remove any dust that may be present and check to make sure it is working correctly by using the test button. If there are no smoke alarms and your home is on one level, fit one to the ceiling **in the hallway** between the living and sleeping areas. If there is more than one floor fit an alarm **at the bottom of the staircase** and one on **each upstairs landing**.

It is worth getting to know the precise layout of your home and preparing a fire escape plan which will enable you to escape quickly and safely should a fire break out and smoke fills rooms and passageways. This is particularly important for young chilldren who may become disorientated in new surroundings. You should familiarise yourself with the various exits and passageways and walk the escape route. It will be much easier to escape when you need to if you have practised the route beforehand.

Check that your fusebox or circuit breaker box have the correctly rated fuses or breakers in place. This will help prevent electric wiring overheating and starting a blaze. If in doubt consult a qualified electrician.

If you have an open fire, ensure that the chimney is swept before lighting the fire for the first time. Excess soot or an old bird's nest could quickly ignite and lead to a fire which can rapidly get out of control.

Be sure to familiarise yourself with the local area so that if you have to call the Fire and Rescue Service, you can give a precise location for your property. Phone boxes, public houses and road junctions etc. are useful landmarks for our firecrews to use. This is particularly important if your home is on a long road or in a particularly rural area.

You can help us even further by making sure your property displays a house number, which is clearly visible from the road. This will help our crews locate your home quickly in an emergency. If you have a fire hydrant within your property it will also help us if you could trim back hedges and grass so that marker posts and hydrant covers are easily seen.

If you would like free advice and information on home fire safety please contact your local fire station or alternatively, if you would like to receive a free information pack on how to protect your home from fire, please contact the Surrey Fire and Rescue Service on: 01737 242444, during office hours quoting reference no. MV1.

Remember in the event of fire:-

GET OUT
GET US OUT
STAY OUT

c) Front door requirements

- solid hardwood construction, preferably 2" thick or more
- one good quality cylinder lock, fitted 1/3rd way down from the top
- a five lever mortice deadlock, fitted 1/3rd way up from the bottom
- door chain fitted between the above
- spy hole if otherwise solid door
- hinge bolts 4"-6" below top and above bottom hinge
- ideally 3" or 4" hinges of good quality

d) Rear or side door

- solid hardwood construction, preferably 2" thick or more
- five lever morticed sashlock to centre of door
- hinges and hinge bolts as for front door
- 2 morticed security bolts fitted about 12" from the top/bottom of the door

e) Door frames

- as important as your door they should be of hardwood construction and rawl bolted or screwed to the brickwork

f) French windows and patio doors

- often a favourite weak spot for burglars
- supplement manufacturer's locks where appropriate
- fit morticed security bolts acting into top and bottom sill
- lock to the centre where possible and appropriate

g) Windows

- locks are available for all sorts of windows and must be key operated
- for safety and convenience all locks should use the same key

h) Security lighting

- internal and external, use on timers or sensors

i) Keys

- remove from their locks when not in use

j) Property marking

- mark valuables with post code followed by house number or name, preferably with UV marker pen or die stamp

k) Smoke/Burglar alarms

- a smoke alarm is cheap and essential, a burglar alarm is expensive and optional, both will help your peace of mind

Cubitt & West
SURREY~SUSSEX~HAMPSHIRE

INVITATION

You are cordially invited to receive an up-to-date *Free Market Appraisal.*

Cubitt and West, one of Surrey's leading Independent Estate Agents, would be pleased to provide you with accurate and professional advice on the current sale or rental value of your property. This invitation is extended entirely without obligation.

Reply to Steve Atterbury

179 High Street
Dorking RH4 1RU
Tel: 01306 883399

3 North Street
Leatherhead KT22 7AX
Tel: 01372 373780

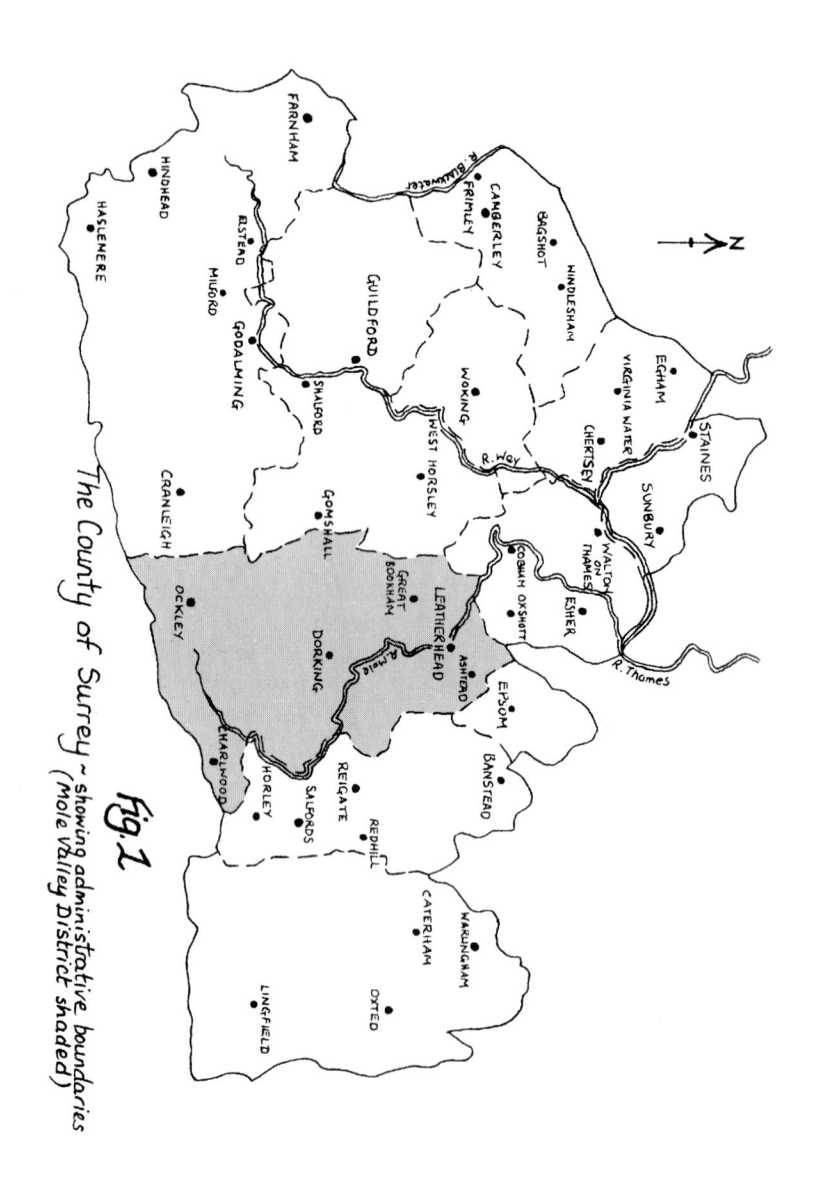

fig.1 The County of Surrey ~ showing administrative boundaries (Mole Valley District shaded)

ABOUT SURREY

LOCATION

Surrey's greatest asset is probably its natural location in England, encompassing an urban landscape on its northern borders with London gradually becoming more rural towards the outskirts. However, even where close to London, Surrey boasts proximity to magnificent **Richmond Park, Wimbledon Common** and **Bushy Park** providing the 'best of both worlds' for many.

Despite being a comparatively small county of only some 650 square miles, Surrey's variety in landscapes is remarkable and much of its attraction. There are many areas of **outstanding natural beauty**, in steep glens, wooded hills and vast open land with wonderful, sweeping views. Deep in its countryside it is not hard to appreciate why this attractive county has, in fact, the largest number of trees of any county in England.

Rural Surrey boasts the area of the **North Downs**, *which despite being so close to central London, have remained totally unspoilt. Here it is possible to find any home of your choice from pretty terraced cottages to fine majestic houses, all within easy reach of comprehensive amenities. There has been and always will be, a solid demand for homes within Surrey's extensive commuter area.*
Guildford, *Surrey's county town, is typical of the area, where modern living and excellent shopping facilities combine with sympathetic historic restoration. Other notable shopping centres of similar proportion are* **Woking, Redhill, Staines** *and* **Kingston**, *although all the major towns have an extremely good variety of shops. Historical places to visit are too numerous to mention but* **Hampton Court Palace** *on the banks of the Thames is probably the most famous.*

N.B. It is interesting to note that the **County Boundary** of Surrey and the **Postal District** of Surrey are not one and the same and may therefore cause confusion. In fact Surrey used to stretch as far into London as Southwark and Penge! Now even Kingston and Richmond are absorbed within the boundary of Greater London and not within the county. It is all the more ironic therefore to find the ***Headquarters of Surrey County Council***, outside the County itself - in Kingston!

ORIGINS

Surrey relied on the growth of London for its origins, which became established with the invasion of the Romans in 43 AD. There is no evidence to suggest London existed before then as no major Iron Age settlement has been revealed, but soon after the arrival of the Romans the city grew to a thriving centre in only 10 to 15 years.

Surrey was in the middle of the road to Chichester known as **'Stane Street'** (stone road). It passed through Ewell, Dorking and Ockley and some parts of the current A29 still follow its precise route. Other parts are still easily found following the course of bridle paths close to Ashtead and across the Mickleham Downs near Box Hill. Although this road was originally built to facilitate troop movement, when peace was established it then became an important trade route. There is evidence that small towns existed at Dorking and Ewell, and Ashtead was the site of an important villa and tile industry.

Most of the Roman villa estates in Surrey probably concentrated on farming at Titsey, Bletchingley, Walton Heath, Walton-on-the-Hill, Chatley Heath, Abinger, Broad Street, Compton, Chiddingfold and Rapsley. At Farnham's villa it seems that domestic pottery was also manufactured. The villas may have had their own shrines for worship, but the sites of three small rural temples are known at Titsey, Farley Heath and Wanborough.

There was another road to Silchester, to the west of London, that passed through Staines and there are signs of a military establishment dating from this time in Petters Sports Field near Egham. There were no major towns established in Surrey, but the most important small town was Staines, a key crossing point over the River Thames. In the fifth century AD Roman Surrey became Saxon Surrey when the county, as we know it, really began to first emerge. New discoveries are still happening to tell us more about this interesting period of transition about which little is known.

POTTED HISTORY
Industry

Surrey's general poor soil quality and hilly terrain meant that much of it was left uncultivated for most of its history, even now the county is not particularly famous for its farms. Surrey however thrived on its proximity to London and its own industries developed, in particular around the use of its clean and **plentiful water.** Therefore the county was well known for its numerous **mills;** corn, iron, copper, calico and paper, which were spread along the paths of its rivers. These mills were active in Surrey from the early seventeenth century until 1928 when the last mill closed.

Other industries depended on the use of **local materials**, extractive works were always important in Surrey. The soils of the county divide into two main areas, that north of the chalk downs with soils of the London Basin and acid Bagshot sands, to land to the south taking in the greensands, the gault and the claylands of the Weald. Much of the land is acid and thin or heavy and wooded therefore not suitable for agriculture.

The **glass industry** made use of the local sand, stone and clay, and oak and coppice wood for firing the furnaces. This skill was brought to Surrey by immigrants from Normandy and Lorraine. Another main industry was **iron,** the ore coming from the clay ironstone of the Weald. Other rural works were based on **cloth** (Guildford), **leather and knitwear** (Godalming), **gunpowder** (Tolworth, Ewell and Chilworth) and **fruit and hops** (Farnham). The influence of London is apparent by the dominant reservoirs for the capital's water supply in parts of Spelthorne and Elmbridge.

The **Wey Navigation** was an early example of a canal system, built at the instigation of Sir Richard Weston of Sutton Place and opened in Guildford in 1653. It is notable for its early use of pound locks and for the survival of one of its wharfside cranes, the treadwheel crane at Guildford.

A distinction for Surrey is the **Surrey Iron Railway** (1803) which was the earliest public railway in Britain running from Wandsworth to Croydon, with its extension to Merstham and Godstone, the course of which may still be found.

A series of **Admiralty Semaphore towers,** some of which still remain at Cooper's Hill, Chatley Heath and Pewley Hill were devised by Sir Home Riggs Popham in 1816 and were used between London and Portsmouth during 1822 -1847.

Coming into more modern day history, **Brooklands** was a major aircraft centre in the early part of the 20th century. Later it became the world's first motor testing and racing circuit - home of bouncing bomb creator Barnes Wallis and now a museum. At present one of Surrey's most modern Business Parks is also situated here catering for some of today's industries.

Leisure

Surrey has been very important as a setting for **sporting activities** and leisure in its more recent history. Even in the seventeenth century, the North Downs had gained a reputation as a health resort and a place of recreation. **Horse racing** seems to have taken place from Tudor times and Epsom, Lingfield, Sandown and Kempton Park have long been famous venues. Horse racing at Streatham, Croydon and Gatwick were also once well-known. **Fox hunting** was also a strong tradition, perhaps because of the proximity of several royal palaces and Croydon was probably the main centre in the early nineteenth century. **Cricket** and **golf** also have been widespread and traditional in the county, the latter having some considerable affect on parts of the modern Surrey landscape.

Various parts of the County are still well known for their Victorian houses, in picturesque settings. Many of these properties were built by wealthy Londoners of the time who enjoyed the Surrey air and beauty. Transport developments from the early nineteenth century really started to open up the Surrey countryside for leisure purposes and especially as **a playground for Londoners.** However it seems that leisure in those days was normally only enjoyed by the rich, as there was little time or opportunity for the majority to indulge.

Fashionable towns emerged, such as **Epsom,** which was the first town in England to be developed as a spa for taking purgative waters for medicinal purposes. **Richmond** too became a resort by the Georgian period, famous for its splendid scenery and stunning location on the Thames. Royal and society patronage assured its growing and continuing popularity.

Surrey became increasingly urbanised north of the Downs so the need for accessible **open spaces** increased, some were provided by local authorities or as gifts from landowners. Several of the old commons near London survived because of very strong local efforts which saved them from development. However, well into the twentieth century it was still easy to take a country walk in the attractive countryside of Streatham, Tooting, Merton and Malden before the great housing sprawl of the 1920s and 1930s.

Buildings and Gardens

Most of Surrey's towns and villages have their origins in medieval times; the surviving 13th century undercrofts in Guildford are an example. However, inevitably many of Surrey's historical buildings have been lost with time. One example is Guildford's Friary which was only revealed recently when excavations were completed beneath the new shopping centre there of the same name.

Other great buildings have been lost as well such as Nonsuch Palace at Cheam, although the ruins of **Waverley Abbey** - the first Cistercian house in England - and **Newark Priory** still exist. Of the few castles ever built in Surrey, those at Farnham and at Guildford have fortunately survived, the former remarkably well.

Surrey, which can now be described as one vast 'garden suburb', was once home to several traditional landscape gardens. Such examples as **Claremont** (near Esher) and **Painshill** (near Cobham) have been recently restored and are open to the public. There are also numerous smaller gardens which are open occasionally throughout the year. Normally you can find them advertised within the local press and in some tourist guides.

ROAD AND RAIL COMMUNICATIONS

Surrey is extremely well served by an extensive road and rail network so that the furthest parts of the county are all less than an hour away from central London. Running through the heart of Surrey is the south west quarter of the **M25**, connecting the towns of **Reigate, Leatherhead, Chertsey** and **Staines.** This large **London Orbital Motorway** therefore provides excellent connections between all of the capital's surrounding home counties, and fast roads into London.

The major arterial routes from London in Surrey are the **M3** to the west, the **A3** to the south west, and the **A24** and **M23** to the south. Much of the county is therefore equi-distant between the **Capital** and the **South Coast**, providing some of the finest venues for leisure entertainment of all kinds.

The **M25** continues to dominate both discussion of, and work on, the county's infrastructure needs. Major re-widening programmes are continuing along its length in Surrey. The **A3** has recently been very much improved and in the area of **Hindhead** there are plans for a new tunnel, thus relieving its last major congestion site on the route to Portsmouth.

Examples of fastest commuting rail times to **Victoria/Waterloo:**

From **Godalming** 44 mins, **Guildford** 39 mins, **Dorking** 38 minutes, **Reigate** 37 mins, **Leatherhead** 33 minutes, **Ashtead** 30 minutes, **Epsom** 28 minutes

Examples of road distances to **Central London:**

Godalming 35 miles (A3), **Guildford** 31 miles (A3), **Dorking** 25 miles (A24), **Reigate** 23 miles (A217), **Leatherhead** 19 miles (A24), **Ashtead** 17 miles (A24), **Epsom** 14 miles (A3)

See Fig. 2 Surrey's main road network and Fig. 3 Surrey's main rail network

fig.2

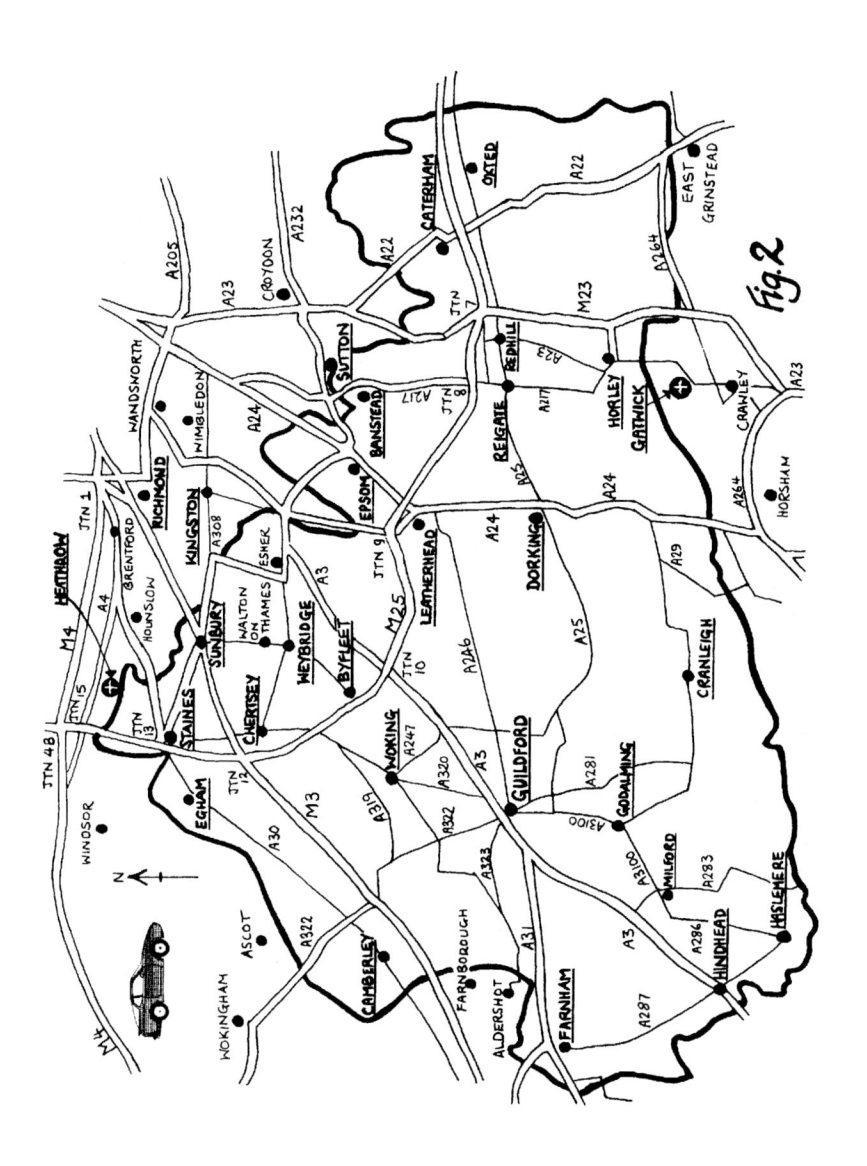

fig.3

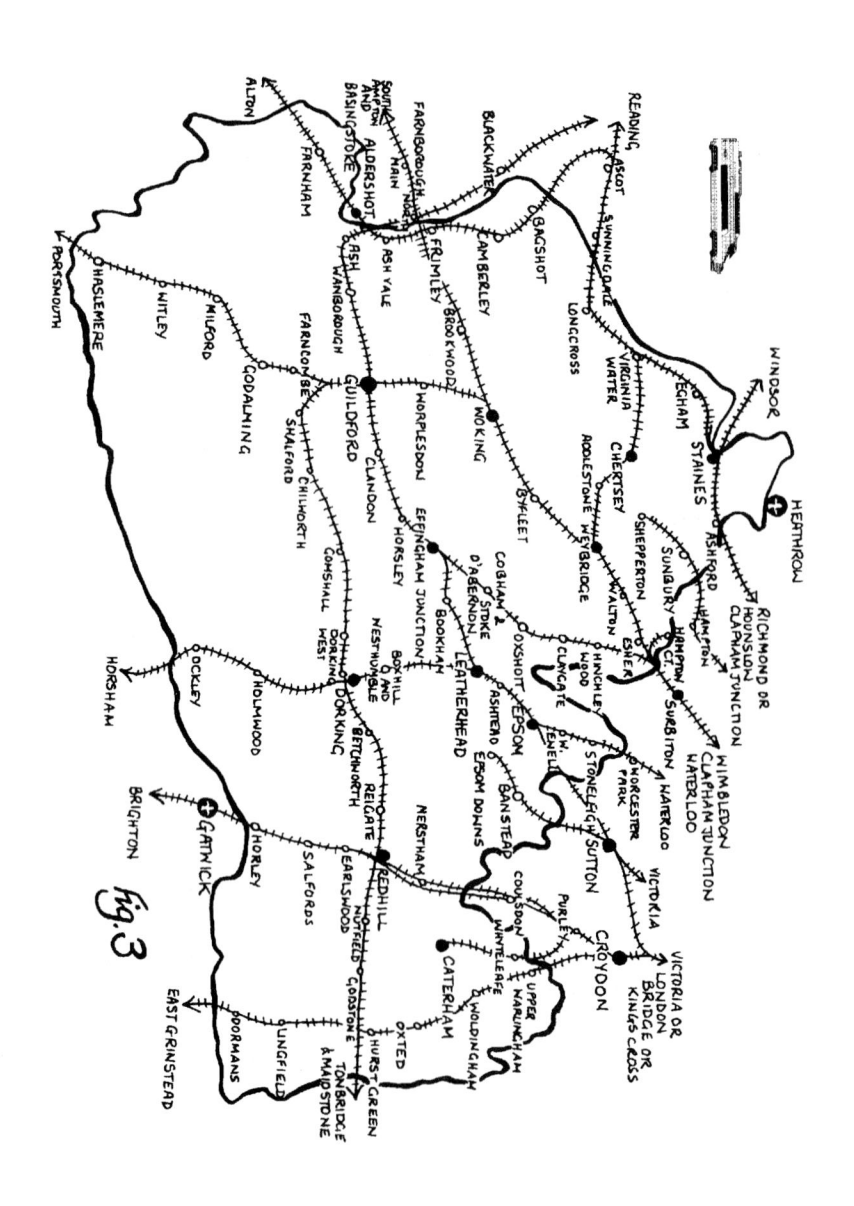

RIGHTS OF WAY - 'OFF ROAD'

The county has some 37,000 acres of land known as open space, 10,000 of which is managed by the County Council. Other bodies such as The National Trust, The Forestry Commission and Hurtwood Control nurture and protect particular open spaces, the majority of which is open and accessible to the public.

Surrey is particularly fortunate therefore to have a large network of public **Rights of Way** meandering through this glorious countryside, often presenting spectacular views. In fact there are about two thousand miles of public footpaths and bridleways which criss-cross the county through its varied scenery of woodland, downland and heathland. It is noticeable, and not surprising that activities which take advantage of these routes are particularly popular in Surrey such as horse riding, rambling and mountain biking. The three longest such routes in Surrey are the North Downs Way, The Greensand Way and the Downs Link.

The North Downs Way

This historic path has been used since the Stone Age by travellers for pilgrimages or for trade. In Surrey it begins near the banks of the River Wey passing the villages of Compton and Puttenham to Guildford, then through woodland along the southern edge of the downs by way of Hackhurst Downs, White Downs and Ranmore Common.

After crossing the River Mole it climbs steeply up the western face of Box Hill keeping to the escarpment above Brockham and Betchworth. It follows the crest of Reigate Hill, climbs past Arthur's Seat, (an Iron Age camp), on to Gravelly Hill and then Botley Hill, (at 867 feet the highest point on the North Downs) above Limpsfield. South of Tatsfield it crosses the county boundary into Kent. Marked by an 'Acorn' symbol, it is a total of 141 miles long from Farnham to Dover. The route in Surrey alone covers 45 miles, however unlike the South Downs Way, not all of it is a public path.

The Greensand Way

A route 105 miles long, of which the 55 miles in Surrey is marked by the letters 'GW'. As its name suggests, it follows the greensand hills from Haslemere to Hamstreet in Kent. It crosses the highest point in south east England on its path at Leith Hill, which is approximately 1000 feet above sea level.

Downs Link

A 33 mile long bridleway which mostly follows the route of a disused railway. At its northern end it starts at St. Martha's Hill and connects the North Downs to the South Downs at Steyning in West Sussex.

There are many rights of way to enjoy and the Pathfinder series of maps produced by the Ordnance Survey at a scale of 1:25,000, are recommended as showing them most accurately. More information about routes, symbols or waymarks may be obtained by telephoning the **Rights of Way Group** on 0181 541 9331. A copy of **Surrey's Environment News** provides details of guided walks and events.Telephone: The Editor, Surrey County Council on 0181 541 9463.

AIRPORTS

Surrey lies between the airports at **London Heathrow** to the north of the county and **London Gatwick** to the south, therefore providing one of the best possible locations for any air traveller. Discussion on a possible 5th terminal for Heathrow is currently underway, though Surrey County Council is against the proposals on environmental grounds. Gatwick may also be a venue for an extra runway within the next ten years or so. *Despite the close proximity of these airports most of Surrey does not suffer acute aircraft noise.* However, some of the smaller rural villages and outlying areas to the west of Gatwick are frequently beneath the flight paths and consideration must be given to this factor when moving home. In particular Charlwood is on Gatwick's doorstep and the villages of Capel, Ockley, Newdigate, Holmwood, Walliswood and Oakwoodhill are also not far away. Bear this in mind especially when considering property prices.

Tip - For enquiries/complaints about noise from Gatwick - Tel: 0800 393070

BUSINESS INVESTMENT

Historically Surrey residents relied on London for employment, but more recently it is turning in on itself. Now about 18% of those employed in the county are self-employed and between 1981 and 1991 there was a 12.1% reduction in commuters to the capital. However Surrey's growth in employment only ranks 57th out of the country's 66 counties.

'**Surrey First**' is a pro-active partnership between the county's public and private sectors, incorporating **Surrey County Council, Surrey Training and Enterprise Council (TEC)** and district councils. It also receives support from more than 30 private sector businesses across Surrey who recognise the long-term benefits of new business moving to the area. Originally set up in 1993, Surrey First has announced initial successes of its global marketing campaign where major relocation is being attracted into the area. The local county councils, although not looking for major development, want existing businesses to prosper and for empty workspaces to be efficiently used. There are many examples of large international companies based in Surrey (such as 'Esso' at Ashtead, 'Kuoni' at Dorking and Brown & Root at Leatherhead; further campaigns are planned to attract more.

Recently 'Kimberly-Clark', the hygiene products manufacturer has relocated 100 executives from France and Kent to **Reigate.** The company hopes to create up to 500 jobs over the next few years. These newcomers are in good company, during the past few years 'Sony' and 'Proctor and Gamble' have chosen Surrey for major headquarters and are now based at **Brooklands Business Park.**

However the employment created by high-profile relocations is dwarfed by the county's retail sector. Retailing is Surrey's biggest employer, accounting for 20.7% of the working population, other important sectors include business, property and public services. Surrey's most populous town is **Guildford** (60,000), companies there include the National Grid and pharmaceutical manufacturers Sterling Winthrop. The town is also home to one of the county's leading science parks owned by the **University of Surrey. Surrey Research Park** is known for its work in bio-technology, pharmaceuticals and information technology. **Woking** is the county's second biggest centre with a population of 55,500. The plastics manufacturer ACI Europe UK, steel equipment manufacturer FC Brown, the Martins Printing Group and Crown Financial Management are the major local employers. The communications company 'Nokia' is currently investing £35 million in its base in **Camberley** which will provide significantly more jobs in the area.

NEW HOMES

Provision has been made for the construction of **35,600 new homes** in the county as part of the **Surrey Structure Plan** which is the blueprint for development into the next century. Recent government figures suggest a need for another 17,000 which places pressure on Surrey's Green Belt policy. However the Department of the Environment forecasts the number of Surrey households to reach 483,000 in the next 20 years. Much of rural Surrey has stringent planning restrictions especially in the wealth of Areas of Outstanding Natural Beauty so Surrey County Council is questioning the need for so many new homes. Long term the prosperity of Surrey will be based on the continuing success of London as a major world capital city which is unlikely to reduce. Overall Surrey's population is increasing at about 2.3%, albeit less rapidly than the South East average at 3.2%. The largest growth being in the Woking area.

HOUSE PRICES

On a general basis house prices have lost ground in Surrey since 1988 by an average of -18%, but as with so many 'average' figures this doesn't mean across the board. Generally pre-1920 quality properties have faired much better than average and the more unique character homes have at least held their ground. Brand new homes too, are particularly popular with incentives and part-exchange schemes to make moving more attractive. Once in the market of course, the price disparity between smaller and larger properties remains much the same and for first time buyers undoubtedly the price of homes now are more affordable in comparison with general income, than in many times this century.

Such is Surrey's popularity, that house prices are set to continue to be one of the country's highest, even compared with other home counties. Although the recent recession hit the South East to a great extent, Surrey has traditionally boasted very affluent residents especially in the areas of Virginia Water, Epsom and Guildford, this trend is unlikely to change. A fact which also reflects this is the very large number of independent schools in the County.

For 'prime' Surrey property and estates where 'cash rich' investors may invest without the need for mortgages, generally these types of properties are making significant increases in value. For the more usual 'mainstream' properties requiring mortgaging, the market can be still rather unsteady.

However with the future beginning to look brighter for the economy and employment prospects, any confidence will certainly filter through to the housing market. This may take longer, of course, than some estate agents would like to forecast, but realistically further significant reductions in prices must be becoming less and less likely.

J.B.P. Builders
A
Complete Building Service
Extensions - Alterations - New Houses
Garden Layouts - Plumbing & Heating
Decorating
Inc: J.N. Norton
Plumbing & Heating
Tel 01306 712880 Fax 711648

DORKING

Chalcraft Pool Centre
For All Types Of
Pools & Leisure
Equipment
Installers
Maintenance
Sales
Tel: 01306 713503 Fax: 711648

R.T. OVERTON & SONS LTD
BONDS LANE
MID-HOLMWOOD,
DORKING, SURREY RH5 4HF
GENERAL BUILDER
FAMILY FIRM
ESTABLISHED 1957
Telephone: 01306 888624
Fax: 01306 876252

G.T. HEATING
CORGI REGISTERED
Quality gas central heating, installation and repairs. Bathrooms, showers, tiling. All electrical work undertaken.
Tel: 01306 730648
Mobile 0378 995726

THE NATIONAL TRUST

The National Trust, Britain's leading conservation charity, protects over 5,267 hectares of outstanding country-side in Surrey for you to visit. In the Mole Valley there is: Polesden Lacey, Box Hill and Leith Hill.

You can support the National Trust by joining as a member and benefit from free admission to hundreds of properties. To join, or for further details, please ask at a National Trust property or contact the Membership Department, PO Box 39, Bromley, Kent. BR1 3XL
Tel: (0181) 315 1111

POLESDEN LACEY

Great Bookham, near Dorking
Surrey RH5 6BD
Tel. 01372 458203
Polesden Lacey is a peaceful country estate, set on the Surrey Downs. The house, an elegant Regency 'villa', was luxuriously furnished in Edwardian times by society hostess, The Hon. Mrs Greville. Her collection of furniture, paintings, porcelain and silver is remarkable. Walled rose garden & stunning landscape walks.
Grounds: Open Daily.
House: Open between March and October, (Telephone first to confirm days & hours)

BOX HILL

Nr. Dorking
Tel. 01306 885502
On the edge of the North Downs, rising to 600 feet above the River Mole. Walks and nature trails through extensive wood and chalk downland.
Shop. Information Centre

LEITH HILL

Nr. Coldharbour
18th century Tower on the highest point in South East England. Magnificent views to the North and South Downs. Tower Open: All year at weekends, (occasionally midweek). Refreshments
Photo:
Polesden Lacey Estate

Photo: Leith Hill Tower

INFORMATION CENTRES

TOURIST INFORMATION CENTRES

FARNHAM
Vernon House, 28 West Street, Farnham　　　　01252 715109
GUILDFORD
14 Tunsgate, Guildford　　　　01483 444333
CLACKET LANE,
M25 Service Area, Limpsfield　　East bound　01959 565063
　　　　　　　　　　　　　　　West bound　01959 565615

SURREY COUNTY COUNCIL INFORMATION CENTRES

BANSTEAD LIBRARY
Bolters Lane, Banstead　　　　01737 352958
CAMBERLEY LIBRARY
Knoll Road, Camberley　　　　01276 683626
EPSOM LIBRARY
12/14 Waterloo Road, Epsom　　　　01372 744224
EWELL LIBRARY
Bourne Hall, Spring Street, Ewell　　　　0181 394 0372
GUILDFORD LIBRARY
77 North Street, Guildford　　　　01483 34120
REDHILL LIBRARY
18-20 London Road, Redhill　　　　01737 773204
STAINES LIBRARY
Friends Walk, Staines　　　　01784 463071
WEYBRIDGE LIBRARY
Church Street, Weybridge　　　　01932 856058
WOKING LIBRARY
Gloucester Walk, Woking　　　　01483 771011
BANSTEAD HELP SHOP
The Horseshoe, Banstead　　　　01737 363178
DORKING HELP DESK
Pippbrook, Dorking　　　　01306 885001
REDHILL HELP SHOP
35 Station Road, Redhill　　　　01737 770333

Forest Enterprise, an arm of the Forestry Commission, is responsible for managing the nation's forests. In the Mole Valley area this includes Pasture Wood, Highridge, Redlands and Buryhill.

For a number of years, Forest Enterprise has been practising "Multi-purpose Management". This means that in addition to the original and prime purpose of producing timber from sustainable sources, a considerable effort is now put into wildlife conservation, landscaping, public access and recreation.

Wildlife Conservation

Species diversity is of great importance and to encourage this, plantings are now of diverse tree species, rides and pathways are widened, shrubs and wildflowers planted at the edges and dead trees allowed to stand, where they can in safety. All this encourages various species of insects. Dead wood is allowed to rest where it falls, providing homes for invertebrates as it rots. More insects mean more food for birds so they too prosper in the forests.

Landscaping

These days when felling takes place it is usually done in relatively small patches or compartments. Replanting is carried out with wavy edges to the compartments, and with different species to give a variation in the colour of the forests when viewed from a distance. Variation is also provided by planting hardwoods next to ditches and other watercourses.

Public Access

The public have the freedom to roam in all of the forest owned by Forest Enterprise. In many there are waymarked trails to follow. Car parks are provided, notably at Highridge where the car park is now much improved.

Recreation

The forest lends itself to many recreational pursuits from cycling to husky racing, form archery to wayfaring. Permission for any organised activity must be obtained from the District Office. Forest Enterprise also has an education service staffed by rangers, complete with a Forest Classroom at Alice Holt Woodland Park near Farnham. Rangers are able to run courses in any of the District's forest for groups large or small.

Please use and enjoy your forest, it is an ever changing organism for us all to cherish.

For further information, contact the District Office on 01420 23666

SURREY COUNTY COUNCIL

LOCAL INFORMATION

Surrey County Council
County Hall, Penrhyn Road,
Kingston upon Thames KT1 2DN   0181 541 8800

Surrey County Council has nearly 1000 service outlets throughout the county. Some useful contact numbers are listed below. If you need a number which is not listed, phone the switchboard on 0181 541 8800.

Adult Education - area office	01372 386851
Archives and Records	0181 541 9065
Business and Economic Information	0181 541 9602
Casualty Reduction (Road Safety)	01737 249224
Countryside Information	0181 541 9463
Education	0181 541 9501
Elderly and Disabled Bus Passes	0181 541 9407
Fire and Rescue HQ	01737 242444
Gipsy Matters	0181 541 9036
Leisure and Tourism	0181 541 9477
Libraries-Leatherhead	01372 373149
-Dorking	01306 882948
Planning	0181 541 9409
Public Relations	0181 541 9082
Register Office for Births, Deaths & Marriages	01372 721747
Rent Officer	01483 577619
Rights of Way	0181 541 9331
Roads and Footpaths	0181 541 9947
Social Services	0181 541 9641
Surrey Information Service	0181 541 9099
Surrey Traveline	01737 223000
Trading Standards	01306 513000
Waste Disposal	0181 541 9105
Youth Service - area office	01737 243661

Caring For Our County

Its big business securing vital services for over one million people in Surrey - essential services people in and around Ashtead, Capel, Dorking and Leatherhead use every day.

Last year Surrey County Council:
- educated over 105,500 children
- answered 33,522 '999' calls
- helped over 18,000 social services clients
- financially supported over 200 bus routes in the County
- managed 10,000 acres of Surrey's countryside
- loaned out over 2 million books and audio visual
- looked after 3,000 miles of roads
- dealt with 18,000 enquiries from traders and consumers
- registered over 35,800 births, deaths and marriages

Have you received the A-Z guide of local services?
Produced in partnership by Surrey County Council and Mole Valley District Council it is your essential guide to public services in Mole Valley.

SURREY COUNTY COUNCIL
County Hall,
Kingston upon Thames
KT1 2DN

Telephone 01306 885001 or 0181-541 9082 for your free copy.

SURREY COUNTY COUNCIL arranges services for over one million people in Surrey every day. Wherever you are in Surrey, you'll find near you a library, a school, a fire station, a youth club, a family centre, a highway improvement scheme, a countryside trail, a home for the elderly.

High quality services which touch your life and the lives of your family and friends every day.

365 days a year Surrey County Council aims to get value for money in everything it does and to make Surrey a quality place in which to live and work.

SURREY COUNTY COUNCIL PUBLICATIONS

Who Does What? - guide to local authority services, A-Z of Services in Mole Valley, Caring for our County, Council Tax, How to get to County Hall, How to have your say, Countywide, Your County Councillors, Surrey Citizen's Charter, Monthly Programme of County Council Meetings, Annual Report (£2.50 incl.: p&p), Places to Visit in Surrey, What's On In Surrey, Surrey's Environment News, Surrey Bus and Train Guides

All the above may be obtained from the County Council
Telephone: 0181 541 9082 / 9099

MOLE VALLEY DISTRICT COUNCIL INFORMATION

Mole Valley District Council
Pippbrook, Reigate Rd, Dorking RH4 1SJ   01306 885001
Emergency Council service (outside office hours)   01372 376533

The District Council look after the services which have a more local emphasis like housing, environmental health, local planning, refuse collection, leisure and other amenities. If you require a number which is not listed, telephone the switchboard. *Tip* - The Mole Valley is a 'District' as opposed to a 'Borough' Council, because it has a chairman rather than a mayor, did you know the difference?!

Air Pollution and Bonfires		01306 879226
Allotments		01306 879299
Building Control/Regulations		01306 879264
Car Parks		01306 879190
Community Transport		01306 879377
Community Alarm		01306 276573
Council Housing	applications	01306 879209
	rents	01306 879222
	repairs	01306 888810
Council Tax	see table	01306 885001
Electoral Registration		01306 879138
Housing Grants		01306 879226
Noise nuisance		01306 879226
Pest control		01306 879226
Planning		01306 879261
Recycling (collections from home in urban areas)		01306 879190
Refuse Collection		01306 879203

COUNCIL TAX BANDS AND CHARGES 1996-97

Council Tax is the way that residents help to pay for the services that the local council provides. Each council sets the level of the council tax for its own area, but the amount payable depends on the value of the property relative to others in the local area. There is one council tax bill for each dwelling which is usually payable by the owner-occupier or tenant.

Valuation Band	Range of Values
A	Up to £40,000
B	£40,001...... £52,000
C	£52,001...... £68,000
D	£68,001...... £88,000
E	£88,001.....£120,000
F	£120,001...£160,000
G	£160,001...£320,000
H	More than....£320,000

Approximate Mole Valley Charges for 1996

Bands:	A	B	C	D	E	F	G	H
(1)	£307	£358	£409	£460	£562	£665	£767	£921
(2)	£28	£33	£38	£42	£52	£62	£71	£85
(3)	£42	£49	£56	£63	£77	£91	£106	£127

(1) = Surrey County Council Charge
(2) = Surrey Police Charge
(3) = Mole Valley District Council Charge

Add (1) plus (2) plus (3) for the annual charge, also allow for local Parish charges which add a further figure to the **total bill**. They vary between approximately £40 for Band 'A' properties to about £140 for Band 'H' properties

TOWN AND VILLAGE FACILITIES
'AT-A-GLANCE'

To help you in your choice of area, listed below are the towns and villages of the 'Mole Valley' - the area covered by this guide. The following section introduces them all in more detail.

Key: * Indicates 'limited' services or facilities
'State' or 'Ind.' under Schools shows the numbers of state or independant schools in the immediate area
'Train Stn' showing 'Yes' indicates within about one mile's distance
'Golf Course' showing 'Yes' indicates very local

	DORKING	LEATHERHEAD	ASHTEAD	BOOKHAM	FETCHAM
BUSES	YES	YES	YES	YES	YES
TRAIN STN	YES	YES	YES	YES	YES
PRIMARY SCHOOLS	7 STATE 2 IND.	4 STATE 2 IND.	4 STATE 2 IND.	4 STATE 1 IND	2 STATE
SECOND'Y SCHOOLS	3 STATE	2 STATE 1 IND.	2 IND.	1 IND.	
SHOP(S)	YES	YES	YES	YES	YES
POST OFF.	YES	YES	YES	YES	YES
PUB(S)	YES	YES	YES	YES	YES
CHURCH(S)	YES	YES	YES	YES	YES
ACCOMM'N	YES	YES	YES	YES	YES
SPORTS GR	YES	YES	YES		
REC. GR.	YES	YES	YES	YES	YES
GREEN					
CRICKET GR.		YES	YES		
GOLF C'SE	YES	YES			
THEATRE		YES			
LIBRARY	YES	YES	YES	YES	
STABLES	YES	YES		YES	
PETROL	YES (24 HR)	YES (24 HR)	YES	YES	YES

	ABINGER COMMON	**ABINGER HAMMER**	**BETCHWORTH**	**BROCKHAM**	**CAPEL**
BUSES	YES*	YES	YES	YES	YES
TRAIN STN		YES*	YES*		YES
PRIMARY SCHOOLS	1 STATE 1 IND.	1 STATE	1 STATE	1 STATE	1 STATE
SHOP(S)		YES*	YES*	YES*	YES*
POST OFF.		YES	YES	YES	YES
PUB(S)	YES	YES	YES	YES	YES
CHURCH(S)	YES		YES	YES	YES
ACCOMM'N	YES		YES	YES	YES
SPORTS GR				YES	
REC. GR.	YES	YES			YES
GREEN	YES	YES		YES	
CRICKET GR.		YES	YES		
GOLF C'SE			YES	YES	
PETROL			YES		YES

	CHARLWOOD	**COLDHARBOUR**	**HEADLEY**	**HOLMBURY ST. MARY**	**HOLMWOOD**
BUSES	YES*		YES	YES*	YES
TRAIN STN					YES
PRIMARY SCHOOLS	1 STATE			1 STATE 1 IND.	
SHOP(S)	YES*		YES*		YES*
POST OFF.	YES		YES	YES*	YES
PUB(S)	YES	YES	YES	YES	YES
CHURCH(S)	YES	YES	YES	YES	YES
ACCOMM'N	YES			YES	YES
SPORTS GR				YES	YES
REC. GR.	YES				YES
GREEN				YES	YES
CRICKET GR.			YES	YES	YES
GOLF C'SE			YES	YES	YES
STABLES			YES		
PETROL				YES	YES (24HR)

	LEIGH	MICKLEHAM inc WESTHUMBLE	NEWDIGATE	OCKLEY	WESTCOTT
BUSES	YES*	YES*	YES*	YES*	YES
TRAIN STN		YES		YES	
PRIMARY SCHOOLS	1 STATE 1 IND.	1 STATE	1 STATE	1 STATE	1 STATE
SECONDARY SCHOOLS		1 IND.			
SHOP(S)	YES*	YES*	YES*	YES*	YES*
POST OFF.	YES	YES	YES	YES	YES
PUB(S)	YES	YES	YES	YES	YES
CHURCH(S)	YES	YES	YES	YES	YES
ACCOMM'N		YES	YES	YES	YES
SPORTS GR		YES			
REC. GR.		YES	YES		YES
GREEN	YES			YES	YES
CRICKET GR.				YES	YES
GOLF C'SE		YES		YES	
STABLES			YES		YES
PETROL	YES			YES	

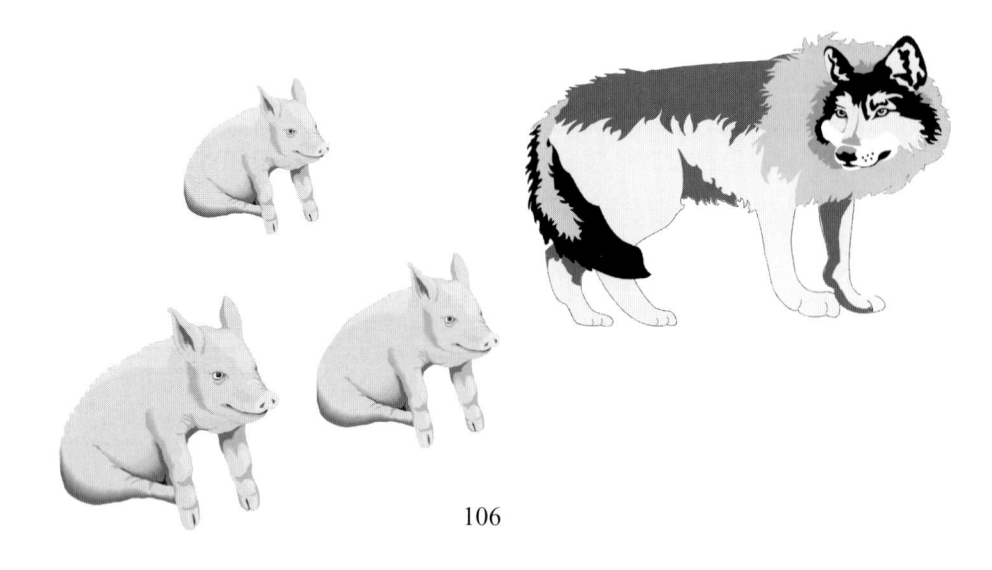

106

"Welcome to the Mole Valley one of the safest areas of England and Wales and a very pleasant and tranquil place to live and work.

Surrey Police works with the community to ensure Mole Valley stays safe and the efforts of the past 12 months have revealed a 12 per cent drop in recorded crime.

This success is based on a geographical approach to policing developed by Surrey Police. As a result, teams of police officers are responsible for individual areas. This gives rise to ownership of problems and the officers work with the community to solve them. The aim is to treat the causes of crime as well as the symptoms.

In developing methods of crime prevention we work in partnership with communities and outside agencies, including *Police and Community Partnership Groups and Neighbourhood Watch Groups.*

There are three Police and Community Partnership Groups in Mole Valley. Members of the public and police officers make up these groups and there is one each for Dorking and Leatherhead, and a third, the Rural Group, for the villages in the southern half of the district.

These groups have already organised major initiatives to raise drugs awareness among parents as well as highlighting the importance of crime prevention for homes and motor vehicles.

They have also been instrumental in the recruiting of parish special constables. These are volunteers who supplement and support the local policing service.

At the present time 110 separate Neighbourhood Watch schemes are running in the area, helping to reduce the amount of crime.

For those of you not familiar with Neighbourhood Watch, it is a self help scheme whereby householders undertake to improve the security and identification of their property.

This not only deters the burglars, but also keeps down home insurance premiums. The scheme also requires neighbours to keep an eye on each others' property and asks them to report any suspicious activity to the police.

The members of the schemes receive training detailing the information the police require, so when you phone in, all your calls can be dealt with quickly and in the most appropriate way.

Neighbourhood Watch has proved to be an effective deterrent to burglars, as well as resulting in many arrests. So if you move to an area that is not yet covered the police will be happy to assist you to set up a scheme.

Surrey Police also runs a *Crimestoppers* scheme by which a person can talk to the police informally and without identifying who they are. To use the service call 0800 555 111, you could be in line for a reward.

There is a full time Police Crime Reduction Officer serving the Mole Valley, who will be only too pleased to advise you on all aspects of security. It is a free service and for more details you can contact the officer on Dorking (01306 882284) or Leatherhead (01372 372255)"

Superintendent Andy Richardson, Mole Valley Division, Surrey Police

■ **SURREY** ■
POLICE

Dorking High Street *Photo courtesy of Surrey County Council*

TOWNS AND VILLAGES OF THE MOLE VALLEY

The Mole Valley is one of the most beautiful Districts in Surrey, through which the River Mole meanders from its source in Sussex north towards the Thames at East Molesey. Its course follows one of the few natural gaps in the **North Downs**. The high grounds of **Box Hill** and **Leith Hill** are also great features in the 100 square miles of the District where numerous quaint villages and smart residential areas may be found. **Dorking**, in the centre and **Leatherhead** further north, lie at either end of the river's path through the Downs. These two Surrey towns provide residences for two thirds of the District's 80,000 population.

As the District lies mid-way between London and the South Coast it is ideally situated for commuters with varied leisure interests and offers good road and rail links to the Capital and South Coast resorts. The Reading-Tonbridge rail route gives access to Wales, the West Country and the Midlands without having to go via London.

The Thameslink service is available from Leatherhead and Heathrow *and* Gatwick Airports *are very accessible. The* **M25** *(Junction 9) at Leatherhead passes through the District so that the country's motorway network is within ten minutes drive from Dorking and about thirty minutes drive from the furthest outlying villages.*

Most of the District lies within the Green Belt and employment within the area is mainly office and retail based with some light industry and research establishments. The **National Trust** cares for most of the open spaces, many of which are designated as '**Areas of Outstanding Natural Beauty**'. There are many unspoilt villages of great charm especially in the southern part of the District, affording fortunate residents a tranquil, rural lifestyle within striking distance of London and all modern amenities.

N.B. - *Television and Radio signals are not wholly consistent throughout the area, which can be frustrating for the use of televisions, radios, pagers and mobile phones. Improvements are always being made with the erection of new masts, where planning permission allows. Some of the District receives television from the Basingstoke transmitter, thereby providing Southern local programmes and news.*

Fig. 4

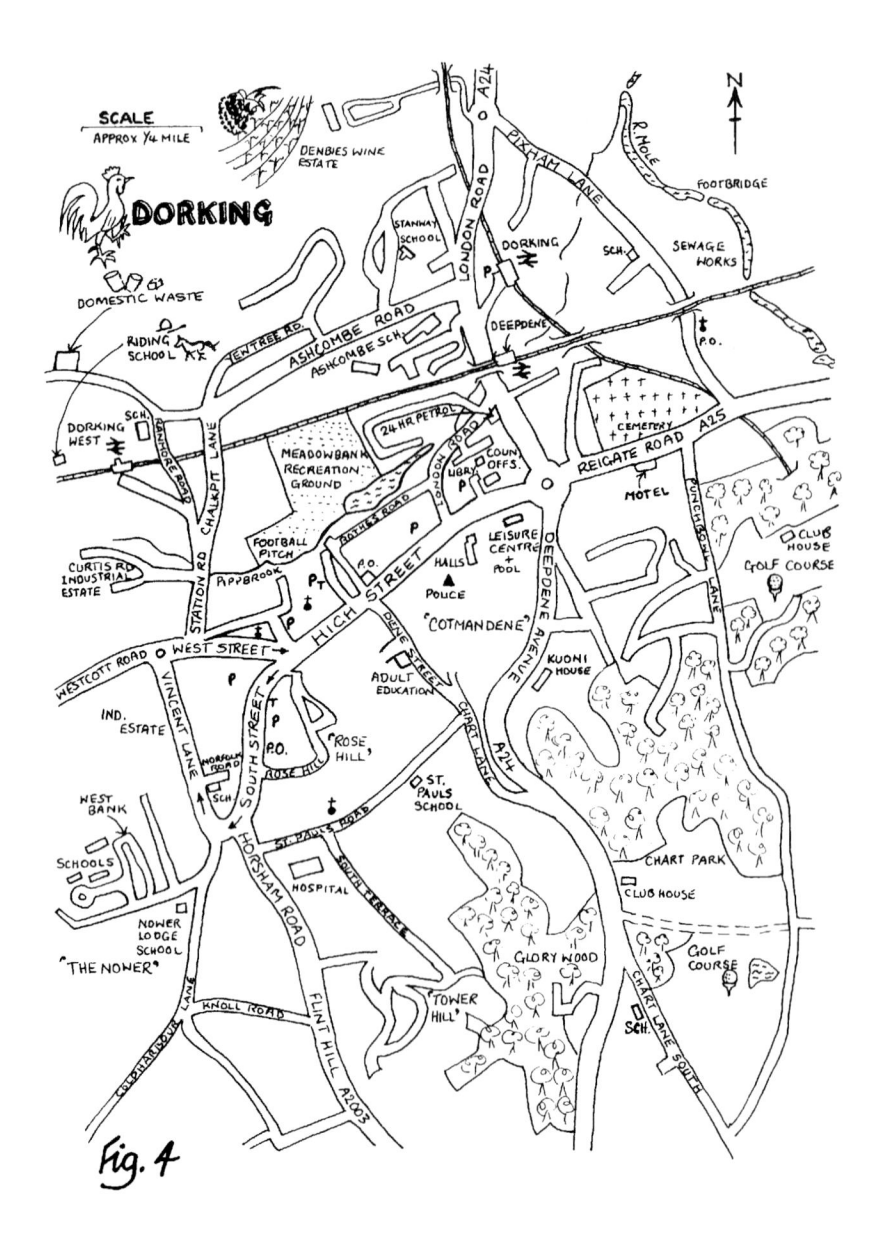

DORKING *See 'Mole Valley' Map and 'Town' Map (Fig.4)*

LOCATION

By some described as the 'Heart of Surrey', situated on the major junction of the A25 and A24 cross roads. About 13 miles *East* of *Guildford,* 6 miles *West* of *Reigate* and 5 miles *South* of *Leatherhead,* low lying in the *Mole Gap* between the *North Downs* and *Greensand ridge.*

✓

Attractive traditional country town. Unspoilt rural location. Good road and rail connections, North/South and East/West.

✗

Limited shopping and leisure facilities by today's standards, definite room for improvement.

OPINION

Dorking will always be a favourite spot, retaining old fashioned charm within an easy proximity of London. More compact than either *Guildford* or *Leatherhead* and liked better by many, it has a unique character and a good variety of homes from which to choose.

THE TOWN AND SURROUNDINGS

Dorking town's unspoilt 'country character' is kept by its natural setting between the neighbouring high ground of woodland, fields and vineyards. The rather antiquated town centre itself is alive and busy, probably because of the fierce resistance to any local out-of-town superstores. The streets are traditional too, with areas of raised pavements to the south side of the *High Street* and much well-kept street furniture.

Immediately to the south of the town centre, on the higher ground, are the larger and more expensive properties surrounding the open spaces of the *Cotmandene* and *Rose Hill* with the more modest terraced housing just to the north and south of the *High Street.*

To the north of the town the ground falls away behind the church to a stream known as *Pippbrook,* a tributary of the *Mole,* which flows through the recreation ground to an old millpond. Although *Dorking* is in the valley of the River Mole the town is not usually liable to flooding. Further north again on the slopes of the downs is *'Denbies'*, England's largest wine estate, boasting 250 acres of vineyards and open to the public.

Calvert Road (near *Stanway School*) marked on the map) is also an area to find the town's more prestigious houses, some of which have a lovely outlook over the vineyards of Denbies. However on weekdays, the amount of car parking in these roads is particularly noticeable due to the overflow from Dorking British Rail Station.

Nestling within its attractive Surrey landscape then, *Dorking* has little to its detriment being a traditional, unspoilt and uncrowded country town with plenty of open space. The population of *Dorking* is about 23,000.

LOCAL TELEPHONE BOOKS

British Telecom - Guildford and West Surrey Area Book No. 530.
See the back of your current Phone Book or dial 150.
Yellow Pages - Gatwick Area, Book No. 22.
Telephone Orders   0800 671444.

TRANSPORT

Dorking has been a popular town for commuters for many years because of its good communications. Rail transport to London, however, can be a little tedious because of the amount of slow train services which stop at most of the stations on the line.

ROADS

The *A25 (East/West)* - outside the town this is a traditional two lane open country road (beyond surrounding village borders it is mostly subject to national speed limit restrictions). It is a well used road, but seldom congested. Town centre traffic is normally busy, because it does not have a by-pass for traffic on the A25.

During rush hours there are frequently queues of traffic approaching *Dorking* from both east and west which can delay a journey by up to 15 minutes. *Chalk Pit Lane* and *Ashcombe Road* carry a lot of the through traffic away from the *High Street* to the north.

The *High Street* undulates and splits into two as a 'Y' shape at the western end onto a one-way system, the southern branch reaching down to the A24 again at *North Holmwood* and the western branch providing the incoming traffic from *Guildford* and the neighbouring villages along the A25.

The ***A24 (North/South)*** - generally an open country road and in many parts a dual carriageway (outside town mostly subject to national speed limit restrictions). Like the A25 it is subject to congestion at rush hours approaching *Dorking,* in particular travelling north in the morning.

N.B. At weekends, especially on Sundays and in the better weather, motorcyclists in particular congregate at 'Rykas' a family restaurant near the Burford Bridge Hotel on the A24. This means that the A24 itself becomes somewhat of a local 'race track,' (despite constant attention by the local police) particularly in the area of the *'Mickleham Bends'*; it is helpful for other road users to be aware of this beforehand.

RAIL

Dorking, rather unusually for a country town, has three separate railway stations being at the site of two crossing railway lines.

Dorking Station, a relatively modern station on the *London* to *Horsham,* Network South Central line. Approximate typical rail times: 7 mins *Leatherhead,* 13 mins *Epsom,* 50 mins *Victoria,* 55 mins *Waterloo,* 1 hr 5 mins *London Bridge*. Going south: 16 mins to *Horsham* on a fast train.

Customer Information Telephone: 0171 928 5100

Station Car Park at *Dorking:* Currently £1.50 per day.

Dorking Deepdene and **Dorking West** on Thames Trains' *Reading/Guildford* to *Redhill/Gatwick/Tonbridge* line. Approximate typical rail times from *Dorking Deepdene:* 15 minutes *Redhill,* 30 minutes to *Gatwick*, 20 minutes to *Guildford*, 1 hour to *Reading*. (*Dorking West* is covered by slower stopping trains).

Customer Information Telephone: 01732 770111. *Dorking Deepdene* Car Park is shared with *Dorking* Station (3 minutes walk). *Dorking West*, the other side of town, has its own separate car park.

The whole of Network South East Railway Services are depicted in the front section of 'Yellow Pages'. Further information may be obtained on many maps, booklets and leaflets obtained from most railway stations.

BUSES

Bus Timetables/Enquiries/Maps from Surrey Traveline: Tel. 01737 223000. Copies of timetables are available from local libraries, council offices throughout Surrey or by post from the County Council at County Hall, Kingston upon Thames, KT1 2DY.

TOWN CENTRE CAR PARKING

There are Short Term and Long Term car parks in Dorking.

Typical Charges: Short Term 10p for 1 hour, 30p for 2 hours.

Long term £1.50 per day.

SHOPPING

Dorking town has a variety of traditional shops catering for most local needs. There is an attractive modern complex at *St. Martin's Walk* (in the shadow of the parish church of the same name) with sufficient local parking at modest cost. This old market town still holds its market on Fridays, which is located on the upper level of the car park to *St. Martin's Walk*.

Dorking is also famous for its wealth of antique shops which are mostly found in the narrow *West Street*. Regular car boot sales are held in *Dorking Station* car park on Sundays and frequently on Saturdays there are auctions for antiques and furniture behind *Dorking Halls*. Currently there is mixed opinion about the possible future site of a larger supermarket in the area. The main post office is located centrally on the *High Street* opposite *Dene Street* (Tel: 01306 740018).

PLANTERS COUNTRY PINE

3,500 sq. ft. showroom Extensive range of English Country Pine Furniture always in stock. Our workshops offer a made to measure and design service for traditional furniture in new and antique reclaimed pine. Fitted kitchens and bedrooms custom-built. Hand painted furniture our speciality.

Mon - Sat   9.30 - 5.30
Sundays by appointment
**40 West Street, Dorking, Surrey
RH4 1BU
Tel: 01306-886080
Fax: 01306-887265**

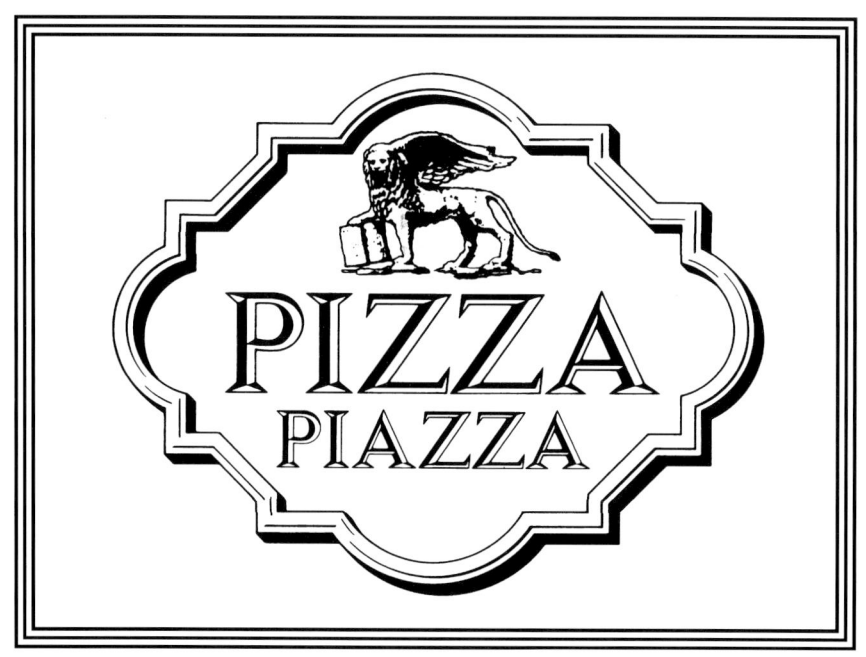

PIZZA PIAZZA

£50.00 OFF

COMPUTER SYSTEMS

WORTH OVER £1000

UPON PRESENTATION OF THIS VOUCHER

MCL SOLUTIONS LIMITED
15/19 SOUTH STREET
DORKING

THE COMPLETE SOLUTION

MCL SOLUTIONS LIMITED

- COMPUTER SYSTEMS & NET WORKS
- COMPUTER MAINTENANCE & REPAIRS
- SYSTEM UPGRADES
- DOCUMENT IMAGE PROCESSING
- MULTIMEDIA SYSTEMS

THE COMPLETE SOLUTION FOR ALL YOUR COMPUTING NEEDS

M.C.L. SOLUTIONS LIMITED
15/19 SOUTH ST, DORKING,
SURREY RH4 2LE
TEL: (01306) 742182
FAX: (01306) 742519

NOVELL

25% OFF

This voucher entitles the holder to a 25% discount off the total bill.

(Minimum bill £5.00, maximum bill £100)
Not in conjunction with any other offer.
Valid till August 1997 at Dorking Piazza.

We have the pleasure of offering you a complementary bottle of Italian House Wine when two or more people each order a main course. 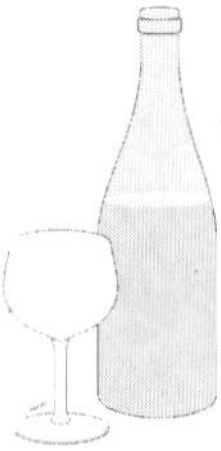
Hand this voucher in when you request the bill.
Not in conjunction with any other offer.
Valid till August 1997 at Dorking Piazza.

PIZZA PIAZZA

PIZZA PIAZZA, 77 SOUTH STREET, DORKING
SEVEN DAYS A WEEK, 11 a.m. - 11.30 p.m.
Telephone
01306 889790

Local high street shops are listed (with their telephone numbers and locations shown) in the front of 'Yellow Pages'.

COUNCIL OFFICES

The distinctive council offices, known as *'Pippbrook'*, were built of red brick, to an attractive modern design in 1984, and can be found to the east end of town on the *Reigate Road* before the roundabout at the junction of the A24 (Tel: 01306 885001).

COMMERCIAL

There is a good supply of local employment, the more well known employers being Friends Provident, Mortgage Trust, UNUM Ltd., Biwater, British Gas, Kuoni Travel, Johnson Brothers Ltd., Croxton and Garry, the Department of Transport and Philips Electrical. The concentrated light industrial side of Dorking has been deliberately confined to the west of town in *Vincent Lane* and *Curtis Road*.

LEISURE

The present Leisure Centre and swimming pool (Tel. 01306 887722) are opposite the Council Offices on the *Reigate Road*. The main Library (Tel: 01306 882948) is situated just behind the Council Offices. Dorking Halls for entertainment (Tel: 01306 889694) may also be found almost next door to the Leisure Centre (*N.B.* This will be closed for refurbishment most of 1996). Dorking Museum, open Wednesdays, Thursdays and Saturdays is off *West Street* (Tel: 01306 883429). The town does not provide a cinema or theatre as such, the nearest being in *Leatherhead* or *Guildford*.

SCHOOLS

The two largest, *Ashcombe School* and *Sondes Place* are found in *Ashcombe Road* and *West Bank* respectively. Inevitably they will affect the nearest housing with extra traffic and noise during term times. *Ashcombe School* is a large secondary school and renowned to be one of the best for examination results locally; it is featured in 'The Daily Telegraph Schools Guide'.

NIGHT LIFE

Confined to local public houses, restaurants and Dorking Halls.

HOSPITALS

Dorking Community Hospital (Tel. 01737 768511) is situated just off the *Horsham Rd*, it is not an Accident and Emergency Hospital.

Nearest Accident and Emergency Hospital at East Surrey Hospital, Three Arch Road, Redhill, Surrey (Tel. 01737 768511).

POLICE STATION

In *Moores Road*, just south of the *High Street* (Tel. 01306 882284)

FOOTBALL PITCH

To the north of the town centre at the bottom of *Mill Lane*.

RECREATION GROUND

At the end of *Mill Lane* with a small playground.

ALLOTMENTS

Enquiries to Mole Valley District Council (Tel. 01306 879229).

CEMETERY

Reigate Road junction with *Pixham Lane*, Dorking (Tel. 01306 883769).

SEWAGE WORKS

These are to the east of the A24 off *Pixham Lane*.

REFUSE TIP

On *Ranmore Road,* discreetly set away from the town centre and any housing.

GIPSY SITES

In Dorking at *The Park* and *Conifer Park,* a total of 5 pitches. In **Mickleham** there is a site in *Cowslip Lane* for 2 pitches.

AIRCRAFT AND TRAFFIC NOISE

Dorking is not subject to noticeable aircraft noise and is not likely to be in the foreseeable future, even with the possible second runway at *Gatwick.* Noise from traffic is very localised and must be assessed in each individual case, obviously properties closest to the A24, A25 and through routes will generally suffer the most.

DENBIES
ENGLAND'S LARGEST WINE ESTATE

Tourist Board

AWARD WINNING
visitor attraction

"THE ULTIMATE WINE EXPERIENCE"

- ◆ AUDIO VISUAL PRESENTATION
- ◆ 3-D FILM
- ◆ PEOPLE MOVER THROUGH THE WINERY
- ◆ TOUR AND TASTING
- ◆ REFRESHMENT AREA AND SHOP
- ◆ GROUP BOOKINGS WELCOME

Open 7 Days a week

All year round

Denbies Wine Estate, London Road, Dorking, Surrey RH5 6AA
Telephone: 01306 876616   Fax: 01306 888930

ONE FREE TOUR AND TASTING
When accompanied by another paying adult.
A saving of £4.50
Please bring this voucher with you.

BE IN THE KNOW...
with Dorking Chamber of Commerce

Do you know what's happening in Dorking ?

As part of our service to members we provide:

Quarterly and general meetings to discuss specific and important issues keeping members informed of local activities

Regular newsletters to update members on current matters

Regular mailouts spearheading prominent issues

Networking and social forums to discuss local business issues and to encourage trade amongst fellow members

The promotion and advancement of Dorking as a regional centre of commerce

Representations of the views of the business community at local government, county council and national levels

Participation in the town centre management of Dorking and its development to protect members' interests

BE IN THE KNOW...
JOIN YOUR CHAMBER TODAY

Contact: Terry Collins, T M Collins, 70 High Street, Dorking
Telephone: (01306) 880790

HISTORY

Dorking is the largest town in the District situated at the southern end of the *Mole Gap* and also in the *East/West* valley known as the *Vale of Holmesdale*. The town has been established since Saxon times and is directly on the route of the famous Roman Road *'Stane Street'* which extended from *London* to *Chichester*. More recently *Dorking* developed as a coaching stage and prosperous agricultural market town. In the centre of the *High Street,* dating in parts from the 15th century, there is still a coaching inn, now called the 'White Horse Hotel'.

Opposite is *St. Martin's Church* which was built to the designs of *Henry Woodyer*. It has a 210 feet spire built in 1868-1877 to the memory of *Samuel Wilberforce,* Bishop of Winchester, who was killed by a fall from his horse nearby in an area locally known as *Abinger Roughs* in 1873. In the south porch there is a square bronze relief by *David McFall* which commemorates the composer *Ralph Vaughan Williams* (1872-1958) who spent his boyhood at *Leith Hill Place*. Apparently many of the older town's buildings have caves beneath them and the deepest at 75 feet can be visited on application to the *Dorking Museum*. The 'Burford Bridge Hotel' beneath *Box Hill*, once called the 'Hare and Hounds' in the 12th century, is reputed to claim that Nelson stopped here on his way to the Battle of Trafalgar in 1805.

Deepdene, to the east of the town, takes its name from the estate owned by the famous Surrey based Howard family in the 17th century and where beautiful terraced gardens were a great feature. First mention of *Dorking* can be found in the *Domesday Book* and there is evidence to support the fact that it was a settlement long before, as Stone Age tools and an Iron Age site have been found.

The Romans introduced to the town an unusual 'five clawed' breed of fowl, the 'Dorking Cock', which has since become a symbol of *Dorking* and is still bred locally to this day. An example of the cock can be found in the *Dorking Museum* in *West Street*, apparently it was a popular breed throughout the 19th century, *Queen Victoria* was said to favour *Dorking* eggs above all others and certainly *Dorking* was admired for its poultry market. Also from the Museum, guided tours of *Dorking's* caves in *South*

Street may be arranged, interpreted as a gentleman's folly, they were used as wine cellars until the 1960s.

To the south of town there are open spaces at *Rose Hill* and *Cotmandene,* the latter being an early home of cricket and where once *Daniel Defoe* (1660-1731) wrote of learned physicians singling it out for 'the best air in England'.

LIVING IN THE BEAUTIFUL MOLE VALLEY

Should you be lucky enough to live in the southern part of the Mole Valley, not only will you be living in some of the finest parts of Surrey, but you will have the satisfaction of knowing that the Dorking and District Preservation Society is doing its best to protect and maintain the environment for yourselves and your successors.

Established in 1929
REGISTERED CHARITY No 246806

The Society, which is a registered charity established in 1929, is based in Dorking, that pleasant country town nestling under Boxhill with a history going back to pre-Roman times, and takes in that part of Mole Valley from Mickleham to the Sussex border, over half of which has been designated an area of "great landscape value" or an area of "outstanding natural beauty".

The Society currently boasts some 1100 individual members and some 40 corporate subscribers. Its various activities include the Dorking Museum, a local history group, the custodianship of the Dorking caves, all planning applications in the area are vetted, footpaths and bridleways are checked. There is a project to reinstate the once famous Deepdene Garden and each year there is a Best Development competition jointly sponsored by the Society to encourage high standards and good practice.

Why not join this worthwhile organisation by getting in touch today with the
Hon. Secretary, Peter Hawkes,
at 15 Yew Tree Road, Dorking, Surrey RH4 1ND.
Tel: 01306 883699.
The annual family membership is £5 a year.

the Rug centre

ONE OF THE BEST SELECTIONS IN THE SOUTH OF ENGLAND

*An enormous range of handmade RUGS and KELIMS
Large carpets, runners, saddlebags, etc. - over 25 years experience -
Insurance valuations and repairs - Free home trials
The Rug Centre Ltd.
68 South Street, Dorking, Surrey RH4 2HD
01306 882202*

fig. 5

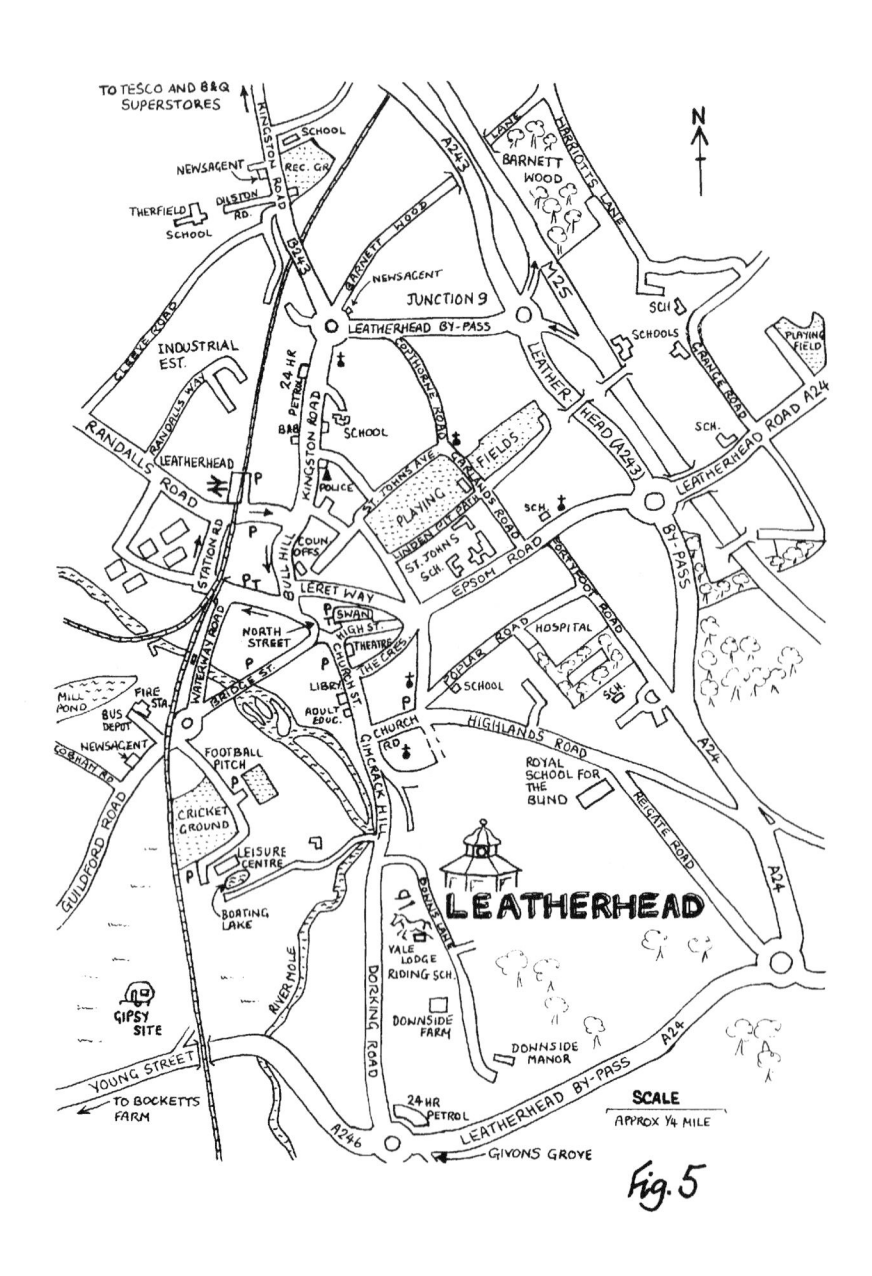

LEATHERHEAD *See 'Mole Valley' Map & 'Town' Map (Fig. 5)*

LOCATION
Five miles *North* of *Dorking* on the A24 and on higher ground, nearest neighbours are *Fetcham* and *Great Bookham* to the *West* and *Ashtead* to the *East*. Most convenient for the M25 at junction 9.

✓

Excellent public transport and road connections. Comprehensive shopping and leisure facilities. Theatre in town. Good schools selection.

✗

Sprawling industrial estates. Town centre lacking in character.

OPINION
Leatherhead is a town combining old and new, somewhat unsuccessfully in my opinion. There is no real 'bustling heart' to the centre, which in the main, cannot be described as quaint or traditional. Despite the good choice of lovely homes around town, especially to the south and east, the overall impression can be drowned by the extensive local authority housing and business parks mostly to the north and west.

THE TOWN AND SURROUNDINGS
On the bright side Leatherhead town centre is free of through traffic and has a nucleus of shops in and around the *Swan Centre*, but at the same time it is rather unremarkable. Somehow the pedestrianised old roads have lost their character and the selection of shops are nothing special. A local business woman and long time resident remarked to me that "Leatherhead should make more of its proximity to the River" and I tend to agree. This lovely natural feature so close to the centre is rather forgotten, making more of it would certainly improve the ambience of the whole town.

Away from the centre progressing northwards and past the train station, unfortunately the landscape doesn't improve. The northern part of town spreads into an unwieldy area of industrial and council estates. *Randalls Road,* stretching north west from the centre, leads to many business parks, as does the *Kingston Road* going north. However, in contrast, the south of *Leatherhead* is really quite charming and here, near the church, may be found the older terraced cottages and bigger, more prestigious homes.

Fetcham, over to the west of the river, is *Leatherhead's* closest neighbour. Low-lying along *Cobham Road* and gradually climbing uphill towards *Great Bookham*, it is a generally pleasant residential area with mostly modern styled homes. The population of *Leatherhead* is about 42,000 and *Fetcham* about 8,000.

LOCAL TELEPHONE BOOKS

British Telecom - Guildford and West Surrey, Book No 530.
See the back of your current Phone Book or phone 150.
Yellow Pages - Gatwick Area, Book No. 22.
Telephone Orders on 0800 671444.

TRANSPORT

Exceptionally well placed for all communications, a real selling point!

ROADS

Leatherhead's close proximity to **Junction 9** of the **M25** has meant a great boost in the town's popularity with easy road communications for residents and businesses alike. The slightly unusual two locations for Junction 9 allows for one roundabout (northside) to cater for anti-clockwise traffic slipping on and off the motorway and the other roundabout (southside) for clockwise traffic to do the same. For this reason, traffic directions on the two roundabouts on the A243 can be confusing at first for new users.

This year there are also extensive ongoing roadworks at this location which have altered the appearance of the landscape with three blue distinctive towers rising high into the sky and a range of portacabins stretched out over what was otherwise open land. I expect this is temporary, although the re-widening programme of the M25, which has caused them, will take several years.

Formally situated around the junctions of the A243, A244, A245 and A24, *Leatherhead* had already become established at their convergence. With the building of the A243 by-pass and then the new access roads to the M25, the local network of faster roads is very comprehensive.

RAIL

Leatherhead has an old central station that is at the split of the lines from *London* to *Dorking* and *London* to *Guildford*. The Network South Central Service and South West Trains Service both use this station.

Leatherhead Station Approximate rail times: 6 mins *Epsom,* 40 mins *Victoria,* 45 mins *Waterloo,* 1 hour to *London Bridge,* 24 mins to *Guildford.*

Customer Information Telephone: 0171 928 5100

Small Station Car Park: £1.50 per day

Overflow in Long Term Car Park: £1.00 per day.

The whole of Network South East Railway Services are depicted in the front section of 'Yellow Pages'. Further information may be obtained on many maps, booklets and leaflets obtained from most railway stations.

BUSES

Comprehensive services. Bus garage in Guildford Road, opposite Leisure Centre.
Bus Timetables/Enquiries/Maps from Surrey Traveline: Tel. 01737 223000. Copies of timetables are available from local libraries, council offices throughout Surrey or by post from the County Council at County Hall, Kingston upon Thames, KT1 2DY.

TOWN CENTRE CAR PARKING

There is very good provision for car parking generally in *Leatherhead* both long and short term. Main facilities for shoppers at the *Swan Centre* (380 spaces, free after 6.00 p.m., access via *Leret Way*) and in *Church Street* and *Randalls Road* for Pay and Display open-air parking:
10p for 1 hour, 30p for 2 hours.   Long Term: £1.00 all day.
Free car parks at *Tescos* and *B&Q* superstores out of the town centre.

SHOPPING

Good facilities for shopping in *Leatherhead* include the well known superstores *Tesco* and *B&Q* at the northern end of the *Kingston Road* and the central, comprehensive *Swan Centre*. The *Swan Centre* was built on the site of the old *Swan Inn* from which it takes its name. Nowadays shops and services such as *Sainsburys, Next, Menzies, Thomas Cook* and *Boots* may all be found there. *Leatherhead's* old, small *High Street* has been pedestrianised around the *Swan Centre* and up to the *Thorndike Theatre*.

COUNCIL OFFICES

The Red House Council Offices were acquired by the former *Leatherhead* Council around 1949. Formally the building had been a private house (Belmont Lodge), a hospital (during the first World War) and a hotel during the 1920s. Close by, the *Red House Gardens* provide two hard tennis and netball courts and an attractive short cut to the railway station.

COMMERCIAL

Leatherhead has large industrial sites and business parks to the north and west of the town centre where many industries are established, both big and small. It is famous for a concentration of modern research establishments, but all sorts of trades are represented here. Some present businesses are 'The Pyrene Company', 'Magnet', 'Convex' and 'Encore' Computers, 'Legal and General' and 'The Fairmount Group'.

LEISURE

The modern *Thorndike Theatre* (Tel. 01372 377677) in *Church Street*, despite being an unimpressive building from the outside, is one the best and most popular playhouses in Surrey. *The Library* (Tel. 01372 373149) and *Local Museum* (restricted opening) may both be found in *Church Street*. The *Leisure Centre*, open every day of the week and one of the biggest in the country, also has a *Water Park* alongside for boating during the better half of the year. (Tel. 01372 377674). *Leatherhead* is also particularly well placed for a choice of local golf courses and riding establishments.

SCHOOLS

There are three first schools, a middle school and two secondary schools in and around the town, offering a good selection within the state system. Leatherhead residents, however, are particularly well placed for a choice of independent schools. The *Downsend* group of independent pre-preparatory and preparatory schools are all close by, as is *St. John's School* for boys in the *Epsom Road* and *Parsons Mead School* for girls on the Ashtead side of the M25. It is also interesting to note that The Royal School for the Blind, '*see*Ability' is located in *Highlands Road* and its residents form part of the local community.

*see*ABILITY ROYAL SCHOOL FOR THE BLIND

Realising the potential of people who are blind and have other disabilities

***see*ABILITY** - a unique charity headquartered in Leatherhead, Surrey. Further proof that Mole Valley is the place to be for social awareness as well as general amenities.

***see*ABILITY** - is the operational name for the Royal School for the Blind, an independent charity founded in 1799 to provide residential accommodation and training for young people who were blind to enable them to lead more independent lives through the learning of a craft or trade.

Today the charity remains unique in the field of blind welfare because of its expertise in dealing with those who are multi-disabled. Its Leatherhead operations continue to offer residential and day services for over 130 people in a range of flats and houses, with community rehabilitation services to people in their own homes.

***see*ABILITY** was adopted as the charity's operational name in 1994 to emphasise its positive attitude to disability and its aim to make people who are blind and multi-disabled obtain greater independence and to achieve their maximum potential.

Residents are blind often as a result of accident or trauma, and ***see*ABILITY** has a special unit for those with high physical needs.

***see*ABILITY** also runs a sheltered workshop in Bermondsey, South London and a community home in Guildford. Plans are in hand to launch a major appeal to build the first home in the UK for young blind people with short life expectancy, especially those with juvenile Batten's disease.

Much of the charity's activity is dependant not only upon voluntary income but also voluntary work. Tasks include driving, visiting, helping with daytime activities.

If you would like to get involved and meet other people we would be delighted to hear from you.

Please call Ruth Wellden on 01372 373086 Extn. 326.

NIGHT LIFE

The *Thorndike Theatre* provides frequent entertainment, but there are no night clubs or cinemas as such in the town.

HOSPITAL

Leatherhead Hospital, Poplar Road (Tel. 01372 384384) - not Accident and Emergency.

The closest Accident & Emergency Hospital is *Epsom District Hospital,* Dorking Road, Epsom (Tel. 01372 735735).

POLICE STATION

44 Kingston Road, *Leatherhead* (Tel. 01306 882284).

FIRE STATION

On the *Fetcham* banks of the *River Mole* opposite the *Leisure Centre.*

BUS STATION

Next to the Fire Station.

FOOTBALL PITCH

West bank of the *River Mole* near the *Leisure Centre.*

RECREATION GROUNDS

One in *Fortyfoot Road* with a Bowling Green and small children's playground, another further north and east of the *Kingston Road,* which is much used serving the most densely populated area of town.

ALLOTMENTS

Enquiries to Mole Valley District Council (Tel. 01306 879299)

CEMETERY

Cemetery and Crematorium off *Randalls Road.*

SEWAGE WORKS

At *Randalls Road* junction with *Oaklawn Road.*

REFUSE TIP
On *Randalls Road*, next to the Sewage Works.

GIPSY SITE
Salvation Place off *Young Street* is the largest pitch in the District.

AIRCRAFT AND TRAFFIC NOISE
Leatherhead is not near any airport so aircraft noise is minimal. Although the *M25* is very close, it is in a deep, unobtrusive cutting between *Leatherhead* and *Ashtead* town before rising above the *A243* within distant view of some of the houses and industrial estates to the north of *Leatherhead*.

HISTORY
Leatherhead has Saxon origins and the name comes from 'Leodridan' mentioned in *King Alfred* the Great's will, it is derived from the old English 'Leode' (people) and 'Rida' (riding path or ford, a reference to the crossing point on the Mole where the bridge is now).

Two local manors belonged to *Edward the Confessor* and two others to *King Harold*. Later the *Leatherhead* estate was given to *Walter de Merton* to enable him to found a college. *Merton College* still is a large landowner in the area.

In 1758 the small town of *Leatherhead* became more established and gained much of its trade because of its critical position on the *Epsom to Guildford* turnpike road. Here, at the gap in the North Downs, *Leatherhead* became a significant junction. Historically *Leatherhead* is most notable nowadays for its road and railway bridges, including a water pumping and treatment plant on the banks of the *River Mole*. A tannery also stood on the upstream side of the bridge until the 1870s. It is worth stopping to look at the recently restored and most attractive 18th century road bridge, which arches above numerous medieval stone piers across the *River Mole*. This bridge was first built in 1783 by *George Gwilt* on the site of a previous ford. This wide and shallow part of the river had been a well established crossing point for centuries. Nearby as well, the famous landscape architect *"Capability" Brown* built an 18th century shell bridge which can still be seen on a signposted riverside walk.

The 16th century *'Running Horse'* public house is a cream painted Tudor building just up from the river banks and is the town's oldest pub. Another old property is *Hampton Cottage*, a half timbered building in the town centre and now a museum. One of its modern exhibitions features *Donald Campbell*, the racing driver, who once lived in *Leatherhead*. He later died on Coniston Water in 1967, when the speedboat in which he was travelling overturned at 300 mph.

The *Church of St. Mary and St. Nicholas*, with its very rare double dedication, was almost certainly built by *Edward the Confessor*. It dates back as far as 1200 and has many unusual historic features. The church is a large flint building standing in an attractive setting at the south end of *Church Street* and the imposing tower, built in the 15th century, is very much a local landmark. *The Mansion* (also in *Church Street* and built around 1730) is the largest old building in the town, apart from the church, with its public garden dropping away to the banks of the *River Mole*.

The introduction of the railway in the 19th century led to the town's growth as a residence and is still important today. *Leatherhead's* two fine brick bridges which carry the *Dorking* line and the *Effingham Junction* line over the *River Mole* were built in 1863 and 1885 respectively.

If you have information about any crime, phone

Surrey
CRIMESTOPPERS
0800 555 111

- **Your call is free**
- **You do not have to give your name**
- **You may receive a reward**

Uniting against crime

CRIMESTOPPERS TRUST is a registered charity number 297500

> "Fire and Iron Gallery is a Mecca for metal maniacs."
>
> Miranda Innes, COUNTRY LIVING

Fabulous presents made by leading international jewellers and metalsmiths, beautifully displayed in the characterful outbuildings of a Grade II* listed 1450 farmhouse. Parking is plentiful, easy and free. Commissions are welcomed, and a full repair and restoration service is offered

LOCKS
CANDLESTICKS
SCULPTURE
JEWELLERY
FURNITURE
WIND CHIMES
FIRE BASKETS
CURTAIN POLES
GATES
MIRRORS
LIGHTING
FIRE BACKS
BOWLS

Have you discovered Fire and Iron yet?

Fire and Iron Gallery
Rowhurst Forge
Oxshott Road
Leatherhead
Surrey
KT22 0EN
Tel: 01372 375148

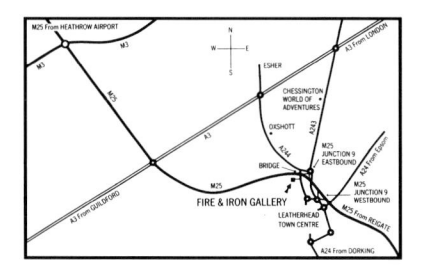

OPEN
MONDAY TO
SATURDAY
10 a.m. - 5 p.m.

SOUTH·EAST ARTS

CRAFTS COUNCIL Selected

fig.6

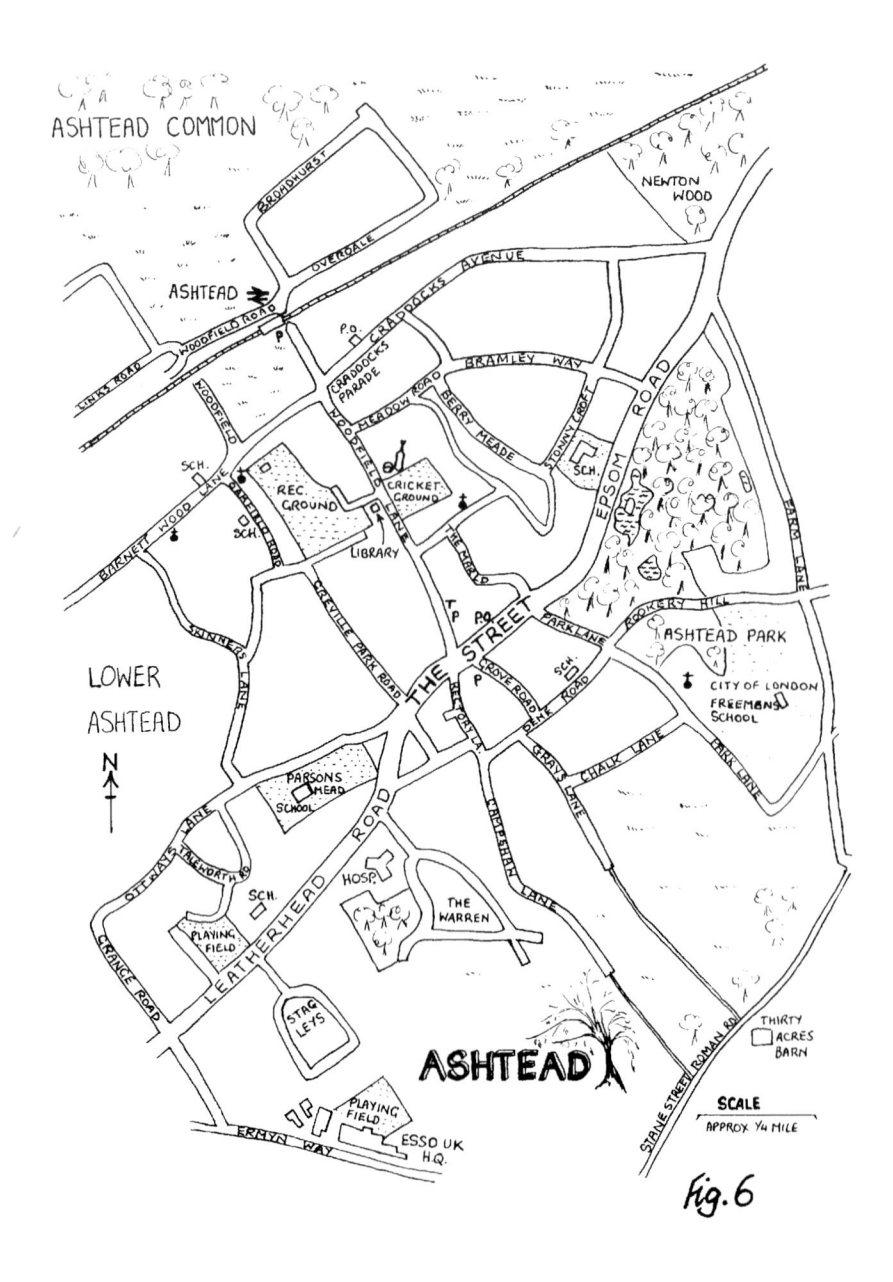

ASHTEAD *See 'Mole Valley' Map and 'Town' Map (Fig. 6)*

LOCATION

Just over 1 mile *North East* of *Leatherhead* on the A24 towards *Epsom,* situated on higher ground.

✓

Excellent independent schools selection. Very attractive setting. Own train station. Good road connections. Good bus services. Village atmosphere.

✗

Limited shopping on busy main high street.

OPINION

Ashtead is one of the last villages so close to *London,* to be surrounded by so much glorious open countryside. Some of the residential side roads are narrow and rather hazardous, but lead to a wealth of attractive homes.

THE VILLAGE AND SURROUNDINGS

Ashtead's residential roads, which stretch to the north and south sides of the A24, are mostly a network of quiet country lanes lined with homes of all different shapes and sizes, with a definite 'country village feel'. The village is sandwiched between two lovely areas of open space - common land to the north and sweeping fields to the south. The railway line is also on the northern perimeter adjacent to *Ashtead Common* whereas to the south *Campshaw Lane* and *Grays Lane* end as bridlepaths leading to the old *'Stane Street'* Roman Road.

In the area of *Shepherds Walk,* at the southern end of *Farm Lane,* the landscape is truly rural and the close downland of *Epsom* racecourse is apparent. To the west of *Park Lane,* there are some beautiful large homes in very attractive settings. Many residential plots in the area are of a generous size, affording the luxury of pleasant gardens and few are subjected to any busy traffic. The overall ambience of *Ashtead*, with its quaint narrow lanes, is that of a leafy, quiet pleasant area with a current population of about 13,000.

LOCAL TELEPHONE BOOKS

British Telecom - Guildford and West Surrey, Book No 530.
See the back of your current Phone Book or phone 150.
Yellow pages - Gatwick Area, Book No. 22.
Telephone Orders 0800 671444.

TRANSPORT

Like *Leatherhead,* its larger neighbour, *Ashtead* is very close to the country's motorway network at junction 9 of the M25. Popular for commuters, with its own main line station, *Ashtead* would probably be considered by the majority, to be within a reasonable car journey of *London* as well.

ROADS

The main *A24 (South West/North East)* runs through the middle of Ashtead. This long old road, starting near the *South Coast*, carries on north to *London* ending at *Clapham Common* at the junction with the *A3*. It is mostly subjected to a 30 mph speed limit around *Ashtead* and has the character of a normal undivided two lane carriageway. Traffic is mostly slow moving through *'The Street'* area and there is a pelican crossing in the centre of town.

Most local traffic uses the road to connect the *Leatherhead* and *Epsom* areas, faster through traffic to most parts of *London* would generally use the A243 or A3.

RAIL

Ashtead is on the main line to *London,* which serves to keep the town high on the list of desirable commuter areas. Trains from both *Dorking* and *Guildford* run through *Ashtead*.

Ashtead Station is located away from the main high street and is found up *Woodfield Lane* near *Ashtead Common.* Approximate typical rail times: 5 mins to *Epsom,* 37 mins to *Waterloo,* 58 mins to *London Bridge.*

Customer Information Telephone: 0171 928 5100. Station Car Parking: Currently £1.00 daily, £18 monthly, £50 quarterly, £180 annually, some free 'on street' parking nearby.

The whole of Network South East Railway Services are depicted in the front section of 'Yellow Pages'. Further information may be obtained on many maps, booklets and leaflets obtained from most railway stations.

BUSES

Good services to Epsom and Leatherhead areas.

Bus Timetables/Enquiries/Maps from Surrey Traveline: Tel. 01737 223000. Copies of timetables are available from local libraries, council offices throughout Surrey or by post from the County Council at County Hall, Kingston upon Thames, KT1 2DY.

TOWN CENTRE CAR PARKING

The most convenient car parks are to be found in *Woodfield Lane* and *Grove Road*, both are pay and display at 10p for 1 hour and 30p for 2 hours. Longer times are available.

SHOPPING

Basic shopping facilities in the form of small shops line *'The Street'* with all the 'Big Four' Banks represented. In *Craddocks Avenue* near *Woodfield Lane* is a further parade of shops and a post office. *Leatherhead* and, more especially *Epsom,* provide the more extensive and comprehensive shopping required.

COMMERCIAL

There is no main industrial area in *Ashtead,* local employers at Esso House and Ashtead Hospital can be found south west of the centre.

LEISURE

Leatherhead's extensive facilities are the nearest source of leisure entertainment for Ashtead residents, however there is a local library, football pitch, squash club, recreation area and cricket ground in the village. As with *Leatherhead, Ashtead* residents have a good choice of golf and riding establishments close at hand. Also famous *Epsom Racecourse* is within two miles to the east. Just to enjoy some fresh air, *Ashtead Park* and *Ashtead Common* are pleasant venues, with a network of footpaths and bridleways.

SCHOOLS

There are several *non-fee* paying primary and middle schools within the boundaries of the village, but especially with regard to independent schools *Ashtead* residents are almost spoilt for choice. *The Downsend* schools can be found to the west of town, as well as *Parsons Mead* school in *Ottways Lane* and *The City of London Freemen's* school in *Park Lane.*

NIGHT LIFE

Restricted to local restaurants and public houses in the immediate vicinity.

HOSPITAL

Ashtead Hospital, The Warren, Ashtead. Tel. 01372 276161 - Not Accident and Emergency.

The nearest Accident and Emergency Hospital is Epsom District Hospital, Dorking Road, Epsom, Surrey. Tel. 01372 735735.

POLICE STATION

See *Leatherhead.*

FOOTBALL PITCH

Ashtead Football Club has its home on the Recreation Ground to the south of *Barnett Wood Lane.* Access to the Recreation Ground may also be gained from *Woodfield Lane, Greville Park Road* or *Oakfield Road.*

ALLOTMENTS

Enquiries to Mole Valley District Council (Tel. 01306 879299).

CEMETERY
Randalls Road in Leatherhead (Tel. 01372 373813).

SEWAGE WORKS
See *Leatherhead.*

REFUSE TIP
See *Leatherhead.*

AIRCRAFT AND TRAFFIC NOISE
Like neighbouring *Leatherhead* there is no airport close by to cause noticeable aircraft noise. Traffic noise would be mostly confined to homes bordering the A24 and generally not considerable in any event.

HISTORY
Previously an agricultural village, *Ashtead* was developed in the 1930s and since then there has been a huge growth of modern housing here. It is now separated from *Leatherhead,* its larger neighbour, by the strong dividing line of the M25 and from Epsom by half a mile of unspoilt countryside. Because of these divisions it has retained a village identity, centred around the main shopping parade on *'The Street'* which is part of the busy A24.

Most of the old village buildings have now gone, apart from a group of almshouses on the corner of *Farm Lane*, built in the 18th century and recast by the Victorians. *'Park Farmhouse'* and *'Ashtead House'* are two splendid 18th century houses further up *Farm Lane,* the latter *'Ashtead House'*, now being the *City of London Freemen's School*. This large three storey yellow brick mansion was designed in 1790 by Joseph Bonomi.

Ashtead Park is situated to the east of the village and immediately south of the main *Epsom Road* on the A24. The entrances are from *Rookery Hill* and the *Epsom Road*. This natural parkland was once part of the original grounds belonging to the *Manor House of Ashtead*. When *Sir Robert Howard* bought the estate in the latter part of the 17th century the present park was laid out and enclosed. The soil being mostly London Clay, the park is prone to holding surface water and there are two ponds, in particular, which support a wide variety of wild life. *The Island Pond* was reclaimed by the *Leatherhead and District Angling Society* and now contains carp and perch, providing excellent fishing.

Ashtead Common covers 500 acres of land north of the village. Covered by a network of paths, it is a fine open space of woodland, bracken heath and pasture. The Common is noted to be an ancient oak pollard woodland, where the trees were continuously cut back on a rotational basis, to encourage the growth of more young branches. Some of the oaks may be 400 years old and they provide a habitat for lichens, mosses and liverworts, as well as for many native birds.

In the 1st or 2nd century AD a Roman villa and tile factory were built at the site of *Ashtead Common* and only recently discovered in 1926. It is thought that *Ashtead* was then an important centre in the tile industry, indicated by the evidence of bonfire kilns and large clay pits. This site had a villa bath house complex linked by its own branch road to nearby *Stane Street*. Various types of tiles were made for under floor and wall heating systems, for herringbone pattern floors and for roofs.

FOR INFORMATION ON LOCAL

BEAVERS, CUBS, SCOUTS AND VENTURE SCOUTS

CONTACT

THE COUNTY ADMINISTRATOR: MARIAN COZENS,
TELEPHONE: 01483 203451
SURREY COUNTY SCOUT COUNCIL

FOR INFORMATION ON LOCAL

RAINBOWS, BROWNIES, GUIDES, RANGERS ETC.
LEATHERHEAD DIVISION CONTACT
MRS HELEN CARR, TELEPHONE: 01372 458171

DORKING AND LEITH HILL DIVISION
(including Dorking and Leas and Southern Dorking Weald Area)
CONTACT: MRS ROSEMARY GODDARD, TEL. 01306 711259

Do you enjoy squash?
ASHTEAD SQUASH CLUB
4 heated courts,
and all the following items for your enjoyment:

2 all weather tennis courts,
a licensed bar with exceptional food services,
a pool table,
and a full size snooker table.

We also offer a wide range of memberships including:
full squash, tennis, social events,
junior coaching and various club leagues.

To take advantage of our wonderful facilities,
contact our membership secretary on 01372 272865,
or call the club after 6 pm any day.

Ashtead Squash Rackets Club,
39 Skinners Lane,
phone: 01372 272215

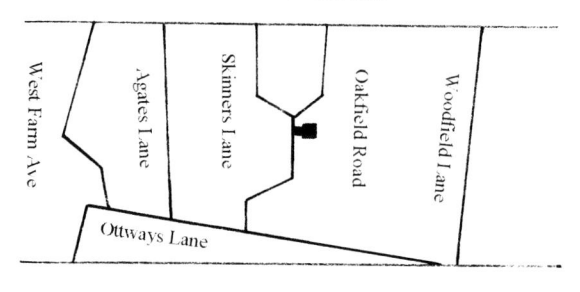

Fig. 7

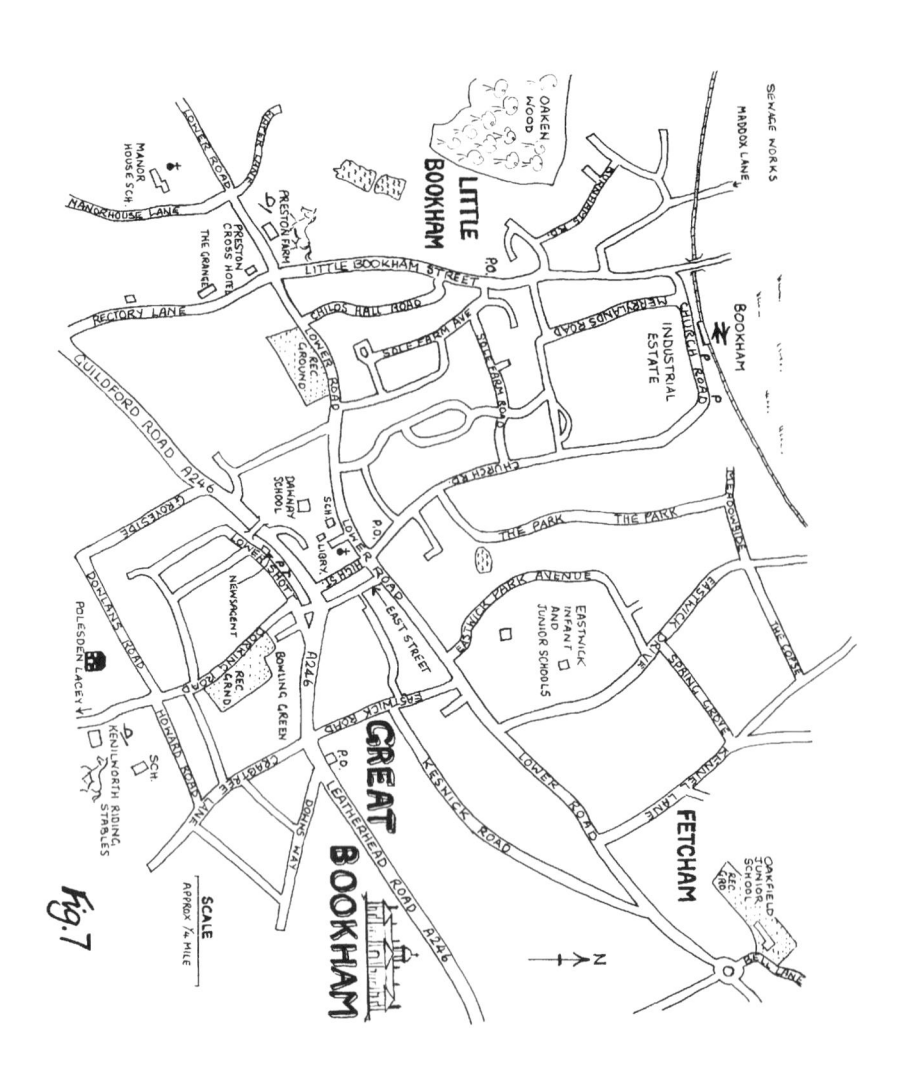

GREAT & LITTLE BOOKHAM

See 'Mole Valley' Map and 'Town' Map (Fig. 7)

LOCATION
The villages are approximately 2 - 3 miles *West* of *Leatherhead* on the A246 road to *Guildford*.

✓

Own train station. Attractive elevated setting. Unspoilt quaint village centre. Good school selection, particularly for girls. Easy road connections.

✗

Limited shopping.

OPINION
Both these villages (which are often collectively known as *'Bookham'*) are ever popular with *London* commuters. *Great Bookham* is by far the more substantial of the two and forms the heart of an attractive large residential area. The neighbourhood sucessfully combines good local facilities with the character of a village atmosphere. Positioned on an elevated setting, it has lovely open countryside on the doorstep.

THE VILLAGE AND SURROUNDINGS
Bookham has a good selection of homes, some terraced cottages of different ages, many bungalows and then the bigger plots for larger detached houses. It is fair to say, that in many ways, as *Ashtead* is to the east of *Leatherhead* so *Bookham* is to the west. The population of *Bookham* is about 11,000.

Fetcham is generally the rather more sprawling residential area between *Great Bookham* and *Leatherhead,* within which there are some lovely houses. However, for this reason it has a different atmosphere from *Bookham* and despite shops and a post office in *Cobham Road*, there is no true village centre. This part of the *Cobham Road*, closest to the railway bridge, is less attractive, but the shops are convenient for the local residents. *'The Bell'* Public House, local school and recreation ground are found in *Bell Lane*. The population of *Fetcham* is about 8,000.

LOCAL TELEPHONE BOOKS

British Telecom - Guildford and West Surrey, Book No 530.
See the back of your current Phone Book or phone 150.
Yellow pages - Gatwick Area, Book No. 22.
Telephone Orders 0800 671444.

TRANSPORT

Comprehensive and convenient facilities for both road and rail passengers.

ROADS

The *A246 (East/West)* - a normal undivided two lane carriageway giving good access to the villages, subject to 30 mph speed limit in the immediate vicinity, but with parts towards Guildford which are dual carriageway and subject to the national speed limit for faster driving. *Lower Road* (running parallel to the north) is also a busy local cut through.

RAIL

The station is similar in location and type to *Ashtead* although being beyond the split at *Leatherhead,* trains only service South West Trains' *London/Guildford* line. The railway here connects *Leatherhead Station* to that at *Effingham Junction* another popular and convenient station. **N.B.** A word of warning, in particular, about these quieter stations and that is **'Remove your valuables from your cars'**.

Bookham Station serves both villages and is next to a small industrial estate on the outskirts of the area adjacent to *Bookham Common.* Approximate typical rail times to London would be the same as *Leatherhead's* allowing for an additional five minutes or so. Typical rail times to *Guildford* about 19 minutes.

Customer Information: Tel. 0171 928 5100.

Car Parking at the Station: Free - (unless your car is broken into!)

The whole of Network South East Railway Services are depicted in the front section of 'Yellow Pages'. Further information may be obtained on many maps, booklets and leaflets obtained from most railway stations.

BUSES

Several local routes and services.

Bus Timetables/Enquiries/Maps from Surrey Traveline: Tel. 01737 223000. Copies of timetables are available from local libraries, council offices throughout Surrey or by post from the County Council at County Hall, Kingston upon Thames, KT1 2DY.

TOWN CENTRE CAR PARKING

There is free, unrestricted street car parking near the shops in the *High Street* if you can find a space. If not, there is a nearby free car park in *Lower Shott*, across the main A246 road.

SHOPPING

Confined to local shops bordering the *High Street* including two small supermarkets and *Lloyds, National Westminster* and *Midland Banks*. There are three post offices in the area, one centrally placed at the end of *Church Road,* closest to the *High Street*, one on the *Leatherhead Road* towards *Leatherhead* on the left hand side and the other near *Bookham Station* in *Little Bookham Street*.

COMMERCIAL

There is a small industrial estate next to the station.

LEISURE

There is a village library in *Townshott* (Tel. 01372 454440) and a good choice of local riding stables and golf courses, including the particularly well known *Effingham Golf Club*, just over the District boundary towards Guildford. Other outdoor sports facilities are provided at the *Chrystie Recreation Ground* in *Dorking Road* (south of the A246) and on the *Lower Road Recreation Ground*. Otherwise *Leatherhead's* leisure facilities would be the most comprehensive local choice.

SCHOOLS

Again there is a good selection of schools in the immediate area ranging from the *Eastwick Schools* around *Eastwick Park Avenue, Dawney County* in *Griffin Way* and slightly further west in *Lower Road* is the *Howard of Effingham School*. For independent girls' schools there is *Manor House School* to the west of the village on *Manorhouse Lane* and to the south *St.Teresa's* on *Effingham Hill*.

NIGHT LIFE

Confined to local public houses and restaurants and the facilities of *Leatherhead*.

HOSPITAL

There is no hospital in the immediate vicinity, **the nearest Accident and Emergency Department** is at Epsom District Hospital, Dorking Road, Epsom (Tel. 01372 735735).

POLICE STATION AND FIRE STATION

See *Leatherhead*.

ALLOTMENTS

Enquiries to Mole Valley District Council (Tel. 01306 878299).

CEMETERY

See *Leatherhead*.

SEWAGE WORKS

Near *Bookham Station* to the north of the area in *Maddox Lane*, bordering the common.

REFUSE TIP

See *Leatherhead*.

AIRCRAFT AND TRAFFIC NOISE

Nothing to highlight or draw to your attention, obviously traffic noise will be most closest to the A246, *Guildford/Leatherhead Road*.

HISTORY

Probably one of Surrey's most famous houses, *'Polesden Lacey'* is found just south of the village centre in *Polesden Road*. Belonging to the *National Trust* and the location of their Southern Region Headquarters, this elegant house dates mainly from the 1820s. The house and grounds were given to the Trust in 1942 by the Hon. Mrs. Ronald Greville as a memorial to her father the Rt. Hon. William McEwan. Both the building and its 1000 acres of parkland and gardens are open to the public.

Also owned by the *National Trust* to the north of the village and station are the 500 acres of the *Bookham Commons*. The majority of the soil here is London Clay, which means there are plenty of marshy areas ideal for water loving plants and animals; for this reason they are of *'Special Scientific Interest'*.

Although surrounded by post-war housing, *Great Bookham* retains its small scale village character. At the main cross roads, the Parish Church of *St. Nicholas* dates from the 11th century and the rector here from 1769 until his death in 1820 was *Jane Austen's* godfather, the *Rev. Samuel Cooke*. The *'Royal Oak'* public house, opposite the church, is 17th century and some of the cottages around the village are even earlier dating from the 1500s.

Great Bookham's attractive village shopping centre is in the middle of a 'Conservation Area' and there is another such Area in neighbouring *Little Bookham* centred around *Preston Cross*. Here several 17th century cottages may be found nestling amongst more modern styled sympathetic housing.

FETCHAM

Included under *Bookham* because it is difficult to define any boundary, *Fetcham* dates back to Saxon times, although little of its present day appearance would suggest this. Of historical interest now is *St Mary's Church* containing Roman tiles within its west wall and a fine font which dates from 1632. Behind this building is *'Fetcham Park'*, an 18th century mansion. The area once supported a well established ale and beer industry and in the times of the *Domesday Book*, five mills were in the vicinity.

Abinger Hammer — *Photo Courtesy of Surrey County Council*

Leigh — *Photo Courtesy of Surrey County Council*

THE RURAL VILLAGES

Parish News Magazines. Common among many of the rural villages are 'Parish News' monthly publications. These are sometimes delivered to homes in the area on receipt of a small annual payment and, if you are new to the area, can be found out about through the local Parish Council Clerk. Many residents find them very useful for local news and information about their villages and they undoubtedly enhance a community spirit. They may also be discovered on sale in places such as village stores, local newsagents, churches, doctor's surgeries or public houses.

Public Houses and Local Shops. Generally Mole Valley's rural public houses are not open all day and shops may observe early closing one day a week, which in most cases is Wednesday. It should be appreciated too, that shops such as village stores and newsagents may close for lunch. Locally (and understandably), prices of comparable goods are often more expensive. Petrol prices are a noticeable example of course, and fuel is unlikely to be available 24 hours a day, off the beaten track!

The District's Country Lanes. Many country lanes are subject only to the national speed limit, but experience shows that in most places, nothing like the top speed of 60 mph, may normally be achieved. Unfortunately some of the lanes in the Mole Valley are amongst the most dangerous you may ever travel on, owing to people driving too fast in places they cannot see to be clear. Adding to the trouble, are the whims of wild deer, foxes, rabbits, pheasants and other wildlife who are liable to cross the road without warning causing all sorts of chaos!

Always remember too, that even in the villages the lanes often have no street lighting or footpaths. This makes driving more hazardous and even short walks along these roads are undesirable, especially with young children.

Horses. Horses are kept all over Surrey and must also use the roads sometimes, they need extra allowances to be made for them, especially with the speed and size of today's traffic. Not all horses react the same way in traffic, it is best to expect the worst! Try not to be impatient, they existed as a form of transport long before the internal combustion engine. Perhaps because of this, believe it or not, they still have 'absolute right of way'.

Modern Utilities. Some of the more remote areas of Surrey will not be connected to the gas supply or mains drainage. Most people quickly adapt to the alternatives and in some cases find them preferable. Remember also the expense of private sewage disposal is offset by not having to pay the water board for the service.

One added hazard of living in more remote areas is the raised probability of power cuts which may sometimes be extremely inconvenient. You are not normally entitled to any compensation for any unscheduled power cuts over short periods, no matter what disruption and inconvenience they may cause. Whilst mentioning electricity there are a surprising lack of ugly pylons in the District which is fortunate for residents.

VILLAGES' NOTICE BOARD

CAPEL NEWSAGENCY - For newspapers, groceries, chemistry, video and off-licence. Free local deliveries. Fresh bread daily. Football pools.
Open 6am-6.30pm Monday to Saturday. 6am-3pm Sunday.
We also sell National and Instant Lotteries. Tel: 01306 711021

M.J. BYRNES
(GARDEN MAINTENANCE)
Overgrown gardens tidied
Strimming Hedge cutting
Flymowing
Roses and Shrubs pruned

Glenside,   **01306 888388**
Westcott Green,
Dorking, Surrey   Est. 1987

ROSES STORES, MICKLEHAM

Try your local shop and post office with a select range of goods and personal service. We sell ham on the bone, bacon sliced to order, freshly ground coffee in addition to general groceries, stationery and haberdashery.

Deliveries by arrangement
Tel: 01372 372377

ABINGER (ABINGER COMMON) *See 'Mole Valley' Map*

LOCATION

Abinger is about 6 miles *South West* of *Dorking,* set on very high ground, off the A25. See also *Abinger Hammer* below.

✓

Good primary school choice. Most attractive location. Excellent riding/walking country. Church and public house.

✗

Not one shop!   Remote train station.   Infrequent buses.

OPINION

One of the loveliest places to live and relax in the world - except for some English weather of course! A tranquil, secluded village, very rural and steeped in history. A *'must'* to have a car and forget any night life! If you love fresh air, wonderful views and country pursuits then this is the place for you.

THE VILLAGE AND SURROUNDINGS

Local homes surround the church, the local *'Abinger Hatch'* public house, the village hall and first school, but there are no shops. Set high on the *Greensand Ridge* amidst thick woodland and rolling fields, *Abinger* is exceptionally picturesque. Some modest terraced housing may be found in the area alongside character cottages and larger homes.

Lutyens, the great Surrey architect, built *Goddards* in 1898 as a hostel for young women and later made additions when it was converted into a house. This property is situated overlooking the large village green near *Hollow Lane.* **Abinger Bottom** sits deep in a valley to the south of the Common, all that is here are some charming cottages. The total population of the whole of *Abinger* is extremely small.

LOCAL TELEPHONE BOOKS

British Telecom - Guildford and West Surrey No. 530
See the back of your current Phone Book or Tel. 150
Yellow Pages - Gatwick Area, Book No. 22.
Telephone Orders 0800 671444

TRANSPORT

Abinger is remote, which is part of its greatest charm, so most residents rely heavily on private cars make them four wheel drive when possible!

ROADS

The A25 is about one mile north of the village and the best approach road from it is *Hollow Lane*, which inclines up to the green through a deep cutting, on a fairly wide, but twisting road.

RAIL

The nearest main line train station is *Dorking*. *Gomshall* Station and *Dorking West* are on the Thames Trains *East/ West* line - see the *Rail* section under *Dorking*.

The whole of Network South East Railway Services are depicted in the front section of 'Yellow Pages'. Further information may be obtained on many maps, booklets and leaflets obtained from most railway stations.

BUSES

There is a bus route close by along *Hollow Lane*, but as with most villages, the service is infrequent.
Bus Timetables/Enquiries/Maps from Surrey Traveline: Tel. 01737 223000. Copies of timetables are available from local libraries, council offices throughout Surrey or by post from the County Council at County Hall, Kingston upon Thames, KT1 2DY.

SHOPPING

The nearest village shops are in Westcott and more extensive facilities can be found in *Dorking*.

SCHOOLS

Belmont Preparatory School is set close to the village and there is a good local first school and adjoining nursery.

NOISE

There is very little traffic in the village and most people would not remark upon what little aircraft noise may occasionally be heard.

PARISH COUNCIL INFORMATION

Clerk to the Parish Council: Mrs. J. Bolton, Blue Hills House, Abinger Common, Dorking RH5 6HZ. Tel: 01306 730759

HISTORY

Described as the oldest village in England, since it was inhabited as long ago as 5000 B.C., *Abinger* (shown on today's maps as *Abinger Common*) is a delightful beauty spot on the north slopes of *Leith Hill*, the highest point in South East England. The village green boasts a canopied Victorian well and there is a picturesque 17th century public house *'The Abinger Hatch'* opposite *St. James's Church*. The church, built in the 12th century, has been rebuilt twice since a bomb exploded near it in 1944 and lightening damaged it 20 years later. In the Middle Ages the church was a stopping off point for travellers along the *Pilgrims' Way* and it still retains a medieval look.

Once a year, in June, the Abinger Fair is still held to which the villagers traditionally wear medieval costume. The fair was famous in the middle ages for pilgrims putting on plays for villagers, in return for their food and lodging. Outside the church gate are the old village stocks and to the other side is the manor house, with a 'motte' (a small Norman earthwork), probably constructed by a knight soon after the Norman Conquest. The hamlet of **Sutton** to the west of *Abinger* has two old farm houses, one is *'Sutton Place Farm'*, built around 1700. Another, named *'Fulvens'*, was built earlier and is renowned to be one of the best farms in the county. The visitor will find *'The Volunteer'* public house's location here quite charming.

The hamlets of **Friday Street** and **Broadmoor** nearby, are deep on the northern slopes of *Leith Hill*, both are worth discovering and very picturesque. At *Friday Street*, there's the *Stephan Langton Inn*, sited just above the old mill pond, which served a cornmill in the late 16th century and possibly a gunpowder mill earlier. Tradition claims that *Stephan Langton*, the first *Archbishop of Canterbury*, was born here around 1150. Later he sided with the barons against *King John* and was famous for finally witnessing the signing of the *Magna Carta* at *Runnymede*. Now only a cottage remains beneath the dam and adjacent cottages are mostly of tiny proportions. The ponds, waterfalls and water courses run down hill towards *'Wotton House'*, home of the Evelyns, so renowned in this parish.

ABINGER HAMMER *See 'Mole Valley' Map*

LOCATION
About 5 miles *West* of *Dorking* on the A25 beneath the area of the *North Downs* known as *'White Downs'* and *'Netley Heath'*.

✔

Local pub, a few shops and first school. Nearby train station at Gomshall with limited service. Good bus services.

✗

Busy through road for nearby housing. No immediate choice of schools. No real village centre.

OPINION
A pretty spot on the busy A25, but there is little to this village. It is most memorable for its very photographed clock which hangs out above the road on the 'S' bend (blink and you might just miss it!). If you like *Triumph Stags* you may already know this village, its well-known specialist garage is adjacent to the green.

THE VILLAGE AND SURROUNDINGS
There are a few village shops and the local post office on the main A25 at the junction with *Felday Road*. Otherwise this once busy, industrial village

now only has a school, *'The Abinger Arms'* public house, a tea rooms, a couple of rural industries and Martin Grant Homes' Head Office. Some of the larger houses fronting onto the north side of the road are noticeable and appealing for their old brickwork and beams. Houses further down *Felday Road* are scattered on large plots, some on elevated ground and mostly backing onto farmland, but there is not a lot of choice in type or price range.

Abinger Hammer Village Hall is set to the south of the A25 on high ground above the cricket pitch and local produce may be enjoyed from the Tilling Bourne Trout Farm and Kingfisher Watercress Beds, both easily found on the main road. The population of Abinger Hammer is about 2,000.

LOCAL TELEPHONE BOOKS

British Telecom - Guildford and West Surrey No. 530
See the back of your current Phone Book or Tel. 150
Yellow Pages - Gatwick Area, Book No. 22.
Telephone Orders 0800 671444

TRANSPORT

More accessible than some villages, but most would find it necessary to have a car.

ROADS

The main A25 passes through the village *east/west*. In the immediate vicinity it is a 30 mph limit, but national speed limits apply in both directions quite soon.

RAIL

The station at **Gomshall**, although within walking distance, offers rather a restricted service between *Guildford* and *Dorking*.

Customer Information Telephone: 01732 770111. The whole of Network South East Railway Services are depicted in the front section of 'Yellow Pages'. Further information may be obtained on many maps, booklets and leaflets obtained from most railway stations.

BUSES

The main A25 runs through the village which is a bus route between *Dorking* and *Guildford*.

Bus Timetables/Enquiries/Maps from Surrey Traveline: Tel. 01737 223000. Copies of timetables are available from local libraries, council offices throughout Surrey or by post from the County Council at County Hall, Kingston upon Thames, KT1 2DY.

SHOPPING

Almost equi-distant between *Dorking* and *Guildford,* the village offers very little shopping itself. There are the watercress beds, some farms, a forge, a couple of antiques and 'junk' shops, the *Tillingbourne Trout Farm* and one little combined general store and post office.

SCHOOLS

There is a primary school in the heart of the village.

NOISE

Only from the A25 major through route.

HISTORY

Abinger Hammer was once the industrial neighbour of *Abinger.* As its name suggests, the village was an established iron working area in Tudor times (and later), when the *Tilling Bourne River* was dammed to form hammerponds, now in use as watercress beds. It is a very attractive spot and famous for the Victorian 'anvil clock' which juts out above the road. There is still a blacksmith and forge a few yards from the clock serving at least to remind visitors of the village's history. So apart from the proximity of the A25, it is mostly a quiet rural area with a pretty green, through which the *Tilling Bourne River* now meanders.

TO ADVERTISE IN THIS SPACE
IN THE NEXT EDITION CONTACT
THE 'GOOD *move* GUIDE
Tel: 01306 731122
Fax: 01306 731444

The new Musical Bed is a copy of a French antique which Simon Horn admired on a visit to the Dordogne. Based on a Louis XVI style, the Musical Bed is hand carved from solid wood and decorated in the French classical style with a musical motif of crossed lyre and flute.

Here the bed has been sumptuously hand painted in cream with decorations picked out in gold leaf. It can also be painted to the customer's own specification. The price of the Musical Bed as shown above starts from £1,992 plus VAT

HEAD OFFICE: Showrooms: 117-121 Wandsworth Bridge Road, London SW6 2TP
Telephone: 0171 731 1279 Fax: 0171 736 3522
FRENCH OFFICE: Chemin Des Amoureux, Zone Industrielle Nord, 35400 Saint Malo, France
Téléphone: 0033 99 82 29 95 Téléfax: 00 33 99 82 29 96

BETCHWORTH *See 'Mole Valley' Map*

LOCATION
About 3 miles *East* of *Dorking* on the A25 road towards *Reigate,* almost equi-distant between these two towns.

✓

Own train station with limited service. Very pretty, but tiny, village centre away from A25. Good road connections. Post Office, shop, pub, church and first school. Close to Dorking and Reigate.

✗

Hazardous country lanes. Relatively low lying. Land excavations are wide spread in the area.

OPINION
More an area, than a village as such, but very worthy of attention and ideally located for the local facilities of *Reigate.* Well within 'commuter' country with particularly pretty spots.

THE VILLAGE AND SURROUNDINGS
A small, but typical Surrey village, the heart of which is located just south of the main A25 and attractive in its setting. The compact village centre is just above the *River Mole* where *The Street* meets *Wonham Lane*. Within view of this junction is the beautiful *St. Michael's Church* set at the end of the cul-de-sac *Church Street*. This church was recently made famous in the film *'Four Weddings and a Funeral'*. In *The Street* close by is *'The Dolphin Inn'*, opposite which is the 300 year old forge, still operating and most appealing.

The general area here, especially around the A25, has long been the site of successful excavation industries. Some pits are in the process of being re-filled and some land reclamation and conservation of industrial features have begun. The population of *Betchworth* is about 1,500.

LOCAL TELEPHONE BOOKS

British Telecom - Guildford and West Surrey No. 530
See the back of your current Phone Book or Tel. 150
Yellow Pages - Gatwick Area, Book No. 22
From: Telephone Orders 0800 671444.

TRANSPORT

As with all of the rural villages, having access to a car is recommended although the main A25 is within easy walking distance where there is a bus route.

ROADS

The main A25 runs to the north of the village centre by about half a mile. At this point it is a fast, wide country road which is the same for most of its length between *Dorking* and *Reigate*.

The *B2032* (which joins the *B2033* - see map), is a busy *north/south* through route which starts as *Station Road* and then eventually climbs up the local well-known and rather dreaded *Pebble Hill Road*. The level crossing, adjacent to *Betchworth Station*, is frequently responsible for local traffic congestion, particularly in the rush hours.

Pebble Hill Road has many sharp bends and is exceptionally steep and narrow, but fast traffic uses it all day long and unfortunately it has been the site of many bad accidents in its long history. Attractive houses set next to this road (and up narrow driveways), are at a slight disadvantage because of its character and local reputation.

RAIL

Betchworth Station on Thames Trains' *East/West Guildford* to *Redhill* line, runs very much to the north of the village and across the A25, making it slightly inaccessible. Faster services start at *Dorking* or *Reigate*.

Thames Trains' Customer Information Telephone: 01732 770111. The whole of Network South East Railway Services are depicted in the front section of 'Yellow Pages'. Further information may be obtained on many maps, booklets and leaflets obtained from most railway stations.

BUSES

Fairly frequent Route 32 between *Dorking* and *Reigate* and beyond.

Bus Timetables/Enquiries/Maps from Surrey Traveline: Tel. 01737 223000. Copies of timetables are available from local libraries, council offices throughout Surrey or by post from the County Council at County Hall, Kingston upon Thames, KT1 2DY.

SHOPPING

There are many garden centres along this part of the A25, one is at the junction with *Station Road*. In the village there is just one little post office and general store in *Old Reigate Road*.

SCHOOLS

There is a County First School in the village and an independent preparatory school close by at *Leigh*.

NOISE

In the proximity of the major roads (including the already mentioned *Pebble Hill Road*) and near the railway line.

PARISH COUNCIL INFORMATION

Clerk to Betchworth Parish Council: Mrs V. Houghton, Brick Field, 20 Kiln Lane, Betchworth, RH3 7LX. Tel: 01737 843342

HISTORY

Betchworth is a picture-postcard village, like its neighbour *Brockham*, lying on the banks of the *River Mole* with the *North Downs* providing a dramatic backdrop. It was once a Saxon village, with a church dating from the 11th century and a noticeable building close by called the *'Old House'* of early Georgian design. In *Betchworth Park*, now a golf course, there are remains of the 15th century *Betchworth Castle* which was built to defend the *Downs*. Although some of the castle's walls still remain most were destroyed or dismantled. (Not open to the public).

Buckland village close by sits astride the *Pilgrims Way* where *St. Mary's Church,* rebuilt in 1860, has a 14th century stained glass window which is probably the best in Surrey. This village, like so many in Surrey, is split in half by the A25, the pond and green to the north side of the road and the church to the south.

Occupants of fast moving traffic along the A25 may be forgiven for hardly noticing this village, but to stop at *Rectory Lane* on the north side of the road is a treat to behold. The picturesque green and the pond (reputed to be a home of terrapins) within this lovely setting, is worth a longer look. Just to the south of the A25, next to the church, is the little shop and post office next to a hairdressers. The population of *Buckland* is only about 600.

PARISH COUNCIL INFORMATION

Clerk to Buckland Parish Council: Mr. H.A. Thompson, 7 Montfort Rise, Salfords, Redhill, RH1 5DU. Tel: 01293 771584

Editor of the Parish Magazine: Mr. R. Wheen, Telephone: 01737 842193

BROCKHAM *See 'Mole Valley' Map*

LOCATION

About half a mile *South* of the A25 and about 2 miles *East* of *Dorking*, a pretty Surrey village on low lying ground bordering the *River Mole*.

✔

Picturesque village green in lovely setting. Good bus services. Good road connections. Pubs, village store, hairdressers, travel agent, church, first school.

✗

Low lying. No immediate train station. Limited schools choice.

OPINION

I particularly like *Brockham,* the village green is very special, it has a lovely open aspect. The surrounding roads offer marvellous views of the nearby rolling countryside, but this 'dreamy' tranquil village is close enough to *Dorking* to keep residents in touch with reality!

THE VILLAGE AND SURROUNDINGS

The centre surrounds a large attractive green, away from the A25, with *Christ Church* to the south side. Pretty houses, old and new, border the green and alongside are two public houses, *'The Royal Oak'* and *'The Duke's Head'*. To the north is the steep back drop of *Box Hill*, rising almost vertically in some places and around the village are numerous bridle and foot paths.

The big playing field immediately to the south of the A25 is now used mostly as football pitches, known as *'Brockham Big Field'* it was once jointly tilled by the villagers. Some of the back roads near this field are the setting for attractive residences to the west of *Brockham Lane*. In general, the whole village is surrounded by large fields and sweeping views and there is much to recommend it.

Brockham is well known for miles around for its excellent fireworks every November to commemorate *Guy Fawkes* Night. The huge bonfire in the middle of the village green taking weeks to build, but just hours to burn!

One point to consider is that because the village is low lying, some roads nearest the *River Mole* and its tributaries may be liable to flooding. There are several shops, a butchers and a hairdressers near the green. The population of *Brockham* is about 2,000.

Strood Green, just to the south of *Brockham,* is also set in a lovely spot. It offers the facilities of a post office, general stores and a rather modern styled public house *(The Spotted Cow)!* Some pretty terraced cottages mingle with a larger amount of local authority and modest priced housing.

LOCAL TELEPHONE BOOKS

British Telecom - Guildford and West Surrey No. 530
See the back of your current Phone Book or Tel. 150
Yellow Pages - Gatwick Area, Book No. 22.
Telephone Orders 0800 671444.

TRANSPORT

Certainly a village better placed than some for reasonable access to public transport. *Strood Green* is the end of the line for the Route 21 bus which follows the village route to *Guildford*.

ROADS

Close and easily accessible to the A25, *Brockham* is not so remote as other rural Surrey villages. With the use of a car therefore, *Brockham's* residents can quickly be in touch with modern day living, whilst home remains a country retreat.

Some of the roads around the village have a particularly unique, appealing character, such as *Old School Lane* and *Bushbury Road*. Whereas many Surrey roads are winding and enclosed, these are different, in that they are no more than an unmarked, tarmac single track with wide green verges and far-reaching views. So rather than being typical of public highways, these lanes are more like long sweeping drives or roads of a private park, crossing over this gently undulating low-lying countryside.

RAIL

Closest main station for London trains is *Dorking*. For Thames Trains *East/West,* either *Betchworth* or *Dorking (Deepdene)*. Please refer to *Dorking* or *Betchworth Rail* sections for typical train travelling times.

The whole of Network South East Railway Services are depicted in the front section of 'Yellow Pages'. Further information may be obtained on many maps, booklets and leaflets obtained from most railway stations.

BUSES

Both *Brockham* and *Strood Green* are on a local bus route, still more buses run on the A25.

Bus Timetables/Enquiries/Maps from Surrey Traveline: Tel. 01737 223000. Copies of timetables are available from local libraries, council offices throughout Surrey or by post from the County Council at County Hall, Kingston upon Thames, KT1 2DY.

SHOPPING

Very limited in the village, confined to a small general stores, a travel agent, a butchers, sports wear shop and hairdressers. The nearest shopping facilities are at *Dorking* and for superstores further distances need to be travelled to *Reigate, Horsham* or *Leatherhead*.

SCHOOLS

The local first and middle school is in *Wheelers Lane*, off the green.

NOISE

Brockham is not affected by noise from road or rail, *Gatwick Airport* is not far away to the south east, but generally aircraft noise is not noticeable.

PARISH COUNCIL INFORMATION

Clerk to the Parish Council: Mrs C. Plumb, Willow Cottage, Mill Hill Lane, Brockham, Betchworth, RH3 7LR. Tel: 01737 843471

HISTORY

The name of the village derives from the badgers that once lived along the banks of the *River Mole* in this area.

Christ Church overlooks the green, dating from the 1840s with a tall, octagonal spire, it was built to the memory of *Henry Goulburn*, a *Chancellor of the Exchequer* who served both *Peel* and *Wellington*. *Brockham* became an ecclesiastical parish, separate from *St. Michael's, Betchworth* in 1848.

In earlier days the green was the local venue for cricket and in Victorian times nearby, there was a Home and Industrial School for orphaned girls. Where the road crosses the *River Mole*, is '*Borough Bridge*', dating back to 1737. Wide enough only for one lane of traffic, this bridge has a large flood relief tunnel in the buttress and a separate pedestrian bridge runs alongside.

CAPEL *See 'Mole Valley' Map*

LOCATION

Six miles *South* of *Dorking* off the A24, on relatively low-lying ground.

✓

Shops, post office, first school, pub, petrol and recreation ground. Good, fast road access and open countryside.

✗

Remember the proximity of Gatwick (within five miles to the east) which adds somewhat to village traffic and noise.

OPINION

An attractive village centre with a small green and pond, although it does not benefit from a particularly remarkable geographic position. The setting of the old *'Crown'* public house next to *John the Baptist Church* is very pleasing and there is quite a thriving local community. The A24 by-pass is within a couple of minutes drive providing excellent road communications north and south.

THE VILLAGE AND SURROUNDINGS

Capel takes its name from the Latin word 'capella' for chapel which was built here in the 12th century. It is a fairly large village with a population of around 3,000 which is spread along the old *London* to *Worthing* road. The relatively new by-pass of course, has vastly improved the immediate environment for most of the homes built alongside the old road.

There is a small post office, general stores, petrol station, public house and church along *The Street*. Local residencies are found stretched along this road and in *Vicarage Lane* where there is also the recreation ground. Opposite the small green and pond is *Laundry Way* where there are some light industrial units.

As the village is very close to the *Sussex* border, it is surrounded by small farms and green fields, so typical of this southern part of Surrey. The *'Surrey Hills Hotel'* is located on the approach road into the village from the north. Further south still are large brick works, near the *Sussex* border, so much a part of the excavation industry of clay in the area.

LOCAL TELEPHONE BOOKS

British Telecom - Guildford and West Surrey No. 530
See the back of your current Phone Book or Tel. 150
Yellow Pages - Gatwick Area, Book No. 22.
Telephone Orders 0800 671444.

TRANSPORT

Useful transport facilities are nearby for such a remote Surrey village.

ROADS

The main A24 by-pass circuits round the village with adjoining access at two convenient roundabouts, both north and south of the village. In the immediate area travelling east/west is more difficult where there is only a network of country roads. Unfortunately for local residents the proximity of *Gatwick* increases traffic through the village.

RAIL

Ockley station is very nearby, but physically across the A24, along *Cole's Lane*. This main line station is on the *Horsham* to *London* line which takes about 11 minutes to *Dorking* where there are connections for Thames Trains running *East/West* - see the *Rail* section under Dorking.

Customer Information Telephone: 0171 928 5100. The whole of Network South East Railway Services are depicted in the front section of 'Yellow Pages'. Further information may be obtained on many maps, booklets and leaflets obtained from most railway stations.

BUSES

There are local buses in the area.

Bus Timetables/Enquiries/Maps from Surrey Traveline: Tel. 01737 223000. Copies of timetables are available from local libraries, council offices throughout Surrey or by post from the County Council at County Hall, Kingston upon Thames, KT1 2DY.

SHOPPING

Not particularly conveniently placed for shopping facilities beyond the village stores and tiny *National Westminster Bank*, which is buried within the forecourt of the petrol station. *Capel* is more or less equi-distant from *Dorking* and *Horsham*. There is a *'Tescos'* superstore in *Horsham* and the other side of *Charlwood*, whereas *Dorking's* shops, spread along the *High Street*, are more traditional.

SCHOOLS

There is a first school in the village.

NOISE

Gatwick Airport is only about five miles east of *Capel,* so this village is close to flight paths normally used for take off with the prevailing south westerly winds. Assessing the level of noise and the frequency of it however, must be left to the individual to establish. I only mention it as worthy of note just in case others have an interest in *not* pointing it out!

PARISH COUNCIL INFORMATION

Clerk to the Council: Mrs Pamela Hinks, Briarbank, Vicarage Lane, Capel, Dorking RH5 5LL Tel: 01306 711051

Editor of Capel and Beare Green Magazine: Mrs. Mary Ede Tel: 01306 711293

This Parish Council is split into three wards: Capel Ward, Beare Green Ward and Coldharbour Ward.

HISTORY

Capel's original name was *'Ewekene'* when it was a tiny hamlet named after a prominent local landowner. Then the few inhabitants were mainly pig breeders whose stock fed on the acorns in the wealden oak forests. Much later when the area became split into parishes, there is first mention of the chapel which gave *Capel* its name. Now *Capel* is the centre of a large parish which stretches south to the Sussex borders and there are several 15th to 17th century cottages, houses and farms in the area. *St. John The Baptist Church* dates from the 13th century, but like so many others in the area was extensively rebuilt in the Victorian period.

Also the village had strong connections with the *Quaker* movement which was brought to the village in 1655 by the *Bax* family. *'Pleystowe'*, in *Rusper Road*, the house of *Richard Bax,* became home and local headquarters to the believers.

In 1755 the road between *Dorking* and *Horsham* was opened and *Capel* was midway. The sheep and cattle farmers of *Sussex* found *Capel* was well placed for refreshment and rest on their way to the markets of *London,* so many ale houses grew up in the neighbourhood. Later the proximity of the *London, Brighton and South Coast Railway* passing nearby at *Ockley* served further to establish the village.

At at the beginning of the 20th century musical traditions outside the church were being encouraged in many ways and in 1904 the *Capel Choral Society* came into being. Concerts and musical evenings formed the chief entertainment of the time and *Capel* was fortunate in having the help of the great English composer, *Ralph Vaughan Williams*, who lived on the parish boundary at *Leith Hill Place*. The *Broadwood* family, associated with the firm that made the famous Broadwood pianos, once lived in the area at *'Lyne House'* in the countryside south east of *Capel.* One of its members, *Lucy Broadwood* travelled the country with *Vaughan Williams* helping him note the folk songs of the time. Many of these tunes have since been incorporated into well known classical works and hymns in particular.

Land development continued in the twentieth century with the building of two housing estates at the southern end of the village. The first, *Carterdale* was built in 1930 and comprised 40 houses, the second, *Bennetts Wood* was built in 1952 and totalled some 60 properties. *Broadwood Cottages* were built between these two dates in 1947 on land donated by *Captain Broadwood.* As early as the 1930s the need for a by-pass was first put to Surrey County Council and some 50 years later in 1982, heavy traffic was at last diverted from the village.

CHARLWOOD *See 'Mole Valley' Map*

LOCATION

Extreme *South East* corner of the District, about 2 miles *South West* of Horley and adjacent to *Gatwick Airport*.

✔

Pretty village location. Post office, pub, general stores, recreation ground and first school. Well placed for fast road communications.

✗

Gatwick Airport on the doorstep with accompanying extra traffic, noise and sometimes even smell!

OPINION

Although airports have to be somewhere, what a pity *Gatwick* happens to be in *Charlwood's* back yard! This village is otherwise pretty and well located, close to the much larger towns of *Horley* and *Crawley*. Without doubt there are some lovely properties in the area. If you can live at ease with your intrusive neighbour and the continued pressure on its expansion, the lower property prices might just attract you?

THE VILLAGE AND SURROUNDINGS

A charming Weald village surrounded by flat agricultural land and some beautiful farmhouses, but dominated by nearby *Gatwick Airport* which undoubtedly affects its desirability as a residential area. At the centre there are a few essential shops, a post office and several public houses, the quaintest being *'The Half Moon'* next to *St. Nicholas' Church*.

Along *Ifield Road* to the south of the village is a small industrial estate, here the aeroplanes especially dominate the environment as they roar overhead into the prevailing south westerly winds. Occasionally even the smell of aircraft fuel may waft across the fields.

Nearby just on the *Horley/Charlwood Road* to *Gatwick* is the local area of *Povey Cross*. Naturally there are a prolific number of hotels here, together with a *'Tescos'* superstore and *Gatwick Park Hospital*. The population of Charlwood is about 2,500.

LOCAL TELEPHONE BOOKS

British Telecom - Horsham Area, Book No. 643.
See the back of your current Phone Book or Tel. 150
Yellow Pages - Gatwick Area, Book No. 22.
Telephone Orders 0800 671444.

TRANSPORT

Within the view of *Gatwick Airport's* runways, the village can hardly be called cut off! In some ways however, most would rather it was! As some compensation though, because of the airport, other transport links nearby are excellent.

ROADS

Junction 9 of the *M23* is about ten minutes drive from *Charlwood*, the *A23* by-pass connection to it even closer. So where roads to the north/south and east are better than average, those to the west revert to typical Surrey country lanes until the *A24/A29* junction at *Beare Green*. The small high street of Charlwood is significantly affected by increased 'through-traffic' owing to the airport.

RAIL

Gatwick Airport is the closest train station (or *Horley* with a less frequent service). Typical rail times, *North* bound: 10 mins to *Redhill,* 25 mins to *East Croydon*, 40 mins to *London.*   *South* bound: 16 mins to *Haywards Heath* and 40 mins to *Brighton.*
Customer Information Telephone: 0171 928 5100. The whole of Network South East Railway Services are depicted in the front section of 'Yellow Pages'. Further information may be obtained on many maps, booklets and leaflets obtained from most railway stations.

BUSES

Bus Timetables/Enquiries/Maps from Surrey Traveline: Tel. 01737 223000. Copies of timetables are available from local libraries, council offices throughout Surrey or by post from the County Council at County Hall, Kingston upon Thames, KT1 2DY.

SHOPPING

Little choice in the village itself where there is a post office, general stores, hair salon, off licence and interiors shop, but the proximity of *Horley* and the larger *Crawley* means that modern shopping is close at hand. Nearby at **Povey Cross** there is a *'Tescos'* superstore off the A217 *Reigate Road*.

SCHOOLS

Charlwood First School is in *Chapel Road* in the village. There are no other schools of note very nearby within the District. The neighbouring *Horley* (Reigate and Banstead Borough) and *Crawley* and *Horsham* in *Sussex* offer a wider choice.

NOISE

Little more needs to be said about the proximity of *Gatwick Airport*, the planes will be quite apparent at most times of the day flying over the fields south of *Charlwood*. This is a big factor and there is no getting away from it, the only thing to be said is that house prices should be cheaper because of it.

LEISURE

Gatwick Zoo, at *Russ Hill* is very popular for the younger visitor with its charming residents and a layout designed to keep children's interest (Tel. 01293 862312). *Lowfield Heath Windmill*, which is within the grounds of the Zoo, is one of the few left in the county. It was a tall post mill, first built around 1760 and last worked by wind in 1880. When it became derelict at its original site near *Gatwick Airport,* it was rebuilt in its present position.

Charlwood is well off for pubs, with the *'Greyhound'*, the *'Rising Sun'* and the *'Half Moon'* all in close proximity. Not to be forgotten, as with much of Surrey, England's love affair with the horse is much in evidence here.

PARISH COUNCIL INFORMATION

Clerk to the Parish Council: Mrs. M. Billinghurst, Page Wood Cottage, Rectory Lane, Charlwood, Surrey RH6 0EF. Tel: 01293 862571

Editors of the local Parish Magazine: Mr and Mrs P. Weakley, 81 Parkhurst Road, Horley RH6 8EX

HISTORY

Charlwood retains quite a number of half-timbered and weatherboard cottages typical of the Weald, including the *'Half Moon Inn'* in the centre. A little further along, is the treasure of the village, the Norman church of *St. Nicholas*, one of the most interesting in the area. *Gatwick* was once famous for a racecourse, especially around the turn of the century, when the one at *Croydon* closed. The natural level ground, once so suitable for this purpose, has given rise to London's second largest airport which continues to increase in importance and capacity.

COLDHARBOUR AND LEITH HILL *See 'Mole Valley' Map*

LOCATION

Four and a half miles *South West* of *Dorking* along *Coldharbour Lane*, the highest point in South East England.

✔

Charming, tiny village. Pub and church. The very best (well drained) riding/walking country in the area with spectacular views. Close to Dorking.

✗

Isolated by its elevated, rural situation and rather exposed to easterly winds. Overrun by day trippers especially summer weekends. Especially remote from public transport.

OPINION

One of the most beautiful spots in Surrey with a natural location affording stunning scenery. Attractive homes are set away from the centre down *Anstie Lane* and *Broomehall Road* giving residents exceptional privacy. A must for a car and even better if its four wheel drive! *Coldharbour* has to be one of my favourite places, for me this local area is the treasure at the end of the rainbow.

THE VILLAGE AND SURROUNDINGS

Although *Coldharbour* is remote and exposed to cold winter winds, this charming village has to be seen to be believed. Travelling out of *Dorking* along *Coldharbour Lane* becomes a bewitching experience as this ordinary country lane climbs higher and higher between high sided banks, lined with tree roots. All year the branches of the trees above form a dark tunnel, enticing the visitor on towards the summit.

Eventually the road opens out into an enchanting hamlet where you will find *'The Plough'* public house and a little further beyond, the church. Around the centre are a variety of terraced cottages and detached houses all of which benefit from the natural beauty of the location and many enjoy wonderful views.

Opposite *'The Plough'* is the start of quite breathtaking countryside, in more ways than one! Climbing sharply up hill a number of paths lead to *'Leith Hill Tower'*, almost a mile further on and not for the faint hearted. The rewards at the end of the climb make it all worthwhile, the immediate scenery and extensive views, both north and south are a wonder to behold. Also, if you visit at the weekend, you will normally find refreshments awaiting you in the tower!

Abinger Road, the continuation of *Coldharbour Lane* is also worth mentioning as it twists through rhododendron and bluebell woodland. At one point an established tree forms an arch over the road which all adds to the magic of this unique spot. The population of *Coldharbour* is less than 1000.

LOCAL TELEPHONE BOOKS

British Telecom - Guildford and West Surrey No. 530
See the back of your current Phone Book or Tel. 150
Yellow Pages - Gatwick Area, Book No. 22.
Telephone Orders 0800 671444.

TRANSPORT

As you will have realised, *Coldharbour* is a secluded Surrey village (probably one of the most secluded) and getting around by public transport is not easy.

ROADS

Coldharbour Lane descends rapidly into *Dorking* from the village centre and for this reason the village is brought surprisingly quickly back into the 20th century. This road is similar in type to all the other approach roads to the village in that they are twisting country lanes, sometimes prone to icy conditions, especially considering the height of the ground and some of the exposed positions.

RAIL

Dorking's services are the closest, see the *Rail* section under *Dorking*.

Customer Information Telephone: 0171 928 5100. The whole of Network South East Railway Services are depicted in the front section of 'Yellow Pages'. Further information may be obtained on many maps, booklets and leaflets obtained from most railway stations.

BUSES

Only a local post bus goes through *Coldharbour*.

Bus Timetables/Enquiries/Maps from Surrey Traveline: Tel. 01737 223000. Copies of timetables are available from local libraries, council offices throughout Surrey or by post from the County Council at County Hall, Kingston upon Thames, KT1 2DY.

SHOPPING

The shopping facilities of *Dorking* town are the nearest.

SCHOOLS

There has been no village school, as such, for several decades, so local children normally start at the schools in other parts of the parish provided in *Ockley* or *Beare Green*. *Belmont Preparatory School* in neighbouring *Holmbury St. Mary* and *Nower Lodge* in *Dorking* are nearby independent schools which complement the choice for residents.

NOISE

Many *Coldharbour* properties overlook *Gatwick Airport*, which can be identified in the distance like a child's toy laid out on a green carpet. However, aircraft noise is seldom very apparent, the main flight paths running to the south of *Leith Hill*.

PARISH COUNCIL INFORMATION

See **CAPEL**.

HISTORY

There was an *Iron Age Camp* at 'Anstiebury', the site of which may be found at the junction of *Coldharbour Lane* and *Anstie Lane*. This was probably one of three used during the period between 150 B.C. and 50 A.D., the other two being at *Holmbury Hill* and *Hascombe*. *Coldharbour*, simply meaning 'shelter from the cold weather' stands at 750 feet above sea level and is therefore one of the highest villages in the county. Although now a peaceful and tranquil spot, some of the worst British battles were fought here, in particular between the Danes and the Saxons in the year 851.

Leith Hill Tower was built in 1766 as a *'Prospect House'* by a local resident, *Mr. Richard Hull*. On a fine day thirteen counties may be seen from the top and, if you are lucky enough, a glimpse of the sea some thirty miles away. After his death, *Richard Hull* was buried beneath the tower when it was then vandalised and fell into disrepair, until 1864 when the *Lord of the Manor, Mr. W.J. Evelyn* restored it and re-opened it for the benefit of the public. Now owned by the *National Trust,* the tower may be enjoyed by the general public for a small fee during opening hours, together with some light refreshments.

Christ Church, to the south of the village, was built by *John Labouchere* from stone quarried from *Leith Hill.* The land it was built upon was donated by the *Duke of Norfolk* and consecrated 1848. The *Labouchere* family once lived in *'Broome Hall'* which is a magnificent property on the southern slopes of *Leith Hill* and now split into several residences. The composer, *Ralph Vaughan Williams'* influence in the area (his home being at *Leith Hill Place)* gave rise to the still strong traditions of choral societies in the area.

HEADLEY *See 'Mole Valley' Map*

LOCATION
Two/three miles *South East* of *Leatherhead* on the B2033 on high ground.

(✔)

Very attractive village centre at the church, stores, post office and pub. Within striking distance of Leatherhead and Ashtead. Regular bus service. Good riding/walking area. Golf course and racecourse on the doorstep!

(✗)

No immediate village school. A favourite with day trippers.

OPINION
Headley is very appealing with plenty to recommend it, within easy commuter distances to *London* it will always be popular. The village is the southern, smaller and more rural neighbour to *Ashtead.* As the presence of the race horse is much in evidence here, if you love this sport this is the place for you!

THE VILLAGE AND SURROUNDINGS
Like *Ashtead* this small village benefits from the close proximity of *Leatherhead* and the M25. Positioned high on the *North Downs* with splendid views, the village is centred around *St. Mary the Virgin Church* and its neighbouring *'Village Hall Stores',* post office and local pub *'The*

Cock Horse'. Meaning 'a clearing in the heather', *Headley* has remained appropriately named as it is still situated within extensive open heathland. The rural environment of this village is excellent for immediate walking and riding.

On the heath's southern fringes is the village area of **Box Hill**, extending along *Boxhill Road* and continuing into *Zig Zag Road* (one of the District's closest impersonations of a Swiss mountain road!). Though rather exposed, this naturally lovely area is cluttered, in places, with slightly ramshackle buildings, mobile homes and caravan sites.

However, there is a stunning viewpoint at *Salomon's Memorial* (563 feet above sea level) which prospective residents to *Dorking* and the southern parts of the District, would find especially interesting because of its panoramic view. A *National Trust Information Shop* and cafe are located here which cater well for visitors. Along *Boxhill Road* itself can be found *'Boxhill Country Stores'*, (including newsagents and post office), the *'Hand in Hand'* public house, day-time petrol and a small row of shops opposite. With generally few residencies the population of this whole area is very small.

LOCAL TELEPHONE BOOKS

British Telecom - Guildford and West Surrey No. 530
See the back of your current Phone Book or Tel. 150
Yellow Pages - Gatwick Area, Book No. 22.
Telephone Orders 0800 671444.

TRANSPORT

Headley is not immediately well placed for access to public transport, the neighbouring town of *Leatherhead* affording residents the best options.

ROADS

The *B2033* runs from the *A24* at the *Beaverbrook Roundabout*, east of *Leatherhead,* straight into *Headley* through *Tyrrell's Wood Golf Course.* From the village, this road gives good access to both *Leatherhead* or, in the opposite direction, onto the *B2032* in the area of *Walton Heath*. The area of *Pebble Coombe* on the *B2033* drops south sharply into the Mole

Valley and is one of the steepest hill roads along the whole of this escarpment. Other local lanes are typically narrow with sharp bends and little vision in places, be careful!

Away from the village centre and towards the north and east of *Headley* runs the stretch of the *M25* between Junctions 8 and 9. Some local roads towards Ashtead go under the motorway which is elevated above the landscape. Somehow the motorway is not very apparent which is fortunate for this lovely area.

RAIL

The nearest train stations are *Leatherhead* (*North/South*) line or *Betchworth* (*East/West*) line. See the *Rail* sections under those places for length of journey times.

The whole of Network South East Railway Services are depicted in the front section of 'Yellow Pages'. Further information may be obtained on many maps, booklets and leaflets obtained from most railway stations.

BUSES

There is a bus route in the village from the A25 through to *Leatherhead*.

Bus Timetables/Enquiries/Maps from Surrey Traveline: Tel. 01737 223000. Copies of timetables are available from local libraries, council offices throughout Surrey or by post from the County Council at County Hall, Kingston upon Thames, KT1 2DY.

SHOPPING

Comprehensive facilities in *Leatherhead,* very little choice in the village, but there is a local post office.

SCHOOLS

Local schools in *Leatherhead* are the nearest.

NOISE

Nothing to which to draw your attention.

LEISURE

There are many stables in the area and the famous *Epsom Racecourse* is not far over the District's boundary. *Headley* has its own cricket ground and pavilion on the east side of *Headley Common Road*, set opposite the heath which itself is now owned and maintained by the *National Trust*. As previously mentioned too, there is *Tyrrell's Wood Golf Course* on the outskirts of the village towards *Leatherhead*.

The *'Cock Horse'* public house is in a particularly attractive and elevated setting in the village centre.

PARISH COUNCIL INFORMATION

Clerk to the Parish Council: Mrs. A. Vimpany, 35 Harrowlands Park, Dorking, RH4 2RA. Tel: 01306 741502

Editor of the Parish Magazine: Mrs Denise Wotton 01372 377327

Clerk to Box Hill Neighbourhood Council: Mr. H. Etheridge, 18 The Orchard, Ashurst Drive, Box Hill, Tadworth KT20 7LP. Tel: 01737 844379

HISTORY

One of the area's more interesting homes is the 18th century house *'Headley Grove'* which, standing to the south of the village, was once the home of *Sir Malcolm Campbell*. Another of the more famous houses in the village is the combined forces rehabilitation centre at *'Headley Court'*. It was originally a turn-of-the-century mansion and is well sign-posted in the area along *Headley Road*. On the continuation of the same road, which eventually becomes *Church Lane*, is the church of *St. Mary the Virgin*, built in the 1850s. The oak panelling in the nave is said to come originally from *London's Newgate Prison* which was demolished in 1902 and replaced by the *Old Bailey*.

It is apparent from historians that this area supported flocks of sheep during the 18th century and the daughter of a local reverend, *Emily Faithful* who was born in 1835, became printer and publisher to *Queen Victoria* after establishing a printing press in London.

Box Hill to the south of *Headley Heath,* was once aptly named *'White Hill'* with reference to the visible chalk escarpments which are still apparent. Now its name refers to the box trees that grow all over the hill, not as some might think because of its shape. Box wood is so dense and heavy that it is one of the few that will not float in water. In 1914 a *Mr. Leopold Salomons* gave a large part of the hill to the nation and now 633 acres are owned and protected by the National Trust.

HOLMBURY ST. MARY *See 'Mole Valley' Map*

LOCATION

Six miles *South West* of *Dorking* on the *B2126,* on the boundary between *'Mole Valley'* District and *'Guildford'* Borough.

Exceptionally attractive village. Excellent first school choice. Pubs, post office, garage, and magnificent church. Superb riding/walking country.

Remote train service, buses infrequent.

OPINION

A charming, sheltered, tiny Surrey village, visited from afar because of its lovely scenery and good choice of local pubs! Perhaps because of this, it is a regular haunt for riders, mountain bikers and ramblers! The more observant of you will notice that *'The Good Move Guide'* is based here, so forgive me if I am a little biased this time! *'Holmbury St. Mary'* (pretty in name and nature) nestles deep in a valley overshadowed by the slopes of *Holmbury Hill* and *Pasture Wood.*

THE VILLAGE AND SURROUNDINGS

About two miles south of the *A25, Holmbury St. Mary* is a delight to behold. After passing low-lying houses, clinging tightly against the left hand side of the road, the little triangular green opens up on the right hand side. Behind the green, majestically embedded in the heavily wooded backdrop of *Holmbury Hill,* is the magnificent *St. Mary's Church.*

Next to the church (as is so often the case!) is a local public house. On this occasion it is the *'Royal Oak'*, one of two in the village, which also overlooks the green and stands at the end of *Felday Glade*. This pretty single track lane, lined with period houses, finishes at a car park, where a huge network of footpaths and bridleways lead over *Holmbury Hill*. This beautiful open countryside, which is in fact private land, is nevertheless kept open for the public's access and enjoyment and managed by *Hurtwood Control* (Tel: 01306 730919). *Holmbury Hill* is second only in height to neighbouring *Leith Hill* on the sandstone ridge, at 857 feet above sea level. From the summit, once the site of an *Iron Age Fort*, a wonderful panoramic view may be enjoyed southwards across the Weald.

'Feldemore' house, to the east of the village standing high on the hill towards *Abinger,* is a typical Victorian residence. Once owned by the *Waterhouse* family of *'Price Waterhouse'* fame, it is now *Belmont Preparatory School.*

LOCAL TELEPHONE BOOKS

British Telecom - Guildford and West Surrey No. 530
See the back of your current Phone Book or Tel. 150
Yellow Pages - Gatwick Area, Book No. 22.
Telephone Orders 0800 671444.

TRANSPORT

Just as it has always been, this village is still remote. Even by today's standards when nearly everyone has access to a car, this part of the Surrey hills retains much of its secrecy. This may be to the village's advantage in many ways, though once discovered it does not seem to deter the large proportion of South West Londoners, in particular, who choose to move here.

ROADS

Hollow Lane and *Felday Road* are approach roads to the village leading south from the A25. They both give reasonably good access on national speed limit country lanes. Although they are both wide enough in most places for vehicles to pass, special caution must be shown along many stretches where the road ahead cannot be seen, especially bearing in mind the roads are local bus routes as well.

It has been known for villagers to have been 'cut off' in particularly adverse weather conditions, but the important access roads receive good attention from the Local Authority whenever necessary, so in all but the very worst snow storm, they remain passable.

RAIL

The most appropriate main line station is in *Dorking*. (*Gomshall* is also fairly close with a restricted service).

See *Dorking Rail* section for typical train journey times and Customer Information. *Gomshall* is on the Thames Trains' *East/West* service.

Customer Information on: 01732 770111. The whole of Network South East Railway Services are depicted in the front section of 'Yellow Pages'. Further information may be obtained on many maps, booklets and leaflets obtained from most railway stations.

BUSES

There are several bus routes through the village, but they offer an infrequent service.

Bus Timetables/Enquiries/Maps from Surrey Traveline: Tel. 01737 223000. Copies of timetables are available from local libraries, council offices throughout Surrey or by post from the County Council at County Hall, Kingston upon Thames, KT1 2DY.

SHOPPING

There is a post office on the outskirts of the village, with limited service and opening hours, on the *B2126*. *Bulmer Farm* sells farm produce and *Holmbury St. Mary* Garage provides petrol and services cars. More comprehensive shopping is found in *Dorking* (which is a little closer than *Guildford*) or going south there are a good range of shops at *Cranleigh* or *Horsham*.

SCHOOLS

Belmont Preparatory School is set high above the village and this impressive school, in lovely grounds, has a widespread good reputation. Facilities include a specialist dyslexia unit called *'Moon Hall'*. There is also the local County First school at *Abinger* nearby.

NOISE

With certain unusual wind directions occasionally aircraft do fly within hearing, but generally only the noise of silence and the bird song will keep you awake!

LEISURE

There are no sophisticated leisure pursuits laid on in the village, but the location is the epitome for horse riding, mountain biking, rambling and other wildlife or country interests.

PARISH COUNCIL INFORMATION

Clerk to the Parish Council: Mrs J. Bourgeois, Wotton Barn, Sheephouse Lane, Abinger Common, RH5 6JS

Editor to the Holmbury St. Mary and Wotton Parish News: Mrs. C. Bird, Tel: 01306 730473

HISTORY

On *Holmbury Hill* there are the earthworks of an Iron Age fort which was excavated in the 1930s and whose artefacts may now be seen in *Guildford Museum*. The site of this ancient fortification was about eight acres and it was a camp for the native Celts since between about 150 B.C. to 50 A.D. This camp was one of three along this ridge of hills, the others were at *Anstiebury* and *Hascombe*.

The GOOD *move* GUIDE welcomes any information that corrects, updates, or might add to its content. We always listen to our readers and try to implement new requirements.
Please let us know and keep in touch!

These sandy heights to the south of the *North Downs Way* attracted groups of *Celts* to settle. These primitive people were led by *Druid* priests and practised religious rites connected with the gods of thunder, war, women's crafts and manly beauty. *Holmbury Hill* was not thickly wooded then and it is likely the surrounding land would have been farmed.

Throughout history the general area has been one of the remotest and wildest in the county, so many smugglers, sheep stealers and poachers took refuge in the hills near here and often the local cottages had large cellars used to hide their contraband.

In Victorian times, the village was very popular as a retreat for wealthy Londoners, so in 1872 when the village was still named *'Felday'*, it was visited by the celebrated Victorian architect *George Edward Street* and his wife. The latter is reported to have exclaimed 'This is heaven's gate!' upon entering the village and it is still easy to understand why. Situated as it is, in the valley at the foot of *Holmbury Hill*, the village is one of the most beautiful in all of Surrey.

Felday was soon renamed *Holmbury St. Mary*, after *George Street* designed and erected *St. Marys Church* in his beloved village, where he then lived with his wife in the house they soon built called *'Holmdale'* in *Holmbury Hill Road*. Unfortunately his wife did not live to see the completed church that was built in 1879, as she died in 1876. In fact, *St. Mary's Church* was to be one of *George Street's* last works, as he also died just two years after it was built. He did live, however, to welcome *Gladstone* and the cabinet of the day, when they once visited his home in the village in 1880. *George Street,* who designed the *London Law Courts,* was obviously a man of some considerable standing, he was later buried in *Westminster Abbey*.

TO ADVERTISE IN THIS SPACE
IN THE NEXT EDITION CONTACT
THE **'GOOD** *move* **GUIDE**
Tel: 01306 731122
Fax: 01306 731444

An Invitation to become a friend of 'The Hurtwood'
Do you enjoy walking?
Are you a lover of nature?
Do you enjoy horse riding?
Are you a keen environmentalist?
Do you enjoy the pleasures of **The Hurtwood**?
If the answer to one or more of our questions is YES,
then we invite you to become a Friend of **The Hurtwood**.

HURTWOOD CONTROL

The Hurtwood covers around 3,000 acres of Forest and Heathland, including Holmbury and Pitch Hills and parts of Winterfold, Blackheath and Farley Heath in Surrey. The public have rights of access over this area and these rights are protected by a voluntary charitable body known as the Hurtwood Control. A full time ranger is employed and included amongst his many duties are clearance of Bridleways and Footpaths, maintenance of viewpoints and car parks, and clearance of the inevitable litter and rubbish. The cost of maintaining and protecting this environment on your behalf is increasing annually, so we appeal to you, who enjoy these amenities, for support:

For further information apply to:
The Secretary, Hurtwood Control Committee - Telephone: 01306 730919

NIRVANA Cycles
It's a state of mind

£20.00 worth of accessories with every bike sold
Large selection of components and accessories
Specialising in building bikes to specification
Bike repairs and wheelbuilding

OPEN   MONDAY - SATURDAY 10.00 - 6.00 SUNDAY 10.00 4.00

2 The Green,
Westcott,
Nr. Dorking,
Surrey RH4 3NH

Tuesday and Thursday 6.30 Training Rides
Sunday 11.00 Social Ride

Tel: 01306 740300

Run by mountain bikers for mountain bikers
MAIL ORDER AVAILABLE

THE 'HOLMWOODS' See 'Mole Valley' Map

LOCATION
Scattered villages situated in a line following the route of the main A24 dual carriageway *South* of *Dorking.*

(✔)

Local train station and regular bus services. Bordering National Trust common. Attractive main village green and church. On or near A24 - good for commuters.

(✗)

Clay soils lead to very wet, holding ground in winter. Localised noise from nearby A24 and some from Gatwick Airport which begins to make its presence felt.

OPINION
North Holmwood, is really a 'South Dorking' residential area and as such benefits from its proximity to the town and its facilities, at the same time bordering open countryside. **Mid Holmwood** is tiny and split in two by the A24, there are some lovely houses here, buried in the woodland. **South Holmwood**, as a centre, is my favourite with an attractive small network of side roads, to the west of the A24. Picturesque victorian and turn-of-the-century terraced houses are nestled here with a backdrop of fields and woodland up to *Abinger Forest* above. There is also *St. Mary Magdalene Church* on an elevated site to the south of the village beyond a young children's play area which is pleasantly situated. For some people's tastes however, the very close proximity of the A24 could be seen as more of a detriment than advantage.

THE VILLAGES AND SURROUNDINGS
North Holmwood, Mid Holmwood, South Holmwood and *Holmwood Corner* are a scattered group of villages set around *Holmwood Common* lying on the east side of the A24. *North Holmwood* is the largest and is separated from *Dorking* only by the physical boundary of the A24. It has

undergone much development recently and there is an extensive modern housing estate off *Inholms Lane*. This estate provides a large choice of homes in different price ranges, but although it is in a pleasing setting and attractively laid out, the properties are rather squeezed together.

The other *'Holmwoods'* are much smaller and some distance apart, most are no more than a group of little cottages. There is a big choice of 24 hour petrol stations in the area and a few restaurants all bordering the A24. Care has to be taken on the approach to the villages from the main road, because of the speed of traffic. The *Holmwoods* have a population of about 2,000.

Beare Green is Holmwood's southern most neighbour although, as a Parish, it is linked to Capel and Coldharbour. The site of the large Beare Green roundabout at the junction of the A29 and A24 was once central to the village. The original green is still flanked by fourteen cottages built over 100 years ago, but the village nowadays manifests itself mostly on the west side of the A24, which is also the location of *Holmwood Station*. The *Old Horsham Road* runs through the centre and there is a small network of residential roads and a little courtyard of shops, known as *Beare Green Court*. To the west, the ground begins to climb steeply up to *'Leith Hill'*.

LOCAL TELEPHONE BOOKS
British Telecom - Guildford and West Surrey No. 530
See the back of your current Phone Book or Tel. 150
Yellow Pages - Gatwick Area, Book No. 22.
From: Telephone Orders   0800 671444.

TRANSPORT
Good road and rail links described below.

ROADS
All the villages have immediate access to the A24, affording a quick, uncomplicated route for commuters in particular.

RAIL
At *Holmwood* there is a railway station (which is really to be found at *Beare Green*), serving this group of villages as well as *Beare Green* and *Newdigate*. The station can be found to the west of the A24, off the old

crescent shaped *Horsham Road*, it is well signposted in the area.

Typical Train Times: 7 mins to *Dorking* then refer to the *Rail* section under *Dorking* for further times to London.

Customer Information Telephone: 0171 928 5100. The whole of Network South East Railway Services are depicted in the front section of 'Yellow Pages'. Further information may be obtained on many maps, booklets and leaflets obtained from most railway stations.

BUSES

As would be expected on such a busy through route, there are several buses in the area.

Bus Timetables/Enquiries/Maps from Surrey Traveline: Tel. 01737 223000. Copies of timetables are available from local libraries, council offices throughout Surrey or by post from the County Council at County Hall, Kingston upon Thames, KT1 2DY.

SHOPPING

Very limited shopping facilities in the villages, with a post office at *South Holmwood* and *North Holmwood* and the little courtyard of shops in *Beare Green*. *Dorking* and *Horsham* are the nearest towns for more comprehensive choice.

SCHOOLS

There is the 'special' *Starhurst School* at the A24 junction with *Chart Lane, North Holmwood* and the *Weald* first and middle school at *Beare Green*.

NOISE

There is a *Fire Station* in *Hardy Close* off *Spook Hill*, *North Holmwood*. The noise from the A24 affects quite a number of homes particularly in *Mid* and *South Holmwood* and *Gatwick Airport* is only some six or seven miles away to the *South East*.

SEWAGE WORKS

Off *Tilehurst Lane, North Holmwood*.

PARISH COUNCIL INFORMATION

Clerk to Holmwood Parish Council: Mrs M. Mansell, Mill View, Horsham Road, Beare Green, Dorking RH5 4RB

Parish Magazine: Mrs Audrey Aitken Tel: 01306 888426

We do it all for you at...

ALL ABOUT THE HOUSE

We supply all types of –
FURNITURE • CARPETS • PICTURES & MIRRORS
CURTAINS & OTHER SOFT FURNISHINGS

We can repair and re-upholster your own valued furniture.
French polishing and restoration of antiques.
Contract spray polishing and repair of modern furniture.

At our Beare Green showrooms we also have a jolly useful gift shop with constantly changing stock from around the world.

Showrooms & Shop: **01306-713094**   Office & Works: **01372 457831**

1 Beare Green Court, Old Horsham Road, Beare Green, Nr. Dorking
(at junction with A24, just north of the Beare Green roundabout)

HISTORY

Since 1956, the 650 acres of *Holmwood Common*, have belonged to the *National Trust*. During its history it was held by *William the Conqueror*, the *Earls of Surrey* and *Dukes of Norfolk*. During the 18th and 19th centuries the common was the haunt of highwaymen and smugglers, especially when a turnpike road ran across it. Also this common area once supported the largest stags in England and plentiful crops of wild strawberries. Now it provides only a mixed woodland environment for various wildlife appreciated by ramblers, horse riders and even fishermen at *Four Wents Pond*.

Part of *'Stane Street'*, the original Roman Road, is preserved in *Redlands Wood*, West of the A24 at *Mid Holmwood*. Beare Green was the site of a popular 17th century teahouse and a Tollhouse both of which were demolished to make way for the London-Wothing dual cariageway in the late 1960s. During the 17th, 18th and 19th century tolls were paid at the Tollgate for all wheeled transport except the Mail Coach. Worth mentioning is the old *'White Hart'* public house in *Beare Green* which presently stands derelict. There are plans to restore this listed building within a possible new development of the site. In 1866 the *'White Hart'* was a brewery producing cider from the local orchards and serving several other public houses.

<u>LEIGH</u> - *(pronounced 'lie') See 'Mole Valley' Map*

LOCATION

Low lying position three miles *South West* of *Reigate* off the A217, or about 5 miles *South East* of *Dorking.* South of the A25.

☑

Public houses, church, general stores, day time petrol and pretty green. Preparatory school and first school.

☒

Infrequent buses, remote rail travel.

OPINION

Open and mostly flat countryside surrounding the village with pleasant views, across fields, in every direction. Similar in character to *Brockham, Betchworth* and *Newdigate,* but even smaller! This area to the east of *Dorking* is generally cheaper than to the west, which quickly has very different scenery. I like this village, although apart from in the immediate area of the church, its position is not especially remarkable.

THE VILLAGE AND SURROUNDINGS

Leigh is a traditional old English Wealden village, situated between *Reigate* and *Dorking* on level, low-lying countryside. There is a triangular village green at the centre overlooked by the delightful *St. Bartholomew's Church* and no Surrey village would be complete without the local public house, which in this case is *'The Plough'*. Further north, along *Tapners Road*, is **Dawesgreen,** an outlying hamlet with the *'Seven Stars'* public house and post office. A small variety of houses around the centre of *Leigh,* give way to larger homes and small farms further out. The population is only about 1,000.

LOCAL TELEPHONE BOOKS

British Telecom - Guildford and West Surrey No. 530
See the back of your current Phone Book or Tel. 150
Yellow Pages - Gatwick Area, Book No. 22.
Telephone Orders 0800 671444.

TRANSPORT

Not particularly well located for easy public transport facilities.

ROADS

Good country lanes approach *Leigh* from all sides and the village is easily accessible with the use of a car. Being low-lying the roads are not particularly prone to the worst of exposed weather conditions, which might be found on neighbouring higher ground. Like other nearby villages, remember roads near the *River Mole* or its tributaries may flood, with extremes of weather.

RAIL

Leigh is badly positioned, in comparison with some, for ease of access to a main line railway station. As already mentioned the village is more-or-less equi-distant from *Dorking* or *Reigate,* the rail facilities at *Dorking* or *Redhill* may be most suitable. *Thames Trains'* final destinations to *Reading* or *Gatwick Airport* may be used from *Betchworth.*

See the *Rail* sections for *Dorking* and *Betchworth* for typical train travelling times from there. From *Redhill,* typical train times are: 20 mins to *East Croydon*, 35 mins to *Clapham Junction* and 45 mins to *Victoria. Salfords* or *Earlswood* are stations south of *Redhill* which offer a less frequent service.

Network South Central Customer Information Telephone: 0171 928 5100. Thames Trains Customer Information Telephone: 01732 770111

The whole of Network South East Railway Services are depicted in the front section of 'Yellow Pages'. Further information may be obtained on many maps, booklets and leaflets obtained from most railway stations.

BUSES

There are bus routes through *Leigh*, the most regular being the route 22.

Bus Timetables/Enquiries/Maps from Surrey Traveline: Tel. 01737 223000. Copies of timetables are available from local libraries, council offices throughout Surrey or by post from the County Council at County Hall, Kingston upon Thames, KT1 2DY.

SHOPPING

To the immediate north of the village is the area of *Dawesgreen* where there is a general stores.

SCHOOLS

Burys Court Preparatory School, off *Flanchford Road* offers an independent education for boys and girls between the ages of 4 - 13 years. There is also a County First School in the village in *Tapners Road*.

NOISE

Although *Leigh* is not very far to the north of *Gatwick Airport*, it is not particularly disturbed by associated aircraft noise as the flight paths do not run this way. There is nothing else to remark upon.

PARISH COUNCIL INFORMATION

Clerk to the Parish Council: Miss H. Taneborne, Oak Farm, Clayhill Road, Leigh, Reigate, RH2 8PB. Tel: 01306 611471

HISTORY

The church of *St. Bartholomew*, to the east side of the green, was originally built in the 15th century, although some parts date back to 1200. It was much restored in the 19th century and has a pretty lychgate dated 1891. Other buildings of note are *'Priests House'*, a lovely medieval building on the south east corner of the green and *'Leigh Place'*, a moated red brick house north of the church on *Leigh Place Road*. Ben Jonson (1573-1637) the poet, dramatist and friend of *Shakespeare* is said to have spent much of his retirement here. A quote of his I recently found was *'O for an engine to keep back all clocks'*, perhaps he found the tiny and timeless village of Leigh was sympathetic to this sentiment!

MICKLEHAM *See 'Mole Valley' Map*

LOCATION

Three miles *North* of *Dorking*, off the A24, on the B2209 beneath the west face of **Box Hill**.

(✔)

Excellent location for quick road connections. Public house, post office, church and stores. Nearby train station. 'Box Hill' independent school and a local first school in the village. Restaurants along A24.

(✗)

Exceptionally busy with tourists (and motorcyclists) in the summer months and weekends.

OPINION

In a dramatic location immediately beneath *Box Hill* this little village is quite a favourite with visitors. Villagers are well placed for commuting.

THE VILLAGE AND SURROUNDINGS

The centre of this little village is protected from the busy traffic of the A24 by a by-pass on the west side. However, some of the out-lying cottages actually border the by-pass alongside two attractive restaurants, *Frascati* and *St. Michaels*. A few of these cottages are in a particularly unique position, set high above this fast, busy road nestling in the steep escarpment. There is a post office and general stores on the *Old London Road* and a Recreation Ground in *School Lane*, but there is little else besides *St. Michael's Church* and the well known public house *'The Running Horses'*. The famous and most attractive *'Burford Bridge Hotel'* lies beneath the backdrop of *Box Hill* just to the south of the village.

Givons Grove, just north of *Mickleham* is a pleasant residential area located within the boundary of the A24 where it corners south of *Leatherhead* towards *Dorking*. The 800 acres of *Box Hill*, so called because of the box trees on its slopes, are rich in wildlife and flowers. Across the A24 *Norbury Park* is an attractive area of farmland with pleasant walks westwards towards *Ranmore*.

LOCAL TELEPHONE BOOKS

British Telecom - Guildford and West Surrey No. 530
See the back of your current Phone Book or Tel. 150
Yellow Pages - Gatwick Area, Book No. 22.
Telephone Orders 0800 671444.

TRANSPORT

As *Mickleham* is only a few hundred yards from the A24, commuters and residents find it quick and easy to get about with the use of a car.

ROADS

The fast, dual carriageway A24 on the 'door-step' of the village, soon links up to the A246 to travel west towards *Guildford,* or the M25 link roads near *Leatherhead.* All these roads are fast and well maintained, although the white painted cross-hatch markings on the south bound carriageway of the A24 are rather unusual. This has been brought about by the large amount of accidents on this stretch of the road (locally named the *'Mickleham Bends'*) to reduce traffic speed. Long-term there are uncertain plans to alter the route of the A24 to the west side of its current location.

The approach road into the village from both north and south is the *Old London Road. Headley Road*, to the east, goes off to the village of the same name, reached within about two miles.

RAIL

The facilities at *Dorking* or *Leatherhead* are very close by, refer to their appropriate *Rail* sections for further information.

The whole of Network South East Railway Services are depicted in the front section of 'Yellow Pages'. Further information may be obtained on many maps, booklets and leaflets obtained from most railway stations.

BUSES

Bus routes do run through the village.

Bus Timetables/Enquiries/Maps from Surrey Traveline: Tel. 01737 223000. Copies of timetables are available from local libraries, council offices throughout Surrey or by post from the County Council at County Hall, Kingston upon Thames, KT1 2DY.

SHOPPING

Well placed for *Dorking's* or *Leatherhead's* facilities, little else close by.

SCHOOLS

Box Hill School, the nearest independent school to *Dorking*, and the local first school are actually located in the village, the former on the *Old London Road* and the latter along *School Lane*. There is a further good choice close by, in *Leatherhead* and *Ashtead*.

NOISE

The very close proximity of the A24 must always be borne in mind.

PARISH COUNCIL INFORMATION

Clerk to the Parish Council: Mrs M. Chisman, Old House Cottage, Mickleham, Dorking RH5 6EH. Tel: 01372 375050

HISTORY

The *Old London Road* leads to *St. Michael's Church* of Norman origins. This church, like so many in Surrey, was mostly rebuilt during Victorian times. In this case the architect was *Ewan Christian* who enlarged it and added a circular turret to the south-east corner. *'Juniper Hill'* and *'Juniper Hall'* are substantial 18th century houses within the village boundaries. The latter is now owned by the *National Trust* and mostly used for field studies. *'The Running Horses'* public house takes its name from the Derby Race of 1828, at nearby Epsom, when two horses *'Cadland'* and *'The Colonel'* were declared joint winners. The poet and novelist, *George Meredith* lived in *'Flint Cottage'*, *Mickleham* for many years and the legendary poet *Keats* also came to *Box Hill* for inspiration for his great poem *'Endymion'*.

NEWDIGATE *See 'Mole Valley' Map*

LOCATION
Five miles *South* of *Dorking,* east off the A24 on low-lying ground.

✓

Pretty village location, church, shops, post office, first school and local garage. On bus route.

✗

Within five miles of Gatwick, not far from the flight paths. Remote train service.

OPINION
Newdigate is a favourite with many people, especially equestrians! Even though the area is rather low lying and subject to holding wet clay, many properties have some substantial acreage included which means horses may be kept at home quite easily. Also the prices here are generally less than comparable properties west of *Dorking.* The proximity of *Gatwick* is a matter for you, I have never thought of *Newdigate* as especially noisy, but the future expansion of the airport is likely to make things worse.

THE VILLAGE AND SURROUNDINGS
Another sprawling Wealden village within the shadows of *Leith Hill* and benefiting from the proximity of the A24. The village has many tile-hung and half-timbered houses, but one may be forgiven for thinking there are more horses than people here!

There is a little post office, general stores, bakery and coffee shop, public house, first school and church at the centre where *Trig Street* and *Village Street* meet. This is the heart of the village which otherwise covers a large area. The population of the village is about 2,000.

LOCAL TELEPHONE BOOKS

British Telecom - Guildford and West Surrey No. 530
See the back of your current Phone Book or Tel. 150
Yellow Pages - Gatwick Area, Book No. 22.
Telephone Orders 0800 671444.

TRANSPORT

Not particularly well placed for easy access, although the fast dual carriageway section of the A24 is within a couple of miles away.

ROADS

The A24's large roundabout at *Beare Green* has a well signposted road to *Newdigate,* next to the *'Duke's Head'* public house, however this is quite a drive south of *Dorking*. The country lane roads to the east of *Newdigate* afford access to *Gatwick Airport* with accompanying busier traffic than might otherwise be expected. Be especially careful in adverse weather conditions and after dark, none are lit.

RAIL

Ockley has the nearest railway station on the Horsham to London line. See the *Rail* section of *Ockley* for more information.

The whole of Network South East Railway Services are depicted in the front section of 'Yellow Pages'. Further information may be obtained on many maps, booklets and leaflets obtained from most railway stations.

BUSES

There are several bus routes in *Newdigate.*

Bus Timetables/Enquiries/Maps from Surrey Traveline: Tel. 01737 223000. Copies of timetables are available from local libraries, council offices throughout Surrey or by post from the County Council at County Hall, Kingston upon Thames, KT1 2DY.

SHOPPING

A little closer to *Dorking* than any other town, but the facilities of *Crawley, Horsham* and *Reigate* are also within about six or seven miles. Shopping is very limited in the village.

SCHOOLS

There is a village first school in *Village Street*.

NOISE

Apart from *Charlwood, Newdigate* is the closest Surrey village to *Gatwick Airport*. Although aircraft noise is not particularly obtrusive, there is still uncertainty over how much future development there will be of the airport. One thing is certain and that is that new routes and more airlines are continuing to originate from Gatwick, so it would be naive not to take this factor into account.

PARISH COUNCIL INFORMATION

Clerk to the Parish Council: Mr. A. Warner, Cheyne Wood, Broad Lane, Newdigate, Dorking RH5 5AS. Tel: 01306 631284

HISTORY

Newdigate's name derives from *'On Ewood Gate'* meaning 'on the road to the yew wood' and its remoteness was described as 'the loneliest place in Surrey' as recently as at the turn of the century.

There has always been a good supply of wood around the village and in 1552, *Christopher Darrell* set up the first foundry allowed in Surrey, to fire an iron works.

St. Peter's Church is only one of two in the county to have an all wooden tower. It probably dates from the 13th century and its tower of 15th century origins contains six bells. *'The Old Six Bells'* public house opposite, was once a haunt of smugglers with cellars, concealing contraband, and one passageway said to lead to the vicarage!

OCKLEY *See 'Mole Valley' Map*

LOCATION
Six miles *South* of *Dorking* on the A29 on low-lying ground.

(✓)

Exceptionally large and spectacular village green. Pubs, post office, first school, stores, farm shops and own railway station. Golf course at Gatton Manor.

(✗)

Village on fast through road A29. Very restricted bus service.

OPINION
Ockley has a lot of character and will always be very popular. The large and open aspect of the village green gives a wonderful feeling of space. The main A29, central to the village, is *Ockley's* only flaw with the amount of through traffic which inevitably uses it.

THE VILLAGE AND SURROUNDINGS
A stunning long open green is the main attraction of the village, which runs next to the famous straight path of *'Stane Street'*. With the attractive backdrop of *Leith Hill* and its tower to the north, *Ockley* is a lovely spot.

Surrounded on all sides by fields and with a duck pond, the village stretches along *Stane Street*, the A29. Unfortunately this old, established Roman Road still carries far too much fast moving traffic through its centre. The four public houses, post office and old tile-hung cottages overlooking the green can easily be missed, without stopping to take a walk. To the south of this green is a small modern housing estate offering modest priced homes, but most houses in the area are period semi-detached or detached properties and often on bigger plots.

Another little beauty spot is along *Cole's Lane* where the picturesque *St. Margaret's Church* and *Ockley Court Farm* may be found. A little further along this road will bring you to *Weare Street* and, in turn, *Vann Lake Road* where there is indeed a large lake, mobile home site and nature reserve to be found at the end. The population of *Ockley* is only around 1000.

Worth mentioning here also are the outlying areas of **Forest Green**, **Oakwoodhill** *(Okewoodhill)* and **Walliswood**, where there are no particular village centres. Some of the loveliest spots in Surrey may be found here, although probably some of the most inaccessible! All are low-lying beneath the *Greensand* ridge to the north and west of *Ockley*. These villages offer a selection of lovely homes which benefit from generally larger plots of land than may be found further north. However, as they are rather inaccessible (and some beneath the flight paths at *Gatwick*) the values are less than may be found closer to London. As a general rule, the further you travel south the more the prices drop.

The *Oke* stream flowing through the area springs up at *Pitland Street* in *Holmbury St. Mary* and at *High Ashes* on *Leith Hill*, before it meets other tributaries to form the north branch of the *Arun* in *Sussex*. The area's public houses, such as the *'Scarlet Arms'* at *Walliswood,* the *'Punch Bowl'* at *Oakwoodhill* and *'The Parrot'* at *Forest Green* are renowned all around the area and worth a visit. *Gatton Manor Country Club* and golf course may be found in this delightful countryside, together with the *Hannah Peschar Gallery and Sculpture Garden.*

LOCAL TELEPHONE BOOKS

British Telecom - Guildford and West Surrey No. 530
See the back of your current Phone Book or Tel. 150
Yellow Pages - Gatwick Area, Book No. 22.
Telephone Orders 0800 671444.

TRANSPORT

Although deep in Surrey countryside, *Ockley* can boast of relatively good communication links.

ROADS

Actually set on the A29 and very close to the A24 which is easily accessible along *Cole's Lane, Ockley* residents have quick access to fast roads north and south. East/west links are not so easy with just a network of country lanes until the A25, A281 or A264 can be reached. *Ockley* is one of the many villages in the south which has been expecting a by-pass in the future, from which it will greatly benefit. However the start date is not imminent and is continuously put back.

RAIL

Along *Cole's Lane*, away from the centre, is the station of *Ockley* on the *London to Horsham* line. Slower stopping trains serve this station which have a travelling time of about 11 mins to *Dorking* and 10 mins to *Horsham*.

The whole of Network South East Railway Services are depicted in the front section of 'Yellow Pages'. Further information may be obtained on many maps, booklets and leaflets obtained from most railway stations.

BUSES

Buses run through the village.

Bus Timetables/Enquiries/Maps from Surrey Traveline: Tel. 01737 223000. Copies of timetables are available from local libraries, council offices throughout Surrey or by post from the County Council at County Hall, Kingston upon Thames, KT1 2DY.

SHOPPING

Horsham is probably the best town to serve the residents of *Ockley*, it is slightly closer than *Dorking* and there is a superstore and larger modern shopping area. In the village, *Ockley Court Farm* has its own shop selling its produce, spring flowers, hanging baskets and homemade goodies. It is also very well-known over a large area for its extensive 'pick-your-own' varieties.

SCHOOLS

There is a first school in the village. For more choice and for secondary schools, residents will have to look further afield. On the road to *Horsham* is *Farlington School*, an independent school for girls, and the famous *Cranleigh School* for boys is not far over the county boundary in the *Borough of Waverley*.

NOISE

Like its 'sister' villages of *Capel* and *Newdigate*, *Ockley* might be rather too close for comfort to the ever expanding *Gatwick Airport*. However, to the visitor, the noise from aircraft is certainly not particularly disturbing, living with them may give a different view point of course.

PARISH COUNCIL INFORMATION

Clerk to the Parish Council: Mrs L. Fletcher, 1 Brickyard Copse, Ockley, Dorking RH5 5TJ. Tel: 01306 627128

The Parish Magazine may be obtained from: The Parish Office, The Rectory, Ockley, Dorking. Tel: 01306 712594

HISTORY

One of the bloodiest battles ever fought on British soil was at *Ockley* when *Ethelwulf of Wessex* met the *Danes* in 851. The battle was fierce and few *Danes* were left to tell the tale on this date more than 200 years before the *Battle of Hastings*.

For more than 2000 years travellers have trodden this path along the road the Roman's first built, now many of the properties adjacent to it are of Victorian and Georgian origins. *St. Margaret's Church* was built around 1700 and extensively restored in 1873.

TO ADVERTISE IN THIS SPACE
IN THE NEXT EDITION CONTACT
THE 'GOOD *move* GUIDE
Tel: 01306 731122
Fax: 01306 731444

WESTCOTT *See 'Mole Valley' Map*

LOCATION
Two miles *West* of *Dorking* on the A25 on the northern slopes of *Leith Hill.*

✓

Charming village set on undulating ground with spectacular views. Good bus service. Church, variety of shops, post office, three pubs, pretty green. Not remote.

✗

Nearest train station is Dorking.

OPINION
Westcott's a favourite if you want a distinct rural village feel, at the same time being within easy reach of a town centre. This little village has the best of both worlds in this respect and it has lots of character with its three pubs *'The Cricketers'*, *'The Prince of Wales'* and *'The Crown Inn'*. There is extensive walking, riding and mountain biking countryside on the doorstep and some particularly lovely views.

THE VILLAGE AND SURROUNDINGS
The main A25 snakes through this popular village which has the benefit of being within walking distance of *Dorking,* but with a personality all of its own. It is small with only essential little shops, but the surroundings are glorious and *London* is quite accessible via the good communication links of *Dorking.*

Because of its popularity, house prices stay relatively buoyant and there is something for everyone within its network of little streets. *Westcott Street* starts at the green and continues into *Balchins Lane*. This is an attractive crescent shaped road running north of the A25, from which bridleways lead over the *Downs*. The roads south of the A25 also offer a fine choice of properties and many lead directly onto country paths. The village is set on a north facing slope with wonderful views towards *Ranmore Common*. The population apparently reaches about 2,000 which is surprising for its apparent small size.

The outlying area of **Wotton**, immediately to the west of this village, is where *St. John's Church* is set amidst stunning rolling countryside. This rather remote church, was once owned by the *Evelyn* family whose most famous member was the diarist, *John Evelyn* (1620-1706). Still owned by the same family is *'Wotton House'* to the south of the A25, set in its own extensive grounds, but not open to the public. The extensive *Wotton Estate* stretches across much of this countryside identifying its cottages and properties with blue and yellow painted doors, examples of which may be seen in nearby *Hollow Lane*.

A popular landmark in the area is the *'Wotton Hatch'* public house which stands out at the top of *Coast Hill*. It marks the end of a single track road, called *Sheephouse Lane*. This lane leads to **Broadmoor,** a tiny hamlet buried deep in *Leith Hill's* woods and bordering the spring of the *Tilling Bourne*.

LOCAL TELEPHONE BOOKS

British Telecom - Guildford and West Surrey No. 530
See the back of your current Phone Book or Tel. 150
Yellow Pages - Gatwick Area, Book No. 22.
Telephone Orders 0800 671444.

TRANSPORT

Being so close to *Dorking* and on the main road between this town and *Guildford,* the village is one of the most convenient for public transport.

ROADS

The A25 is well maintained, though not lit through the village and a 30 mph speed limit applies. Outside the boundaries of the village there is mostly the faster national speed limit. Care must be taken at *School Lane* which has a very blind entrance onto the A25 and is busy at the appropriate times during school terms.

RAIL

Dorking provides the only railway station closest to the village, see the *Rail* section under *Dorking* for further information.

The whole of Network South East Railway Services are depicted in the front section of 'Yellow Pages'. Further information may be obtained on many maps, booklets and leaflets obtained from most railway stations.

BUSES

Westcott is well served by buses, especially in comparison with many of the outlying villages.

Bus Timetables/Enquiries/Maps from Surrey Traveline: Tel. 01737 223000. Copies of timetables are available from local libraries, council offices throughout Surrey or by post from the County Council at County Hall, Kingston upon Thames, KT1 2DY.

SHOPPING

There is a bakers, post office, general stores, newsagent, DIY/hardware shop and three public houses in the village. *Dorking* provides more comprehensive shops close by.

SCHOOLS

There is a first school in the village, *Dorking* and *Holmbury St. Mary* provide further choice.

NOISE

Only close to the A25 and there is the local dairy in *The Burrell*.

HISTORY

'Milton Court', to the East of the village centre, is a fine *Jacobean* house rebuilt by *Richard Evelyn* in the 17th century and now used as offices. The *Holy Trinity Church*, on a knoll opposite a tiny green, was built in 1852 by *Sir George Gilbert Scott* as was the distinctive landmark of *St. Bartholomew's Church*, high on *Ranmore Common*, whose spire can be seen from miles around.

Westcott was the birth place of *Thomas Malthus*, who was a prophet of population expansion and control. He was born in a house called *'The Rookery'*, now demolished, but whose name survives in *Rookery Lane*, on a bridlepath south west of the village.

Ranmore Common, to the north of the village, covers 470 acres of *National Trust* land providing excellent walking and riding country. The eastern side of *Ranmore* drops into the valley, where it supports the vines of the privately owned *Denbies Wine Estate*.

WESTHUMBLE *See 'Mole Valley' Map*

LOCATION
Just to the *West* side of the A24, in the 'Mole Gap' and a half mile *North* of *Dorking*.

(✔)

Train station, pub, very accessible. Attractive residential area. Nearby Burford Bridge Hotel.

(✗)

Many day trippers in the locality at weekends. No real village centre.

OPINION
In comparison with *Mickleham,* its closest neighbour, I personally prefer *Westhumble*. However it has no true identity as a village, being somewhat a satellite of *Dorking*. *Chapel Lane* runs out to the west amidst some of my favourite North Downs scenery leading to *Ranmore Common* and *Polesden Lacey*.

THE VILLAGE AND SURROUNDINGS
Westhumble is a tiny village particularly noticeable from the A24 for *'The Stepping Stones'* public house which can easily be seen just set back from the road. This refers to the stepping stones which physically exist across

the *River Mole* almost opposite. These stepping stones form part of the *North Downs Way*, which has been a well used path for centuries. The village has some lovely houses which benefit from good communication links and beautiful countryside on the door step. *'Chapel Farm'* is to be found to the west side of the village, as may the remains of a 12th century chapel opposite, from which it takes its name.

A little further along *Chapel Lane* and climbing steeply uphill, is the *National Trust's Polesden Lacey*. This area of *Surrey* shows off the *North Downs* at its best. The countryside is extensive and glorious, full of sweeping views, fields, woodland and, in particular, some majestic beech trees. Not to be forgotten is *Ranmore Common Road*, which runs south off *Chapel Lane*, leading to the reward of *Ranmore Commo*n itself found at the top. This area is truly worth a visit and local residents must surely be amongst Surrey's luckiest!

LOCAL TELEPHONE BOOKS

British Telecom - Guildford and West Surrey No. 530
See the back of your current Phone Book or Tel. 150
Yellow Pages - Gatwick Area, Book No. 22.
Telephone Orders 0800 671444.

TRANSPORT

An excellent position for communications.

ROADS

The convenience of the A24 on the eastern edge of *Westhumble* makes commuting from this lovely village easy. The only thing to be said against it perhaps, is that being this easy makes the village fall to the prey of numerous visitors, who are obviously enchanted by it as well.

RAIL

Westhumble and Box Hill is a Victorian railway station of attractive proportions, which is the first stop north of *Dorking*. It is located just in *Westhumble Street*, not far from *'The Stepping Stones'* public house.

Refer to the Rail section of Dorking for more information.

The whole of Network South East Railway Services are depicted in the front section of 'Yellow Pages'. Further information may be obtained on many maps, booklets and leaflets obtained from most railway stations.

BUSES

Bus Timetables/Enquiries/Maps from Surrey Traveline: Tel. 01737 223000. Copies of timetables are available from local libraries, council offices throughout Surrey or by post from the County Council at County Hall, Kingston upon Thames, KT1 2DY.

SHOPPING

Dorking's facilities are the closest, but *Leatherhead* is another alternative to the north.

SCHOOLS

Mickleham's and *Dorking's* schools offer the choice nearby.

NOISE

Only in the immediate vicinity of the railway line or A24.

HISTORY

At the end of the 18th century a colony of French aristocrats, who had escaped from the horrors of the *French Revolution* and were better known collectively as the *'Hugenots'*, came to live in this valley. The most famous of these was *General d'Arblay*, who married the novelist *Miss Fanny Burney*. She was most famous for her book *'Camilla'* and after its success they lived in *'Camilla Cottage'* in *Norbury Park*. Reference to her may be seen by *Camilla Drive* leading to *'Camilla Lacey'*, a housing estate built on the site of this former cottage and by *Burney Road* close by.

The 470 acres of the *National Trust's Ranmore Common* used to be called *Ashcombe Hill* and it was not until fairly recent years that a few houses were built on this exposed spot. One that was, took the name of *Denbies*, after the name of *Denby* who was a local farmer in the area. This mansion was built in the middle of the 19th century by *Mr. Thomas Cubitt*, father of the first *Lord Ashcombe,* who built *Ranmore Church* to the designs of *Sir Gilbert Scott*. It has a tall graceful spire which may be seen for miles around. One of the memorials inside *St. Bartholomew's Church* commemorates three of *Lord Ashcombe's* grandsons killed in the *First World War.*

The famous *North Downs Way* runs east/west across *Ranmore* and down towards *Westhumble,* but there are many footpaths and bridleways with which to enjoy the common. Some lime pits on the slopes of *Denbies* are ancient workings and apparently provided lime for the building of *Somerset House,* the *Bank of England* and *London Bridge.*

DON'T FORGET TO RETURN
the Good *move* Guide
MARKET RESEARCH QUESTIONNAIRE
to enter one of our FREE PRIZE DRAWS:

First Draw in September 1996:
FIRST PRIZE: £200 worth of your choice of furniture from
PLANTERS COUNTRY PINE
Second Draw in February 1997:
FIRST PRIZE: £200 worth of Kingfisher Vouchers valid at the following stores:

WOOLWORTHS   *Superdrug*   **STAPLES** The Office Superstore

B&Q   **COMET**   MVC

IN BOTH DRAWS
SECOND PRIZE will be:
a **£20** dining voucher from **PIZZA PIAZZA**

and **THIRD PRIZE**:
One day's free family pass to
HAMPTON COURT PALACE
(up to five family members, to include two adults).

Duke of Kent School

A Preparatory and Pre-Preparatory school with a reputation for caring

    The Duke of Kent School is as good a reason to settle in Surrey as any. It is a coeducational boarding and day school, owned by the RAF Benevolent Fund but happy to welcome children aged four to thirteen from varied backgrounds.

    Situated within a wooded area of exceptional beauty between Guildford and Cranleigh, it provides a stable, caring and very happy environment in which children are best able to develop their own skills and confidence.

    The style of discipline is modelled on that of the family and no effort is spared to make them feel at home, whether they are day or boarding pupils. Duke of Kent educates less than two hundred children in small classes, but has the facilities you would expect of a much larger school.

For details contact
The Headmaster, Duke of Kent School, Ewhurst, Surrey GU6 7NS.
Tel: 01483 277313 Fax: 01483 273862

SCHOOLS INFORMATION

With reference to the following 'Local Schools Information', the vast majority of children attend non fee-paying state maintained schools. Only a small percentage, although a growing number, attend *fee-paying Independent Schools*.

State Schools
The Education Reform Act of 1988 introduced a *National Curriculum* whereby pupils are assessed at four 'key' stages of their education at the ages of 7, 11, 14, and 16 years. Most state schools are wholly maintained by the local authority, but some schools known as *grant maintained schools* have 'opted out' of this system and are financed directly by the government. Other schools within the state system are *voluntary aided schools* and *voluntary controlled schools:* usually their buildings are owned by a church.

Prior to statutory full time education some children attend nurseries and then compulsory education starts at the beginning of the school term following the child's fifth birthday and ends when he or she is 16 years old. Nurseries in the local area are very often connected to the primary schools from where you can normally obtain further guidance and information.

Broadly speaking children from 5 to 11 years attend *primary schools* and from 11 to 16 years of age attend *secondary schools*. *Primary schools* therefore include:

School	Age Group
Infant	5yrs - 7yrs
First	5yrs - 8yrs or 5 yrs - 9yrs
Junior	7yrs - 11yrs
Middle	8yrs - 12 yrs or 9yrs - 13 yrs
Combined	5 yrs - 11 yrs or 12 yrs or 13yrs

Secondary Schools may have all sorts of different names and age ranges, i.e. *Comprehensive, Grammar,* and *Secondary Modern*, starting at 11, 12 or 13 and ending at 16 or 18 years. The vast majority of these are now *comprehensive* catering for all levels and abilities.

Independent Schools

Generally speaking these schools provide a more academic and traditional education than most state schools, often with an emphasis on competition and sport. Some also offer boarding facilities and many are single sex, especially at the senior level, prior to sixth form. Fees may range between about £4,000 to £12,000 per year, depending on the age of the pupil and the facilities of the school.

The *Independent Schools Information Service (ISIS)* exists to help parents plan the education of their children. Each independent school is a responsible, self-governing community, free to appoint staff, to admit pupils and to use its resources as it thinks best. Within the *independent* sector are the following:

SCHOOL	AGE GROUP
Pre-Preparatory	4 - 7
Preparatory	7 - 11, 12 or 13
Senior	11, 12 or 13 to 16 or 18

The London and South-East Regional Office for ISIS:
3 Vandon Street, London, SW1H 0AN. Tel: 0171 222 7274

Nurseries and Child Care for Babies and Toddlers

A list of Registered Child Minders and information on Playgroups etc. can be obtained from the District Council, although experience shows some details can be rather out-of-date. For further information please see our 'Pre-School Noticeboard' which was up-to-date at the time of going to print!

PRE-SCHOOL NOTICE BOARD

ABINGER COMMON NURSERY SCHOOL
The Evelyn Hall, Abinger Common
Welcome Children
from 2½ to 5 years old.
MONTESSORI TEACHING METHOD
Qualified and Experienced Staff
Own safe garden
Open Monday to Fridays
9.00am to 12noon
Enquiries **01483 275538**
or **01306 730691**

ABINGER HAMMER SCHOOL NURSERY DEPARTMENT
Weekdays 9am to 12noon in the School.
From 3yrs (some admissions 2½) to school age. Co-operative and creative indoor and outdoor play leading into structured learning around 4yrs.
FEES: £3.00 a session
Mrs Jee: **01306 886252**

BARNETT WOOD PLAYGROUP
Happy, varied mornings
of learning and play
Bright, well-equipped premises adjacent to
Barnett Wood Infant School
Open every morning Monday-Friday
Nursery session available for older children
FOR MORE DETAILS CONTACT:
MAGGIE DOUGLASS: 01372 376149

BUTTERHILL PLAYGROUP, DORKING
A friendly environment with qualified staff. Open four mornings each week
Tuesday-Friday
Call Sue McDONALD 01306 880297
For further information or to arrange a visit.

CAPEL PLAYGROUP
MEMORIAL HALL, THE STREET, CAPEL
For children aged 2½ to 5 years
Monday to Friday 9.30am to 12noon
Further details from: Ann Harrison on
01306 711315

BEARE GREEN PARENT & CHILD GROUP
Every Mon. 2 - 4 pm at the
VILLAGE HALL
With a large selection of toys and equipment and a 20 min. music session. We welcome mums, dads, carers and children from birth to school age.
Tel. **01306 713253**

BROCKHAM GREEN DAY NURSERY
We are a charitable organisation providing a happy and well structured pre-school education in a friendly and safe environment.
The Nursery is currently under the supervision of a Nursery Teacher and 3 qualified Nursery Assistants.
For further information contact:
Mrs JONES,
33 Brockham Lane, Brockham, Surrey
Telephone No. 01737 842853

CHARLWOOD PLAYGROUP
We are situated in the grounds of Charlwood First School
in a bright new building.
So why not pay us a visit and met the children and our qualified staff.
We are open every weekday morning and still have some vacancies.
**Phone: Sarah 01293 786363
or Angela 01737 248641**

PRE-SCHOOL NOTICE BOARD

THE NATIONAL CHILDBIRTH TRUST

Hello from Dorking N.C.T! We're a busy branch of the National Childbirth Trust. Offering many activities and much support to parents, parents-to-be, their babies, toddlers and children.

Starting at the beginning, ante natal classes are run by N.C.T. trained teachers, the classes are to prepare parents-to-be for birth and are very informative, relaxing and fun. Following on, we hold weekly 'Bumps & Babes' afternoons, mums with bumps or babes meet in each other's houses for tea and biscuits; we find this a great way to talk about the joys and worries of new babies and to meet other mums in the area; all mums are welcome to these. 'Bumps & Babes' move onto 'Crawlers' - again meeting in each other's houses which are by now toddler-proofed! From 'Crawlers' we can go onto the 'Open House' which is more of a toddler group, presently held at Redlands Community Playlink. We have many varied social events from Christmas parties to Teddies picnics and for parents we hold evening talks and social quizzes and dances. We have a lively magazine packed with information and experiences. We can organise post natal support, have breastfeeding counsellors ready to help and a maternity sales service. We're here to give friendship and support and lots of fun to you and your babes! We look forward to meeting you.

For more information please call Lois Cremmen on 01306 880681

DORKING NURSERY SCHOOL

We are a dynamic, friendly nursery school committed to providing the highest quality Early Years education for all children. It is funded by Surrey County Council and all stafff are qualified teachers or nursery nurses.
For more information please
Telephone 01306 882397

ELMDON NURSERY SCHOOL, ASHTEAD

Stimulating and varied pre-school education in a caring environment, with qualified staff.
Please contact
Mrs Hilary Wilkinson
on 01372 272347

HOLMBURY ST. MARY TODDLER GROUP

Mums, Dads, Mums-To-Be
You are invited!
Day: Tuesday
Time: 10.00am - 11.30am
Venue: The Hollybush Tavern (Holmbury Village Club)
Contact: Kay Scott
01306 730724

HOLMBURY PLAYGROUP

ST. MARY'S CHURCH ROOM, HOLMBURY ST. MARY
Loving care: Provision for full and varied play activities. Preparation for school and parental involvement.
Qualified staff, Froebel N.N.E.B., P.P.A. Supervisors Course
YOUR VILLAGE PLAYGROUP
for 2½ to 5 yr olds.
Mon.-Thurs 9.15am-12.15pm
ENQUIRIES: 01306 621204

PRE-SCHOOL NOTICE BOARD

CYGNET PLAYGROUP
ASHTEAD YOUTH CENTRE
FOR CHILDREN UNDER 5 YRS.
We are a friendly playgroup where children have fun and learn through play and other structured activities
Further Information from
Wendy Smith 01372 277916

ST. JOSEPHS MOTHER & TODDLER GROUP
Come and meet other mums, have a coffee and a chat while the children play. Tuesdays
10.00 - 12.00
St. Josephs Church, Falkland Grove, Dorking. For more information ring
Angela: 01306 742068

PIXHAM TODDLERS
A small mother and toddler group which meets every Thursday,
10.00 - 12.00
St. Mary's Church, Pixham Lane, Dorking
Everyone welcome.
For more information
ring Angela on 01306 742068

NEWDIGATE BABY BELLS MOTHER/TODDLER GROUP
Village Hall, Mons 10.00 am
Toys, slide, books, jigsaws, drinks, biscuits, songs and outings
Mums' nights out too!
Tel. 01293 862451

MINI - MINORS
Minding Children?
In need of support?
Mini-Minors is a Dorking based child minding group, we meet to support, encourage and exchange information. For more details ring: Kay Scott
01306 731160

NORTH HOLMWOOD PLAYGROUP (PRE-SCHOOL)
The pre-school is a registered charity organised by qualified staff. Sessions are structured to cover all aspects of curriculum, promote sharing, co-operation and creativity. Children learn and develop through stimulating play in a caring environment.
Open Monday - Friday 9.30am-12 noon
Contact: Julia Woolard Tel: 01306 883911

JUBILEE NURSERY SCHOOL
RED CROSS HALL, JUBILEE TERRACE, DORKING
A small friendly group of 12 children per morning.
We aim to offer a balanced mixture of play and early learning skills.
Open 5 mornings per week, 9.30 am to 12.30 pm
For more information telephone 01306 889310

PRE-SCHOOL NOTICE BOARD

ST. MICHAELS PARENT & TODDLER GROUP
The Village Hall, Dell Close, Mickleham
All pre-school children, babies and their carers are very welcome to join us we're a small and friendly parent run local group with links with St. Michael's Community Nursery. Activities include a craft table, play dough, singing, home corner, sand-play as well as lots more.
For more information please contact:
Amanda Wadsworth: 01306 743164 or Jackie Rzepka: 01306 886189

THE ST. MARY'S PRE-SCHOOL
Parish Hall, South Holmwood, Dorking
Phone: 01306 740135
Mon-Thurs: 9.30am - 12.30pm
St. Mary's is a well equipped Pre-School providing a fun and stimulating early learning environment for children aged from $2^1/_2$ and has Pre-School Learning Alliance Accreditation.

WALLISWOOD MOTHER AND TODDLER GROUP
Forest Green Village Hall
Tuesday 9.30 am - 11.00 am
New members very welcome.
Please ring Lindsay Budgen
01306 621366

WESTCOTT TODDLERS
Every Monday 1.30 - 3.30 pm
at 'THE HUT' FURLONG RD
£1.00 PER FAMILY
EVERYONE WELCOME
JUST TURN UP OR PHONE
GABBY 01306 888473

ST. GILES PLAYGROUP, ASHTEAD
We are open five mornings per week from 9.15am to 12 noon and offer various regular activities, themed weekly topics, climbing equipment, a book corner, outdoor grounds and lots of learning through play. Ages $2^1/_2$ to school age.
Contact: Jill Heath
01372 272054

HOOKWOOD PLAYGROUP
Charity No. 1022868
At: Memorial Hall, Reigate Road, Hookwood
We are a P.P.A. affiliated pre-school group offering a varied curriculum for $2^1/_2$-5 yr. olds. Open 9.30am-NOON term time.
Cost: £2 per session
Ring: Tina 01293 407722 for more details

LEIGH LOLLIPOPS NURSERY
Open Mon. - Thurs. at Abbots Pass Hall, Leigh
For children from $2^1/_2$ years to school age.
P.L.A./N.N.E.B. Trained Staff
Outings, Music, Dance, Topics, Crafts, Cookery, Structured Activities/Folder work.
Ring **01293 863095**

LOCAL SCHOOLS INFORMATION

Local Education Office (SE Surrey Area)

123 Blackborough Road,
REIGATE
RH2 7DD
Telephone: 01737 774166

Upon application to the Local Education Office, details of the District's State Schools will be sent to you.

State Schools Selection

PRIMARY (*AND MIDDLE)

ABINGER
Abinger Common County,
Abinger Lane, Abinger Common, RH5 6HZ　　01306 730747

Abinger Hammer Village,
Abinger Hammer, RH5 6HZ　　01306 730343

ASHTEAD
Barnett Wood County Infant,
Barnett Wood Lane, Ashtead, KT21 2DF　　01372 272701

Greville County, Stonny Croft,
Bramley Way, Ashtead, KT21 1SH*　　01372 274872

St. Giles C. of E. (Aided),
Dene Road, Ashtead, KT21 1EA　　01372 272017

West Ashtead County,
Taleworth Road, West Ashtead, KT21 2PX*　　01372 272082

BEARE GREEN
Weald C. of E. (Aided),
Beare Green, Dorking RH5 4QW*　　01306 711719

BETCHWORTH
Acorn County First, Betchworth, RH3 7DJ　　01737 843211

BOOKHAM
Eastwick County Infant,
Eastwick Drive, Great Bookham, KT23 3PP+   01372 453672

Great Bookham County,
Lower Rd, Great Bookham, KT23 4DH+   01372 453796

South Bookham County,
Oakdene Close, Great Bookham KT23 4PT+   01372 456533

BROCKHAM
Brockham County,
Wheelers Lane, Brockham Green, RH3 7LA*   01737 843384

CAPEL
Scott Broadwood,
The Street, Capel, RH5 5JX   01306 711181

CHARLWOOD
Charlwood County Infant,
Chapel Road, Charlwood, Horley, RH6 0DA   01293 862302

DORKING
Pixham Primary, (annexe of St. Martins below)
Pixham Lane, Dorking   01306 883548

Powell Corderoy,
Longfield Road, Dorking RH4 3DF*   01306 883373

Redlands C. of E. Infant,
Goodwyns Road, Dorking RH4 2LR*   01306 882013

Sondes Place,
West Bank, Dorking, RH4 3DG   01306 887337

St. Josephs R.C. (Aided),
Norfolk Road, Dorking, RH4 3JA*   01306 883934

St. Martins C. of E. Primary,
Ranmore Road, Dorking RH4 1HW*   01306 883474

St. Paul's C. of E. (Aided),
St. Paul's Rd, Dorking RH4 2HS*   01306 883547

FETCHAM
Fetcham Village County,
The Street, Fetcham, KT22 9RF   01372 373502

LEATHERHEAD
All Saints C. of E. Infant,
Aperdele Rd, Leatherhead, KT22 7QT　　　　01372 812754
St. Mary's C. of E. Infant,
Fortyfoot Road, Leatherhead, KT22 8RY　　　01372 372757
St. Peters R.C. (Aided),
Grange Road, Leatherhead, KT22 7JN*　　　 01372 274913

LEIGH
Acorn County First,
Leigh, Reigate, RH2 8NN　　　　　　　　　01306 611336

MICKLEHAM
St. Michael's C. of E. (Aided),
School Lane, Mickleham, RH5 6EW　　　　　01372 373717

NEWDIGATE
Newdigate Endowed C. of E. (Aided),
Village St, Newdigate RH5 5DJ　　　　　　　01306 631353

OCKLEY
Scott Broadwood,
The Green, Ockley, RH5 5TR　　　　　　　　01306 627234

WESTCOTT
Westcott C. of E. (Aided),
School Lane, Westcott, Dorking RH4 3QF　　　01306 881136

ABINGER HAMMER VILLAGE SCHOOL

Non-fee-paying school for children of 5yrs-8yrs old. In a small group confidence and learning advance together, children are happy and standards high.

Tel: **01306 730343 / 730868**

Headteacher:
Mrs Turner B.Ed.Hons.
The School Trust
(Charity No. 285317)

BARNETT WOOD INFANT SCHOOL

Specialists in early years' education to build a sound academic foundation. Stimulating, happy environment. Extensive facilities including purpose-built library and swimming pool.
For a prospectus, or an appointment to see the range of opportunities and experiences we offer, please phone
01372 272701

MIDDLE

BOOKHAM
Dawney County,
Griffin Way, Great Bookham, KT23 4JJ+ — 01372 456774

Eastwick County,
Eastwick Drive, Great Bookham, KT23 3PP+ — 01372 453277

FETCHAM
Oakfield County,
Bell Lane, Fetcham, KT22 9ND — 01372 374781

LEATHERHEAD
Woodville County,
Woodville Road, Leatherhead, KT22 7BP — 01372 813615

SECONDARY

DORKING
Ashcombe School,
Ashcombe Road, Dorking RH4 1LY — 01306 886312
(Featured in the Daily Telegraph Best Independent and State Schools Guide)

Sondes Place School,
West Bank, Dorking RH4 3DG — 01306 887337

Starhurst School, (Specialist)
Chart Lane South, Dorking — 01306 883763

LEATHERHEAD
St. Andrews R.C. (Aided) School,
Grange Road, Leatherhead KT22 7JP — 01372 277881

Therfield School,
Dilston Road, Leatherhead KT22 7NZ — 01372 818123

(+ Denotes Local Education Office SW Surrey Area, Andrews House, College Road, Guildford, GU1 4QF Telephone: 01483 572881)

Independent Schools Selection
PRE-PREPARATORY

ASHTEAD
Downsend Lodge Ashtead,   Mixed   01372 273778
Ashtead
LEATHERHEAD
Downsend Lodge,
Leatherhead   Mixed   01372 372763
Downsend Lodge Rowans,
Leatherhead   Mixed   01372 372123

Belmont Preparatory School - Holmbury St. Mary

A very happy co-educational preparatory school for children aged 4 - 13 with good weekly boarding facilities from 7 upwards. No Saturday school leads to a full family weekend.

Excellent academic and sporting traditions in a caring, friendly environment. Beautiful grounds set in rural Surrey within easy reach of central London. A magnificent "home from home". The school boasts a sixty acre estate incorporating playing fields, all-weather sports pitch, gymnasium, open air heated swimming pool, tennis courts, new IT room and art studio.

The main building has been completely refurbished with extensive modern facilities.

All children are prepared for senior schools of their parents' choice and our success rate in recent years has been extremely high.

A purpose built dyslexia school, **Moon Hall**, has established itself within the grounds and its pupils interact uniquely and fully wherever appropriate. It has a team of highly qualified and specifically trained staff and its own principal.

Emphasis on broad curriculum and exposure to very wide range of extra-curricular activities.

For further information and prospectus contact the Headmaster's Secretary:
01306 730852

PRE-PREPARATORY AND PREPARATORY

ASHTEAD
Parsons Mead,
AshteadGirls01372 276401
BOOKHAM
Manor House School,
Little BookhamMixed01372 458538
DORKING
Nower Lodge,
DorkingMixed01306 882448
Stanway School,
DorkingMixed01306 882151
EFFINGHAM
St. Teresas,
EffinghamGirls01372 453456
HOLMBURY ST. MARY
Belmont,
Holmbury St. MaryMixed01306 730852
LEIGH
Burys Court, LeighMixed01306 611372

PREPARATORY

LEATHERHEAD
Downsend Lodge Girls,
LeatherheadGirls01372 362668
Downsend,
LeatherheadBoys01372 372197

DOWNSEND SCHOOL

Preparatory school in Leatherhead
for boys 7-13
Separate department for girls 7-11
Pre-preps for children 2½-7 in
Leatherhead, Ashtead and Epsom

- ❏ Broad curriculum   ❏ Superb facilities

- ❏ Caring environment   ❏ Excellent results

*Please telephone for
further information
and a warm
friendly welcome*

Wide area covered by morning minibus services

☎ **Leatherhead (01372) 372197**   1 Leatherhead Road
Leatherhead KT22 8TJ

PARSONS MEAD SCHOOL
GSA 350 GIRLS AGED 3 - 18

Excellent Academic Results
Sixth Form Study Room
Technology Suite
Drama Studio Science Block

Applications are welcome at all ages including Nursery
Parsons Mead School,
Ottways Lane, Ashtead
Surrey KT21 2PE
Telephone: 01372 276407 Fax: 01372 278796

Day Boarding available 7:45 a.m. to 8:00 p.m.
Minibus to/from Ashtead Station
Parsons Mead Exists For The Furtherence of Education

SENIOR SCHOOLS

ASHTEAD
City of London Freemen's,
Ashtead Park,
Ashtead — Mixed — 01372 277933

Parsons Mead,
Ottways Lane,
Ashtead — Girls — 01372 276401

BOOKHAM
Manor House School,
Manorhouse Lane,
Little Bookham — Girls — 01372 458538

EFFINGHAM
St. Teresa's School
Effingham Hill,
Effingham — Girls — 01372 452037

HOLMBURY ST. MARY
Hurtwood House,
Holmbury Hill Road,
Holmbury St. Mary — Sixth Form — 01483 277416

LEATHERHEAD
St. Johns School,
Epsom Road
Leatherhead — Boys — 01372 372021

MICKLEHAM
Box Hill School,
Old London Road
Mickleham — Mixed — 01372 373382

ST TERESA'S

Effingham, Surrey
IAPS/GSA Day and Boarding School for Girls 2 - 18

THE GIRLS' SCHOOL FOR THE 21ST CENTURY

Broad and Balanced Foundations in the

Preparatory School (2-11) prepare your daughter for:

Excellence in the Senior School (11-18)

Outstanding Examination Results.

Virtually all Sixth Formers enter University

including Oxford and Cambridge

A coach pick-up service is available covering a wide area

For further information, please contact the
Admissions Secretary:

Senior School: (01372) 452037

Preparatory School: (01372) 453456

Micklefield School
Reigate

Co-educational from $2^{1}/_{2}$ yrs
Small Classes

New Gym & Classrooms

*A Charitable Trust aiming to
provide a first-class education*

**10 Sommers Road,
Reigate RH2 9DU
Tel: 01737 242615**

DUNOTTAR SCHOOL FOR GIRLS, REIGATE
Ages 4 - 18

HIGH QUALITY GRAMMAR
SCHOOL EDUCATION

OUTSTANDING
EXAMINATION RESULTS AT
GCSE AND 'A' LEVEL

SCHOLARSHIPS

Telephone 01737 761945
for a prospectus

Adult Education Centres

LEATHERHEAD
The Mansion Centre (SACE HQ),   01372 373935
Church Street, Leatherhead, KT22 8DA   01372 386851
Mon - Fri 9.15 a.m. to 5.00 p.m.
Mon - Thu 7.00 p.m. - 9.00 p.m.
Therfield Centre,
Dilston Road, Leatherhead KT22 7NZ   01372 377806
Mon and Tues 7.00 p.m. - 9.00 p.m.

DORKING
Dene Street Centre,   01306 883351
Dene Street, Dorking RH4 2DA
Mon - Fri 9.30 a.m. - 5.00 p.m.
      and 7.00 p.m. - 9.00 p.m.
Ashcombe Centre,
Ashcombe School,   01306 742099
Ashcombe Road, Dorking RH4 1LY
Tues and Wed 7.00 p.m. - 9.00 p.m.

COMPUTER COURSES FOR COMPLETE BEGINNERS

OR

JUST THE ABSOLUTELY TERRIFIED !!!

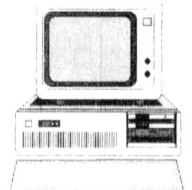

Four x 2 hour lessons (in groups of 5)
for £75.00

CONSULTANCY FOR SMALL BUSINESSES A SPECIALITY

FOR
INFORMATION PLEASE PHONE
01306 712978

SPORTS AND LEISURE FACILITIES

The Mole Valley has a wide range of sporting and leisure interests represented within its boundaries. The following clubs and organisations are just a selection of those which have let us know their most up-to-date contact numbers:-

GENERAL

Leisure Centre
Reigate Rd, Dorking   01306 887722
Leisure Centre
Guildford Rd, Leatherhead   01372 377674
Leisure Centre
Spectrum, Stoke Park, Guildford   01483 444777

SPORTS COUNCILS

Leatherhead Council of Sport and Recreation
Secretary: Mrs V. Hardman MBE   01372 372131
Dorking Sports Council
Contact: Mr D. Clark   01306 889472

SPORTS CLUBS

Abinger Sports Club Pavilion   01306 730389
Contact: Secretary   01737 762975

BADMINTON

Abinger Badminton Club
Contact   01306 730059
Dorking Badminton Club
Secretary: Mike Knott   01306 882995
Fetcham Badminton Club
Contact   01372 454038

BOWLS

Capel and Beare Green Bowling Club
Club Secretary: Mrs. E. Dunsbee   01403 269305
Dorking Bowls Club
Westcott Rd, Dorking   01306 889686
Leatherhead Bowling Club
Fortyfoot Rd, Leatherhead   01372 379804
Pippbrook Bowling Club
Hon. Secretary: Mr. S. Birch   01737 843440

BRIDGE

Abinger Bridge Club
Contact   01483 203234

CRICKET

Abinger Cricket Club
Contact   01306 730309
Ashtead Cricket Club
Woodfield Lane, Ashtead   01372 272912
Dorking Cricket Club
Secretary: Colin Knott   01737 249062
Forest Green Cricket Club
Hon. Sec.: Mr. Tim Ives   01483 268239
Leatherhead Cricket Club
Fetcham Grove, Guildford Rd, Leatherhead   01372 375203
Oakwoodhill Cricket Club
Secretary: Mr. G. Overington   01306 627459
Old Dorkinian Cricket Club
Secretary: D. Wilcockson   01306 883428

CULTURAL ACTIVITIES

Abinger Big Band and Jazz Club
Contact   01306 730010
Dorking Dramatic and Operatic Society
Contact: Mrs Jean Pike   01306 884726

Leith Hill Festival
Chairman: Diedre Hicks   01737 243931
Morris Dancing
'The Rampant Rooster' (Cotswold Style Mixed)
Contact: Sheila Gray   01737 843258

CYCLING

Mountain Biking
Action Packs, The Booking Hall, Boxhill Station   01306 886944
Nirvana Cycles, 2 The Green, Westcott   01306 740300

ENTERTAINMENT

Thorndike Theatre
Church St, Leatherhead   01372 377677
Dorking Halls (closed for refurbishment most of 1996)
Reigate Rd, Dorking   01306 889694

FISHING

Bury Hill Fisheries
Old Bury Hill, Westcott, Dorking   01306 883621

FOOTBALL/RUGBY

Ashtead Football Club
Secretary: Mr. Ralph Gange   01372 276901
Dorking Rugby Club
Kiln Lane, Brockham   01737 843928
Dorking Colts Football Club
Contact   01306 887420
Dorking Town Football Club
Meadowbank, Dorking   01306 884112
Holmbury Football Club
Contact   01306 730693
Leatherhead Football Club
Contact   01372 360151

Old Dorkinians Football Club
Pixham Lane, Dorking   01306 889728
Surrey County Football Association
321 Kingston Rd, Leatherhead   01372 373543

GOLF
See separate sheet

GYMNASTICS/JUDO
Leatherhead Gym Club
Fetcham Grove, Guildford Rd, Leatherhead   01372 377718

KI AIKIDO CLUBS
Coldharbour Ki Aikido Club
Secretary   01306 712978

LIBRARIES
Ashtead
Woodfield Lane   01372 275875
Bookham
Townshott Close   01372 454440
Dorking
Pippbrook House, Reigate Rd   01306 882948
Leatherhead
The Mansion, Church St   01372 373149
Performing Arts Library
Vaughan-Williams House, West St, Dorking   01306 887509

POLO
Hurtwood Park Polo, Ewhurst, Surrey   01483 272828

PONY CLUBS
Surrey Union Pony Club
"Eastfield", Henfold Lane, Beare Green, Dorking, Surrey

THE SURREY SPORTS DEVELOPMENT UNIT

Open since September 1995, The Surrey Sports Development Unit is a joint initiative between Surrey County Council, the University of Surrey and the Sports Council to help facilitate sporting opportunities in the County. The Surrey Sports Development Officer is based there, along with a sports information officer and several sport specific development officers. The unit is open for those involved in sport to use, and facilities include computing and photocopying, a fully computerised information service and a seminar room for meetings and conferences. A reference library contains coaching resource materials, information about raising money for sport and various policy documents to keep you in touch with all the live, sporting issues.

It is hoped that the work and resources of the Sports Development Unit will benefit all sorts of groups; including governing bodies, local sports club members, teachers and coaches. In partnership with the university, the unit staff are developing schemes to involve students in coaching programmes and are setting up a resource centre for sports science. Publications available from the Sports Development Unit include a coaching newsletter "The Surrey Sports Coach" and A Funding Guide for Sport. The unit is set to become the central focus for developing sport in Surrey at all levels, from grass roots to elite performers.

For further information about the unit and how it might help you please contact Laura Harris, **Sports Information Officer, on 01483 32614.**

Other officers based at the unit: James Hayter, Surrey Sports Development Officer: 01483 32614. Andy Challis, Surrey RFU Youth Development Officer: 01483 38514. Simon Twigg, Regional Judo Development Officer: 01483 32614. Dick Taylor, Sports Development Officer for People with Learning Difficulties: 01483 36512. A new Surrey Tennis Development Officer will also be based in the Unit from April 1996.

COLDHARBOUR KI AIKIDO CLUB

- A gentle martial art.
- Learn co-ordination of mind and body
- Relaxation for daily life
- Proper breathing
- Meditation
- It is non competitive, non aggressive
- Affiliated to Ki Federation of Great Britain
- Contact Piers Cooke (4th Dan)
- Tel 01306 712978

RIDING CLUBS

BHS South Eastern Region
Endurance Riding Group Contact: Nita Osborne   01483 272518

RIDING AND LIVERY STABLES

Bridleways Equestrian Centre
Chapel Lane, Bookham   01372 456385
Broomells Farm
Misbrooks Green Rd, Beare Green   01306 711287
Dorking Riding School
Downs Meadow, Ranmore Rd, Dorking   01306 881718
Headley Grove Stables
Headley Common Rd, Headley   01372 376172
Highlands Farm Stables
Headley Rd, Leatherhead   01372 378219
Hooke Farm Stables
Effingham Common, Effingham   01372 454922
Pachesham Equestrian Centre
Randalls Rd, Leatherhead   01372 377888
Partridge Stables
Partridge Lane, Newdigate   01306 631307
Pasture Wood Farm
Holmbury St. Mary, Dorking   01306 730009
Preston Farm Stables
Lower Rd, Great Bookham   01372 456486
Triple Bar Riding Centre
Broadmoor   01306 730959
Vale Lodge
Downs Lane, Dorking Rd, Leatherhead   01372 373184
Wyvenhoe Riding Centre
Guildford Rd, Little Bookham   01372 454339

RIDING INSTRUCTION

Freelance Riding Instructor
Judy Troughton BHSAI   01306 711520

SOCIETIES

Dorking and District Preservation Society
Hon Sec. 15 Yew Tree Rd, Dorking   01306 883699
Dorking Halls Concertgoers Society
Hon Sec. 1 Glebe Road, Dorking   01306 886316

SHOOTING

Newdigate Clay Pigeon Shooting Club   01737 246362
Newgate   01293 871640
Wotton Rifle Club
Contact: Mr. John Symes   0181 642 8966

STOOLBALL CLUBS

Coldharbour Stoolball Club
Contact: T. Ward   01306 711961

SUB-AQUA CLUBS

British Sub-Aqua Club - Dorking Branch
Contact: Peter White   01306 885851
Mole Valley Sub-Aqua Club
based at Leatherhead Leisure Centre
Contact: Keiran Wynyard   0181 337 1914

SWIMMING

Leisure Centre,
Reigate Rd, Dorking   01306 887722
Leisure Centre,
Guildford Rd, Leatherhead   01372 377674

TABLE TENNIS CLUBS

Abinger Table Tennis Club
Contact   01483 203125
Effingham Table Tennis Club
Secretary: Mr Dennis Brunskill   01372 458361

TENNIS/SQUASH

Abinger Tennis Club
Contact 01306 730163
Ashtead Squash Rackets Club
39 Skinners Lane, Ashtead 01372 272215
Bookham Tennis Club
Secretary: Mrs. Waring 01372 459217
Dorking Lawn Tennis and Squash Club
Roman Rd, Dorking 01306 889668
Leatherhead Lawn Tennis Club
Cannon Grove, Fetcham 01372 379619

YOUTH HOSTELS

Tanners Hatch Youth Hostel, Polesden Lacey
Contact: The Warden 01372 452528
Surrey Association of Youth Clubs, Holmbury St. Mary
Contact 01306 730929

Further information about clubs and organisations within the Mole Valley may be obtained via the District Council.

BOWL A MAIDEN OVER!
Forest Green Cricket Club plays weekend non-league matches in a beautiful village-green setting. Pavilion with bar. Excellent wicket. Short boundary! Low match fees. Sociable, pressure-free membership guaranteed.
Contact Tim Ives on 01483 268239

FREELANCE RIDING INSTRUCTOR
JUDY TROUGHTON BHSAI
with 18 years experience. Enthusiastic instruction for all ages and abilities in both dressage and jumping. **Tel: 01306 711520**   Mobile: 0589 101002

SEONA ROSS B.S.Dip - Area Development Officer - London and South East
EXTEND Exercise Training
Movement to Music for the Over Sixties and Handicapped People of all Ages
2 The Betchworth, Reigate Road, BETCHWORTH, Surrey RH3 7ET

LOCAL GOLF COURSES

BETCHWORTH PARK GOLF CLUB,
Reigate Rd, DORKING   Parkland 18 holes   01306 882052
Other facilities: bar, restaurant, changing rooms, tuition,

DORKING GOLF CLUB,
Chart Park, DORKING   Parkland 9 holes   01306 886917
Other facilities: bar, restaurant, changing rooms, tuition, putting green

EFFINGHAM GOLF CLUB,
Guildford Road, EFFINGHAM   Downland 18 holes   01372 452606
Other facilities: club hire, bar, restaurant, changing rooms, tuition, putting green, large practice area, tennis, squash

GATTON MANOR GOLF AND COUNTRY CLUB,
Standon Lane, OCKLEY   Parkland 18 holes   01306 627557
Other facilities: Hotel with en suite conference suites, fishing, tennis, bowls, club hire, bar restaurant, changing rooms, tuition, putting green

LEATHERHEAD GOLF CLUB,
Kingston Road, LEATHERH'D   Parkland 18 holes   01372 843966
Other facilities: practice ground and nets, club hire, bar, restaurant, cafe, changing rooms, tuition, putting green

PACHESHAM GOLF CENTRE,
Oaklawn Rd, LEATHERHEAD   Parkland 9 holes   01372 843453
Other facilities: club hire, bar, restaurant, changing rooms, tuition, putting green

RUSPER GOLF CLUB,
Rusper Road, NEWDIGATE   Woodland 9 holes   01293 871871
Other facilities: club hire, bar, restaurant, changing rooms, tuition

TYRRELLS WOOD GOLF CLUB LTD.,
LEATHERHEAD   Downland 18 holes   01372 376025
Other facilities: club hire, bar, restaurant, changing rooms, tuition, putting green

LOCAL ATTRACTIONS

Bocketts Farm, Fetcham, nr. Leatherhead　　01372 363764
A working farm open to families and
visitors with a barn tea rooms.

Box Hill, nr. Dorking　　01306 885502
National Trust owned and designated as a country
park. Rising to 400 feet above the River Mole.

Chapel Farm, Westhumble, nr. Dorking　　01306 882865
A 200 acre farm suitable for introducing very young
families to farm animals, similar to Bocketts Farm.

Denbies Wine Estate, nr. Dorking　　01306 876616
England's largest wine estate providing excellent
facilities for wine tasting and viewing the wine making
process.

Dorking & District Museum, The Old Foundry,
West Street, Dorking　　01306 743821
Opening Times: Wednesday, Thursday 2 pm - 5 pm
Saturday: 10 am - 5 pm

Fire and Iron Gallery, Oxshott Rd, Leatherhead　　01372 375148
Crafts Council Selected Gallery specialising in contemporary decorative metal-work by leading international blacksmiths and jewellers. Special
exhibitions and demonstrations complement a
permanent display of work.

Gatwick Zoo, Russ Hill, Charlwood　　01293 862312
Animals include otters, penguins, flamingoes and
monkeys to be seen at close quarters.

Hannah Peschar Gallery and Sculpture Garden
Black and White Cottage, Standon Lane, Ockley   01306 627269
A selling exhibition of contemporary sculpture and
ceramics in an unorthodox landscaped garden, by
garden designer Anthony Paul featuring many
architectural plants and lots of water (see back cover).

Leatherhead Museum of Local History
Hampton Cottage,
64 Church Street, Leatherhead.   01372 277611

Leith Hill Tower, Leith Hill   01306 712434
The tower marking the highest point of South East
England, at 1000 feet above sea level it is set
in glorious countryside. At weekends refreshments
are available.

Polesden Lacey, Great Bookham, nr. Dorking   01372 458203
Owned by the National Trust, this Regency villa was
the honeymoon hideaway for King George VI, now it is
home to a fine selection of paintings, furniture and silver
with gardens and lawns worth visiting. Also there is
sometimes an open air theatre here.

SELECT THE RIGHT CLUB
A Special Offer From Gatton Manor
Due to the restructuring and improvement of our club
we are now able to offer annual full golf membership
for just £795.00 (inclusive of of joining fee and VAT)

**Facilities available include
the 18 hole Championship Golf Course,
Hotel, Restaurants and Bars, Conference suites,
Health Club, Fishing and other sports.
There are also a limited number of Corporate Membership vacancies.**

**For further information and membership package contact
Paul Davison or Ray Hussey.**
*Gatton Manor Hotel, Golf & Country Club,
Standon Lane, Ockley, Nr. Dorking, Surrey RH5 5PQ*
Tel: (01306) 627555   Fax: (01306) 627713

LOCAL NEWSAGENTS

ASHTEAD

Ashtead Newsagents,
88 Woodfield Lane, Ashtead — 01372 272506
Forbuoys,
5-6 Craddocks Parade, Ashtead — 01372 272729
Forbuoys,
72 The Street, Ashtead — 01372 276906
Harry's Newsagents,
230 Barnett Wood Lane, Ashtead — 01372 272290

BOOKHAM

Blackmans,
Beckley Parade, Leatherhead Road, Bookham — 01372 452780
A.B. Cox,
10 Grove Corner, Bookham — 01372 452938
Forbuoys,
Church Rd, Bookham — 01372 458123
Glassons,
197 Lower Road, Bookham — 01372 458268

CAPEL

Capel Newsagency,
138 The Street, Capel — 01306 711021

DORKING

Alans Newsagent,
9 Falkland Road, Dorking — 01306 884126
Bradshaws,
94 South Street, Dorking — 01306 882540
Chart Downs Newsagent,
213 Chart Downs, Dorking — 01306 882385
Evans,
10 Hampstead Rd, Dorking — 01306 883369
Forbuoys,
344-346, High Street, Dorking — 01306 884481

Martin, The Newsagent,
155-157 High Street, Dorking — 01306 885639
Station News,
Dorking North Station, Station Approach, Dorking — 01306 882550
Wellers,
201a High Street, Dorking — 01306 882330
Westcott Newsagency,
5 Guildford Road, Westcott, Dorking — 01306 881440
W. H. Smith,
101 High Street, Dorking — 01306 882194

LEATHERHEAD

Channon,
21 North Street, Leatherhead — 01372 373062
John Menzies,
Unit 15, Swan Centre, Leatherhead — 01372 378011
K & G Edwards,
3 Sunmead Parade, Guildford Rd, Leatherhead — 01372 372080
Holiday's Newsagent,
5 Hazel Parade, Penrose Rd, Leatherhead — 01372 454467
One Stop Community Stores Ltd.,
209-211 Kingston Rd, Leatherhead — 01372 372485
PNM Newsagents,
59 Kingston Rd, Leatherhead — 01372 372331
Sky Newsagents,
101 The Street, Fetcham, Leatherhead — 01372 372492

NEWDIGATE

J.C. Bettesworth,
Foresters House, Village Street, Newdigate — 01306 631383

NORTH HOLMWOOD

Forbuoys,
Spook Hill, North Holmwood — 01306 883264

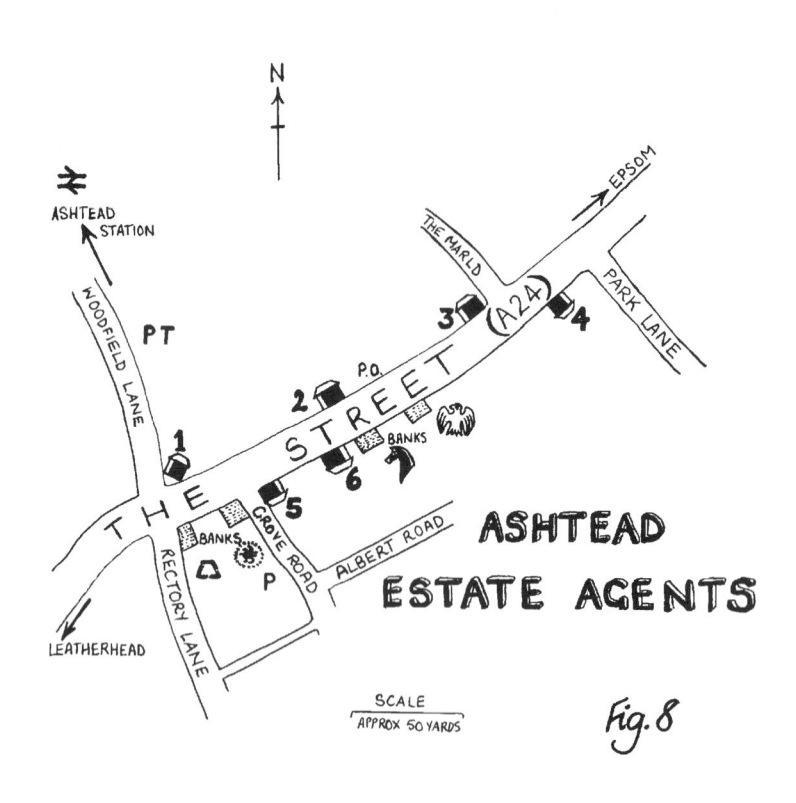

ASHTEAD
ESTATE AGENTS

SCALE
APPROX 50 YARDS

Fig. 8

LOCAL ESTATE AGENTS

ASHTEAD

1 Allan and Partners,
17 The Street, Ashtead *Sales/Lettings* 01372 278877

2 Bairstow Eves,
35 The Street, Ashtead *Sales/Lettings* 01372 276363

3 Elphick Est.Agts.,
71 The Street, Ashtead *Sales* 01372 272321

4 Jackie Quinn and Co.,
118 The Street, Ashtead *Sales/Lettings* 01372 271504

5 Michael Everett and Co.,
58 The Street, Ashtead *Sales/Lettings* 01372 273448

6 Patrick Gardner,
66 The Street, Ashtead *Sales* 01372 271880
 Lettings 01372 360444

As can be seen, *'The Street'* in Ashtead is home to all its local estate agents and therefore they can all be found within a couple of hundred yards of each other. *N.B.* Other agents, outside the village, which may also cover Ashtead, can be found in neighbouring Leatherhead or Epsom.

See Fig. 8 opposite for the numerical location of each estate agent above.

VISITING ASHTEAD ESTATE AGENTS

By Rail

Ashtead is on the London to Dorking/Horsham British Rail line. Customer Information: 0171 928 5100.
'The Street' is about two thirds of a mile from Ashtead Station down *Woodfield Lane*.

By Road

Easily found by road, directly on the A24 and just a short distance from Junction 9 of the M25. Petrol Station in *'The Street'*.

Car Parking P

'The Street' is a busy little high street and subject to restricted parking. There are two local car parks within 50 yards in *Woodfield Lane*, just behind Allan and Partners Estate Agents and in *Grove Road* more or less opposite. Car Parking charges 'Pay and Display': 10p up to 1 hour, 30p up to 2 hours.

Public Toilets T

In *Woodfield Road* Car Park.

Accommodation B & B

See separate section.

MICHAEL EVERETT & COMPANY

ESTATE AGENTS
SURVEYORS
PROPERTY MANAGEMENT
NEW HOMES AND LAND

FOR ALL YOUR LOCAL PROPERTY REQUIREMENTS PLEASE CONTACT US AT:-

58 THE STREET ASHTEAD
01372 273448

Also at Epsom and Walton on the Hill

JACKIE QUINN
01372 - 271504

Thinking of Moving?

Residential Sales
♦
Lettings and Management
♦
Land and New Homes
♦

118 The Street, Ashtead, Surrey

01372 271504

Patrick GARDNER & Co

Estate Agents, Surveyors, Residential Lettings

1 - 3 Church Street, Leatherhead
Your Local Professional Estate Agent

| Residential Letting | Surveys, Probate |
| (01372) 360444 | Valuations, Planning, etc. |

LEATHERHEAD	BOOKHAM	ASHTEAD	DORKING
(01372) 360078	(01372) 452207	(01372) 271880	(01306) 877775

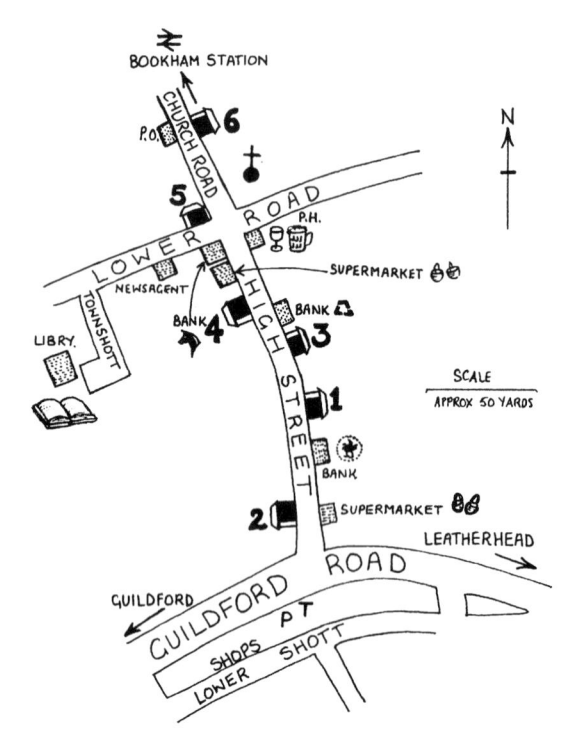

BOOKHAM ESTATE AGENTS

fig.9

BOOKHAM

1 Bairstow Eves,
  19 High Street, Gt Bookham   *Sales/Lettings*   01372 452811

2 Henshaws,
  Rayleigh House,
  32 High Street, Gt Bookham   *Sales*   01372 450255
  (small car park at rear)   *Lettings*   01932 864494

3 Mann and Co.,
  17 High Street, Gt Bookham   *Sales*   01372 453352
                                     Lettings   01483 35211

4 Norman and Huggins,
  6 High Street, Gt Bookham   *Sales*   01372 457011
                                     Lettings   01372 450655

5 Patrick Gardner,
  Corner House,
  Cross Roads, Gt Bookham   *Sales*   01372 452207
                                     Lettings   01372 360444

6 John Wadsworth,
  14/18 Church Road,
  Gt Bookham   *Sales*   01372 450500

7 Gracelands Management,
  (not a shop)
  90 Lower Road, Bookham   *Lettings*   01372 459780

All of Bookham's estate agents are to be found in the small *High Street* and *Church Road* area, within easy walking distance of each other. Estate agents in Leatherhead will also cover the area.

See Fig. 9 opposite for the numerical location of each estate agent above.

VISITING BOOKHAM ESTATE AGENTS

By Rail

Bookham is on the London to Guildford British Rail Line.

Customer Information: 0171 928 5100. The Station is about one mile away from the *High Street*, down *Church Road*.

By Road

Some 10 minutes by car from Junction 9 on the M25. Great Bookham is situated about 2 miles from Leatherhead and some 9 miles from Guildford on the A246. The *High Street* is a small turning off this road, travelling from Leatherhead it is found on the right.

Car Parking **P**

There is free parking in the *High Street* itself, if you can find a space and further free parking in *Lower Shott*, just across the *Guildford Rd*.

Public Toilets **T**

In the *Lower Shott* Car Park.

Accommodation **B & B**

See separate section.

YOU PROVIDE THE HOME...
WE'LL PROVIDE THE BUYER

Our successful sales in your area have created an urgent demand for properties of all types and price ranges. Call in and see us today!

WOOLWICH
PROPERTY SERVICES

250-256 High Street, Dorking,
Surrey RH4 1QT
Telephone: 01306 742308

Woolwich Property Services is a wholly-owned subsidiary of Woolwich Building Society. If you have instructed another agent on a sole agency and/or sole selling rights basis, the terms of those instructions must be considered to avoid a possible liability to pay two commisions.

fig. 10

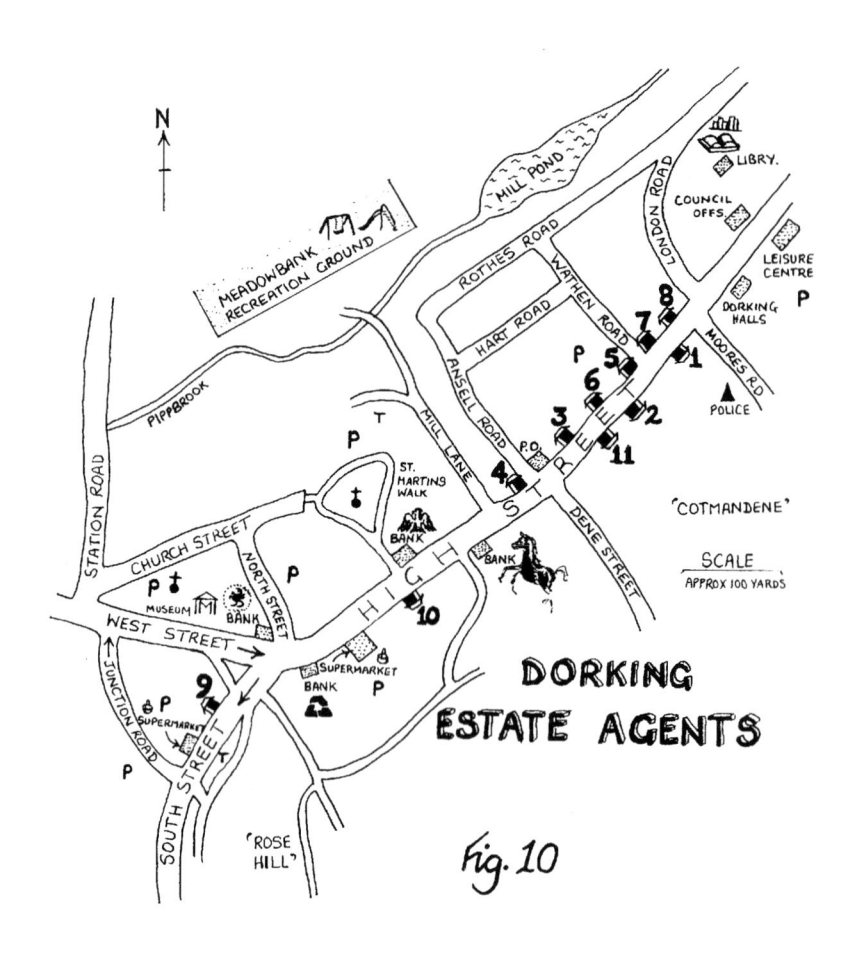

DORKING ESTATE AGENTS

DORKING

1	**Alliance & Leicester,**		
	286-288 High St., Dorking	*Sales*	01306 884404
2	**Black Horse Agencies,**	*Sales*	01306 884699
	266 High Street, Dorking	*Lettings*	01737 221411
3	**Cubitt and West,**		
	179 High Street, Dorking	*Sales*	01306 883399
4	**Halifax Property Services,**	*Sales*	01306 886666
	171 High Street, Dorking	*Lettings*	01737 222858
5	**Hamptons,**	*Sales*	01306 885466
	251 High Street, Dorking	*Lettings*	01483 577577
6	**Mann and Co.,**	*Sales*	01306 741710
	241 High Street, Dorking	*Lettings*	01483 35211
7	**Martin Brown,**		
	253 High Street, Dorking	*Sales/Lettings*	01306 884685
8	**King and Chasemore,**	*Sales*	01306 888080
	275 High Street, Dorking	*Lettings*	01306 742458
9	**Patrick Gardner,**	*Sales*	01306 877775
	16 South Street, Dorking	*Lettings*	01372 360444
10	**White and Sons,**	*Sales*	01306 887654
	104 High Street, Dorking	*Lettings*	01293 785454
11	**Woolwich,**	*Sales*	01306 742308
	250 High Street, Dorking	*Lettings*	01306 877170

Only Patrick Gardner is located is *South Street* away from the *High Street*. **See Fig. 10 opposite for the numerical location of each estate agent above.**

VISITING DORKING ESTATE AGENTS

By Rail

On the London to Dorking British Rail line.
Customer Information: 0171 928 5100
On the Reading to Gatwick, Thames Trains Line.
Customer Information: 01732 770111
Dorking, Dorking Deepdene and Dorking West Stations are all about half a mile from the town centre where the Estate Agents are situated.

By Road

About 15 minutes drive from the M25 Junction 9, situated on the A24/A25.

Car Parking P

On street parking, generally restricted, there are some spaces that are free for short-term periods mainly in *South Street*.
Pay and Display charges: 10p up to 1 hour, 30p up to 2 hours, several to choose from, the most convenient in *Wathen Road, Mill Lane* and behind Sainsburys.

Public Toilets T

In *Mill Road* Car Park (at the entrance) and in *South Street*, beneath *Victoria Terrace*.

Accommodation B & B

See separate section.

HAMPTONS

PRACTITIONERS IN RESIDENTIAL PROPERTY

Hamptons in Dorking provides detailed knowledge on all aspects of the residential property sales market, specialising in fine country and village property with a comprehensive service in the Dorking/Reigate areas.

Our service however is more than local, stretching across England, the Channel Islands and Hong Kong, offering a rich source of potential buyers and contacts.

HAMPTONS

251 High Street, Dorking, Surrey RH4 1YA
Tel: (01306) 885466. Fax: (01306) 743581

HAMPTONS ESTATES LTD: OFFICES IN ENGLAND, SCOTLAND, THE CHANNEL ISLANDS AND HONG KONG, WITH ASSOCIATES IN EUROPE AND SOUTH AFRICA.

Fig. 11

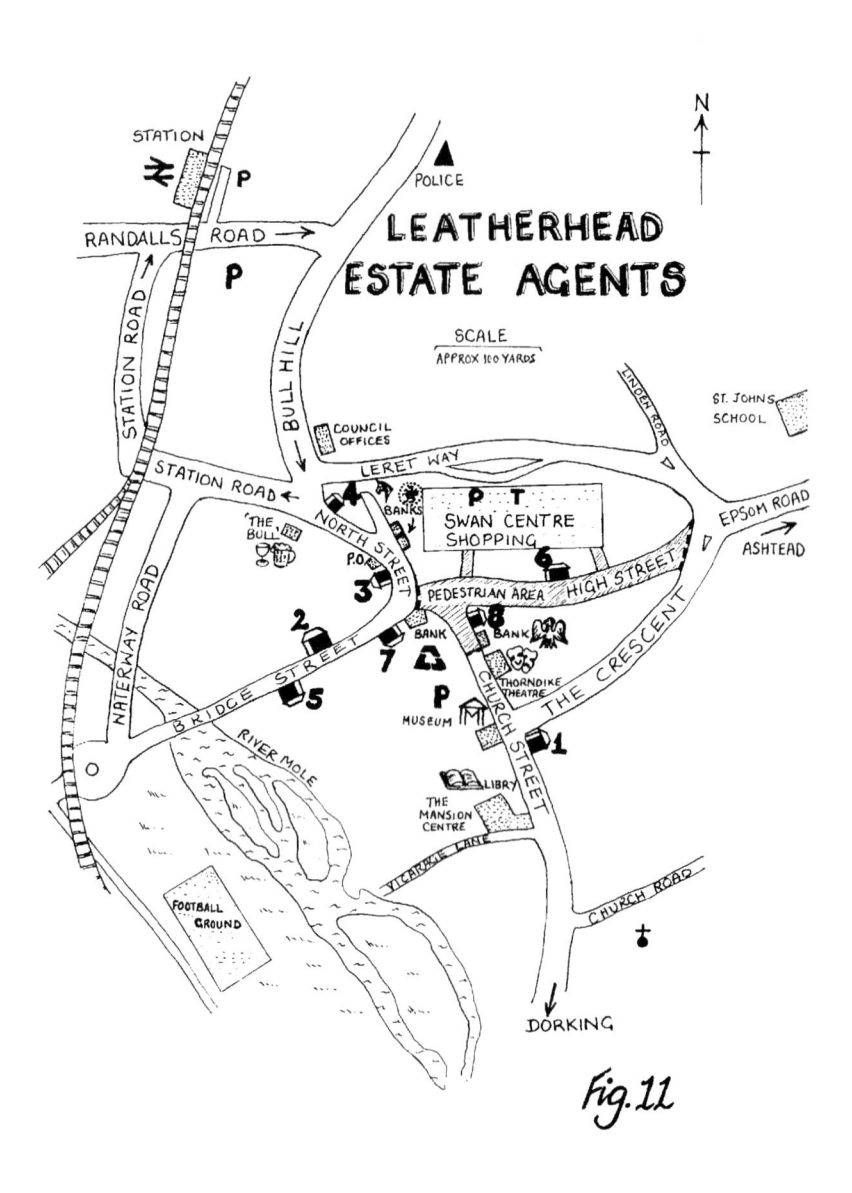

LEATHERHEAD

1	**Bairstow Eves,**		
	29 Church Street, Leatherh'd	Sales	01372 376633
		Lettings	01372 360377
2	**Black Horse Agencies,**		
	6 Bridge St., Leatherhead	Sales	01372 374133
		Lettings	01932 866931
3	**Cubitt and West,**		
	3 North Street, Leatherhead	Sales	01372 373780
4	**Domus Letting Agency,**		
	24 North Street, Leatherhead	Lettings	01372 362555
5	**Douglas,**		
	5 Bridge Street, Leatherhead	Sales/Lettings	01372 379011
6	**Mann and Co.,**		
	39 High Street, Leatherhead	Sales	01372 376071
		Lettings	01483 35211
7	**Norman and Huggins,**		
	3 Bridge Street, Leatherhead	Sales	01372 374806
		Lettings	01372 450655
8	**Patrick Gardner,**		
	1-3 Church Street, Leatherh'd	Sales	01372 360078
		Lettings	01372 360444

All the estate agents are within easy walking distance of each other in the town centre, although they all scattered around in *North Street, Bridge Street, High Street* and *Church Street.*

See Fig. 11 opposite for the numerical location of each estate agent above.

VISITING LEATHERHEAD ESTATE AGENTS

By Rail
On the London to Dorking and London to Guildford British Rail lines. Customer Information: 0171 928 5100

By Road
About 5 minutes drive from the M25 Junction 9.

Car Parking **P**
The most convenient place to park for the Estate Agents would be opposite the Thorndike Theatre off *Church Street*.
Pay and Display charges: 10p up to 1 hour, 30p up to 2 hours.
The Swan Centre parking facilities would be equally as good.

Public Toilets **T**
In the Swan Centre.

Accommodation **B & B**
See separate section.

THE ONE~STOP PROPERTY SHOP

EVERYTHING BUT AN ESTATE AGENT

We offer time saving, independent and flexible new property services designed to suit you.

Fast and friendly, we help you with:

✱ Personalised property portfolios and guided tours to find the right home.

✱ Complete relocation assistance from start to finish.

✱ Home security visits can be arranged.

✱ Property Management service available.

✱ **ADDRESS EXPRESS**
Our fast, free 'change of address' card service
(Free with any other service detailed above, or just £15.00 per 100 cards)

RING: 01306 731122
FAX: 01306 731444

For more details and without obligation

The One-Stop Property Shop is a registered trade mark and subsidiary of The Good Move Guide Ltd.

CHURCHES

Locations and contact numbers
(N.B. sometimes a limited answering service!)

BAPTIST CHURCHES

Ashtead Baptist Church	Barnett Wood Lane	01372 813345
Strict Baptist Chapel	Brockham Green,	01306 882774
Bookham Baptist Church	Lower Road,	01372 459314
Dorking Baptist Church	Junction Road,	01306 876714
Dorking Baptist Chapel	Paper Mews, High St.,	01306 889035

CATHOLIC CHURCHES

St. Michael The Archangel	The Marld, Ashtead	01372 272267
St. Joseph's	Falkland Gr, Dorking	01306 882433
Church of the Holy Spirit	Bell Lane, Fetcham	01372 373387
Our Lady and St. Peter's	Garlands Road, L'head	01372 372278

CHRISTIAN BRETHREN

Hampstead Road Church	Dorking	01306 881255
Kingscroft Road Church	Leatherhead	01372 741119

CHRISTIAN SCIENCE

First Church of Christ Scientist	Moores Road, Dorking	01306 882583

CHURCH OF ENGLAND

St. James, Abinger Common	Abinger	01306 730746
St. Giles and St. George	Ashtead	01372 813354
St. Michael	Betchworth	01737 842102
St. Andrew	Boxhill	01372 377327
Christ Church	Brockham	01306 611224
St. Mary The Virgin	Buckland	01737 842102
St. John The Baptist	Capel	01306 711260
St. Nicholas	Charlwood	01293 862343
Christ Church	Coldharbour	01306 730746
St. Martin's (shared)	Dorking	01306 882875
St. Mary's, Pixham Lane	Dorking	01306 882875
St. Paul's, St. Pauls Road	Dorking	01306 883023
St. Mary's Parish Church	Fetcham	01372 372598

CHURCH OF ENGLAND

Holy Trinity	Forest Green	01306 712594
St. Nicolas	Great Bookham	01372 452405
St. Mary	Headley	01372 377327
St. Mary	Holmbury St. Mary	01306 730285
St. John the Evangelist	Holmwood	01306 882135
St. Mary and St. Nicholas	Leatherhead	01372 362544
St. Bartholomew	Leigh	01306 611224
All Saints	Little Bookham	01372 456752
St. Michael	Mickleham	01372 378335
St. John The Baptist	Oakwood Hill	01306 712594
St. Margaret	Ockley	01306 712594
St. Barnabas	Ranmore	01306 882994
St. Mary Magdalene	South Holmwood	01306 888043
Holy Trinity	Westcott	01306 885309
St. John The Evangelist	Wotton	01306 882495

EVANGELICAL CHURCHES

Evangelical Church	Dorking	Not Listed
Cannon Court Evangelical Ch.	Fetcham	01372 372765

FREE CHURCHES

St. John's Free Church	Westcott	01306 885495

METHODIST CHURCHES

Capel Methodist	01306 882255
Cobham Methodist	01372 372743
Dorking Methodist	01306 882255
Effingham Methodist	01372 372743
Wesley Memorial Methodist	01372 372743

UNITED REFORMED CHURCHES

Bookham United Reformed	01372 452503
Dorking United Reformed	01306 883652
Christchurch United Reformed	01372 378795

SALVATION ARMY

Salvation Army	01306 884485

TEMPORARY ACCOMMODATION
DORKING AND DISTRICT

Dorking Town
Pubs and Guest Houses

Fairdene Guest House, Moores Rd, Dorking	01306 888337
Highbank, 1 Townfield Rd, Dorking	01306 888135
Highgate, Brympton Close, Dorking	01306 882614
5 Rose Hill, Dorking	01306 883127
8 Rose Hill, Dorking	01306 887209
Shrub Hill, 3 Calvert Rd, Dorking	01306 885229
Star and Garter P.H., Dorking North Station, Dorking	01306 882820
The Old Vicarage, 39 St. Pauls Rd West, Dorking	01306 884002
The Pilgrim, Station Rd West, Dorking	01306 889951
The Willows, Mid Holmwood Lane, Dorking	01306 888948
Torridon Guest House, Longfield Rd, Dorking	01306 883724

Motels and Hotels

Travel Lodge Motel, Reigate Rd, Dorking	01306 740361
White Horse Hotel, High Street, Dorking	01306 881138

Self Catering

Pear Tree Cottage, 28 Dene St, Dorking	01306 741503

Abinger
Pubs, Farm and Guest Houses

Crossways Farm, Raikes Lane, Abinger Hammer	01306 730173
Furzenwood, Abinger Lane, Abinger Common	01306 730124
Leylands Farm, Sheephouse Lane, Abinger Common	01306 730115
Mark Ash, Abinger Common	01306 731326
The Volunteer, Water Lane, Sutton Abinger	01306 730798

Betchworth
Farm and Guest Houses

Whitelands, Reigate Rd, Betchworth	01737 842261
Gadbrook Old Farm, Wellhouse Lane, Betchworth	01737 842183

Box Hill
Guest Houses

Danesmore, Pilgrims Way, West Humble	01306 882734
Old House Cottage, Mickleham	01372 375050

Box Hill
Hotels
Burford Bridge Hotel, Box Hill 01306 884561

Brockham
Guest Houses
Kerri Cottage, 54 Brockham Lane, Brockham 01737 843956

Capel
Farm Houses
Ewekenes Farmhouse, Ryersh Lane, Capel 01306 711095
Hotels
The Surrey Hills Hotel, Horsham Rd, Capel 01306 712585

Gatwick Area
Hotels
Stanhill Court Country House Hotel, Charlwood 01293 862166

Holmbury St. Mary
Pubs, Farm and Guest Houses
Bulmer Farm, Holmbury St. Mary 01306 730210
Woodhill Cottage, Holmbury St. Mary 01306 730498
Holmbury Farm, Holmbury St. Mary 01306 621443
The Royal Oak, The Green, Holmbury St. Mary 01306 730120

Holmwood
Guest Houses
Steyning Cottage, Horsham Rd, South Holmwood 01306 888481

Leigh
Guest Houses
Barn Cottage, Church Road, Leigh 01306 611347

Newdigate
Farm Houses
Tanhouse Farm, Rusper Rd, Newdigate 01306 631334
Sturtwood Farm, Partridge Lane, Newdigate 01306 631308

Ockley
Pubs and Country Hotel
Kings Arms, Stane St, Ockley 01306 711224
Gatton Manor Hotel, Standon Lane, Ockley 01306 627555

Walliswood

Guest Houses

Hazels, Walliswood, Surrey — 01306 627228

Westcott

Guest Houses

Corner House, Guildford Rd, Westcott — 01306 888798
The Dene, Hole Hill, Westcott — 01306 885595

LEATHERHEAD AND DISTRICT

Leatherhead Town

Pubs and Guest Houses

Bronwyn, Crabtree Dr, Givons Grove, Leatherhead — 01372 372515
20 Melvinshaw, Leatherhead — 01372 373786
Manston Elms, Kingston Rd, Leatherhead — 01372 374514
Swan Guest House, 39 Kingston Rd, Leatherhead — 01372 376332
The Bull Hotel, North Street, Leatherhead — 01372 372153

Ashtead

Pubs and Guest Houses

91 Broadhurst, Ashtead — 01372 275236
Silver Firs, 7a Leatherhead Rd, Ashtead — 01372 272122

Bookham

Pubs and Guest Houses

Hillcrest, Halepit Rd, Great Bookham — 01372 452257
The Lodge, 2 Park Green, Great Bookham — 01372 459642

Hotels

Bookham Grange Hotel, Bookham Common — 01372 452742
Preston Cross Hotel, Rectory Lane, Little Bookham — 01372 456642

Chessington

Guest Houses

29 Coppard Gardens, off Mansfield Rd, Chessington — 0181 974 1379

Effingham

Guest Houses

Crosslands Guest House, Guildford Road, Effingham — 01372 453479

USEFUL ADDRESSES AND TELEPHONE NUMBERS

HOSPITALS

Accident and Emergency:

East Surrey Hospital, Three Arch Road, Redhill	01737 768511
Epsom District Hospital, Dorking Road, Epsom	01372 735735
Royal Surrey County, Egerton Road, Guildford	01483 571122

Local - Non Accident and Emergency:

Ashtead Hospital, The Warren, Ashtead	01372 276161
Dorking Hospital, Horsham Road, Dorking	01737 768511
Leatherhead Hospital, Poplar Road, Leatherhead	01372 384384

POLICE

(Dorking Division covers the whole of the Mole Valley)

Dorking Police Station,
Moores Road, Dorking — 01306 882284

Leatherhead Police Station,
44 Kingston Rd, Leatherhead — 01306 882284

SURREY CRIMESTOPPERS — 0800 555 111

For receiving anonymous information about any crime.

MAIN UTILITIES AND SERVICES

British Gas South Eastern
Customer Enquiries regarding:

Gas bills/accounts	0645 801802
Servicing and installation	0181 684 6933
Gas Escapes:	
North Surrey District:	
Ashtead, Leatherhead, Fetcham, Mickleham, Headley	0181 648 1001
South Downs District:	
Dorking, Westhumble, Boxhill, Betchworth, Leigh, Newdigate, Capel, Ockley, Westcott, Abinger	01273 693588

British Telecom
Moving Home? (Give preferably 2 weeks notice)   Freephone 150
Enquiries Leatherhead/Ashtead areas:
Delta Point, 35 Wellesley Road, Croydon, CR9 2YZ   0181 666 4321
Enquiries Dorking areas,
Telecom House, Alexandra Road, Aldershot, Hants   Freephone 150

Mercury Communications,
(Residential Sales and Enquiries)   0500 500194
67 Theobalds Rd, WC1X 8SP   0171 971 8500

Seeboard,
Russell Way, Crawley, West Sussex RH10 1UL   01293 562266

Water Utilities,
Thames Water   *Accounts*   0645 200888
Abinger, Ockley, Wotton, Walliswood, Oakwood Hill   0645 200800
East Surrey Water
Other areas in the Mole Valley Borough   01737 772000

HEALTH (DOCTORS AND DENTISTS)
Primary Care Agency, *(formerly Family Health Services Authority)* provides local information
about National Health Doctors and Dentists   0181 399 5133
Health Services Booklet, (from Mole Valley Council)   01306 885001

TV LICENCE
TV Licensing, Bristol BS98 1TL
(quote TV Licence Number)   0117 9763763

POST OFFICE FORWARDING MAIL SERVICE
Redirection Centre,
20 Brandon Street, Edinburgh, EH3 0SP   0345 777888

CITIZENS ADVICE BUREAUX
Dorking 231 High Street, Dorking, Surrey   01306 876805
Leatherhead Wesley House, Bull Hill, Surrey   01372 375522

BUDGET CHANGES AND THE OUTLOOK

Mr. Clarke's November 1995 Budget proved to be very 'non-interventionist' for the housing market. Maybe it could be argued that any short-term sweetners would make little difference anyhow, but there were few specific measures in this budget to help home owners or first time buyers in particular. Perhaps it may be understood therefore, that The Chancellor took the view that policies he judged to be good for the economy were also good for the housing market, making further help unnecessary.

More may have been expected with a general election forthcoming to improve the all important 'feel good factor', but Mr. Clarke was not persuaded. Everyone knows that news over recent years has not been encouraging for home ownership, but it must be recognised that it is misleading to talk about a 'single housing market'. There are still areas and properties which have gone against a general downward trend, some have held a steady price and others have actually gained. In the south of England this is true of parts of Surrey as well as some central London locations, although often confined to bigger or more unique properties.

Overall 1995 was not a particularly encouraging year for the property market either. In comparison with 1994 figures, the number of house sales fell by some 10% to 1.16M which was nearly half the number sold in the boom year of 1988. Some big names also pulled out of house building such as Costain, Mowlem and Lovell and the well known estate agents chain 'Cornerstone' closed after most of their branches were sold.

So why am I optimistic for the year(s) ahead? Basically because people will always want homes and in particular their own homes. In England, reliable research shows that there are hundreds of thousands of first-time buyers approaching the market every year (this is true despite demographic downward trends). This fact, coupled with several years stagnation, has meant that there is a significant queue of would be first-time buyers still waiting in the wings for the 'best time' to buy. As soon as renewed confidence takes hold within this important group, the better news for every home owner and I do not think it is too far away.

GLOSSARY

A.P.R..........Annual Percentage Rate of the total charge for credit. This is the standard way of comparing rates offered by different lenders (laid down by the Consumer Credit Act 1974).

Auction......A means of selling and buying homes as with other items. Explained in more detail under the section 'Where to Find Available Homes'.

Bridging Loan...The loan of money required to complete the purchase of a new home before the funds from the sale of the old home become available.

Chain.......Series of buyers and sellers involved in purchase and sale of properties, dependent upon each other to successfully complete the transactions.

Grade II*.....Listed building of more importance than simply a grade II

M.I.R.A.S......Mortgage Interest Relief At Source. Most mortgage repayments are included in this scheme, so that the mortgagor immediately pays the net amount of interest at once. Any mortgage which does not attract the benefit of interest relief (i.e. a second home) has to be paid outside this system.

N.H.B.C..... National House Building Council, Buildmark House, Chiltern Avenue, Amersham, Buckinghamshire, HP6 5AP (tel. 01494 434477).

Professional organisation which ensures quality control over new house buildings.

'Private Treaty Sale'.....This is the usual type of sale agreement entered into between vendor and purchaser, where an offer is accepted on the open market.

NOTES

NOTES

NOTES

FLOOR PLAN

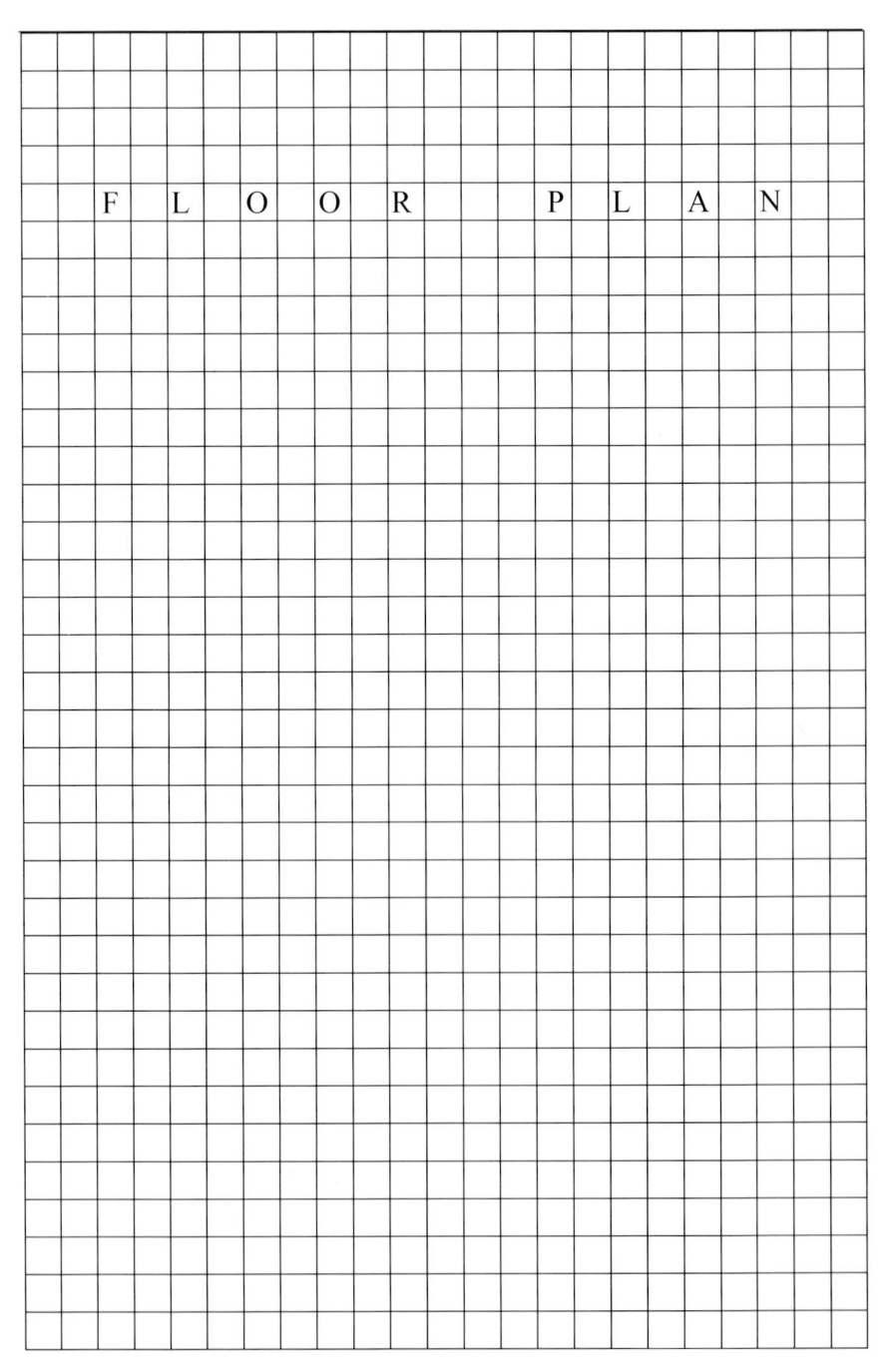

FLOOR PLAN

INDEX TO ADVERTISERS

Outer Back Cover   Hurtwood House School
Outer Back Cover Flap   Hannah Peschar Gallery & Sculpture Garden
Inner Back Cover   Mortgage Trust
Inner Front Cover   Brown and Root

DISPLAY ADVERTISEMENTS

Page	
219	Abinger Hammer Village School
189	All About The House
29	Allied Dunbar
141	Ashtead Squash Rackets Club
219	Barnet Wood Infant School
221	Belmont School
150	Capel Newsagency
95	Chalcraft Pool Centre
226	Computer Courses for Beginners
81	Cubitt and West Estate Agents
119	Denbies
223	Downsend Schools
210	Duke of Kent School
225	Dunottar School
234	Extend Experience Training
133	Fire and Iron Gallery
234	Forest Green Cricket Club
31, 33, 35	Friends Provident
237	Gatton Manor Country Club
95	G.T. Heating
251	Hamptons Estate Agents
272	Hurtwood Park Polo
243	Jackie Quinn Estate Agents
95	JBP Builders
234	Judy Troughton BHSAI
231	Ki Aikido Club
116	MCL Computer Solutions
243	Michael Everett Estate Agents

225	Micklefield School
150	M.J. Byrnes - Gardener
185	Nirvana Cycles
223	Parsons Mead School
243	Patrick Gardner Estate Agents
115-116	Pizza Piazza Restaurant
115	Planters Country Pine
213-216	Pre-School Notice Board
95	R.T. Overton and Sons Ltd.
123	Rug Centre
150	Roses Stores, Mickleham
157	Simon Horn Furniture
18	South Essex Insurance Brokers
63	Southern Travel
225	St. Teresa's School
101	Surrey County Council
255	The One-Stop Property Shop
247	Woolwich Estate Agents

EDITORIALS

Page	
64	British Gas
132	Crime Stoppers
140	Cubs and Guides
122	Dorking and District Preservation Society
120	Dorking Chamber of Commerce
99	Forestry Commission
185	Hurtwood Control
214	National Childbirth Trust
96-97	National Trust
129	Seeability - The Royal School for the Blind
231	Sports Development Council
79	Surrey Fire and Rescue
107	Surrey Police

The Good Move Guide Ltd. gratefully acknowledges the support of the companies and organisations whose advertisements appear in these pages. Without their help we should not have been able to produce this guide. Selective advertising has been sought and we have pleasure in drawing the attention of our readers to their announcements, however The Good Move Guide Ltd. can accept no responsibility for the products or services advertised.

HURTWOOD PARK POLO CLUB
Horsham Lane, Ewhurst Green, Surrey GU6 7SW

Hurtwood Park Polo Club was conceived by Kenney Jones in 1990 after he acquired some additional land to be used as a practice area near his home in Ewhurst, Surrey. The large attendances drawn to the charity matches held subsequently on the practice ground endorsed the idea that a polo facility would be a very popular asset to the area for locals and visitors alike. A significant number of both local and experienced polo players expressed their willingness to join the new club and realising their enthusiasm Kenney purchased further land to build a club offering the very best facilities in the U.K. The new club will combine a listed historic barn with sympathetic architecture and a colonial equestrian theme, to become a graceful centre of hospitality set within sight of the Hurtwood Hills of Surrey. The facilities and ambience of the clubhouse together with the growing interest in the game of polo are expected to achieve a high number of variable memberships. This also presents huge opportunities for corporate entertainment and sponsorship.

Part of Kenney's philosophy is that polo is a family sport and should be more accessible to everyone, the club therefore welcomes all enquiries.

Telephone: 01483 272828 Fax: 01483 272671